FRONTIERS OF
NUTRITION

FRONTIERS OF
NUTRITION

DALLAS E. BOGGS, RD, PHD

The Prudent Diet and Lifestyle

TATE PUBLISHING
AND ENTERPRISES, LLC

Published by Tate Publishing & Enterprises, LLC
127 E. Trade Center Terrace | Mustang, Oklahoma 73064 USA
1.888.361.9473 | www.tatepublishing.com

Tate Publishing is committed to excellence in the publishing industry. The company reflects the philosophy established by the founders, based on Psalm 68:11,
"The Lord gave the word and great was the company of those who published it."

Book design copyright © 2014 by Tate Publishing, LLC. All rights reserved.
Cover design by Carlo nino Suico
Interior design by Mary Jean Archival

Published in the United States of America
ISBN: 978-1-63122-606-9
1. Health & Fitness / General
2. Health & Fitness / Diet & Nutrition / General
14.04.09

Contents

Introduction

Nutrition is the science that deals with the effects of food on the body. Food provides "nutrients," all the absorbable components of what we eat that the body needs in order to fulfill the three main nutritional requirements of good health. Those are (1) the energy we need to keep warm and to help our organs function, as well as fuel for moving and working; (2) specific nutrients that are needed to utilize foods; and, finally, (3) the nutrients that are required for growth of cells and replacement of used-up cells.

Besides the carbohydrates, fats, proteins, vitamins, and minerals that should be included, there is one other so essential it is often forgotten—water. Water doesn't have vitamins; but, depending on its source, it may have some minerals. It should contain fluoride, which is good for teeth and bones. But even if it had no "nutrients," it would still be as vital to life as the air we breathe.

Beyond provision of nutrients necessary for our very existence, fiber (roughage), though not "nutritive," is also important for good health; and we are increasingly aware of the importance of a group of "non-nutritive" substances known as "phytochemicals" in prevention and treatment of degenerative diseases. These components of the foods we eat will be discussed in the appropriate sections of this book.

What we eat, where we eat, and when we eat plays a dominant role in our quality of life—in our social customs, our recreational activities, our aesthetic values, and our very desire to live and enjoy ourselves. Optimum nutrition provides more than the essential nutrients. We could consume adequate amounts of them by mixing a chemical potion in the laboratory and drinking it three or four times a day; commercial liquid or powdered diets can sustain us for a long time; and hospitals can keep us alive for prolonged periods by injecting nutrients directly into the blood vessels. Our suggestions include healthful practices that may preclude the need for such extreme measures.

We are all subject to hazards beyond our control, but we do know how to manage our risks for the major diseases that afflict modern societies. Most of us do not have the incentive to make the necessary changes. We are creatures of habit, and no habits are more ingrained and more difficult to change than our eating habits. Our eating patterns are determined by our families, our ethnic backgrounds, our lifestyles, and perhaps more than anything, our taste preferences. By using the principles outlined in this book, we can still conform to our own individual preferences and those of our families; and, regardless of those aspects beyond our control and whether we are at low, intermediate, or high risk for one or more of the serious nutritionally related disorders, the recommended adjustments will increase your prospects for avoiding them. The higher your risk, the greater your urgency will be.

With adjustments based on your personal profile, you can significantly decrease your risks for nutritionally related diseases such as atherosclerosis, hypertension, obesity, diabetes, cancer, anemia, and osteoporosis. All of us are at some degree of risk for one or more of these afflictions, and more than half of us will die from their complications. None of the diseases is caused solely by poor diet and lifestyle; but, to the extent those factors are involved, you can lower your risks for them without radical changes.

You may need to make some simple adjustments, but it is not necessary to make severe changes that would require you to sacrifice the pleasures of life for a few added years. Quality of life is as important as length of life. Good nutrition and living habits are necessary ingredients for both. We include foods and supplements with protective effects apart from their nutritive values, yet appealing to your individual tastes. You may begin your journey by evaluating your individual risks for the nutritionally related diseases most threatening to your longevity and to your quality of life. Is it worth the effort? Certainly! From a health standpoint, we have nothing to lose—and we can gain a great deal.

Risk Factors

A number of the most serious diseases in our society are related to long-term dietary patterns and our lifestyle. Atherosclerosis, high blood pressure, obesity, cancer, diabetes, chronic vitamin and mineral deficiencies, certain disorders of the gastrointestinal tract, and abnormalities of bones and teeth all fall into this category. Are you at risk for one or more of these diseases? Probably!

Cumulatively, one of each two Americans will be severely affected by one or more of them. Are your chances higher than average? In a few instances the answers may be simple. In most instances, however, the answers are not so clear. They depend on your gender, your race, your ancestry, your lifestyle, your environment, and the diet you have consumed for a long time. Some constituents of ordinary foods can protect us from disease. Others, if consumed in large quantities, can harm us. Our vulnerabilities depend largely on our inheritances.

Let us consider high blood pressure (hypertension). If you are African-American, your risk is higher than if you are white. If you are male, your risk is slightly higher than if you are female. If you have a strong family history of hypertension, your risk increases. If your lifestyle produces constant stress, your risk goes up. If you eat foods that are high in salt, you are more likely to have high blood pressure.

Establishing a precise risk for any individual is nearly impossible. You know without question whether you are male or female and African-American or white. It is much more difficult to ascertain your family history, your lifestyle, or whether you consume a high-salt diet. What constitutes a strong family history? High blood pressure in one distant cousin on your maternal grandmother's side does not. Certainly, if your mother and father, both sets of grandparents, and all your siblings have high blood pressure, you are genetically at high risk for this condition.

But what about the middle ground? One grandparent and an uncle? Both grandparents on your mother's side? One grandparent on each side? What is a stressful lifestyle? Policeman, executive, coal miner, fireman? Going through a divorce? Suffering the loss of a loved one? Finally, do you eat a high-salt diet? How high is high? Most of us do not have any idea how much salt we consume. Salt is everywhere. It is introduced into our food supply through all kinds of processing. Canned peas may contain one hundred times as much salt as fresh peas.

It is easy to establish your risk compared with the average person's. To classify yourself at high, moderate, or low risk, take into account your sex and your race, and carefully assess your family background, your lifestyle, your environment, and your diet.

Your Sex

Perhaps as many as one-half of all American women are depleted to some extent in at least one of the vitamins or minerals. Men (after the adolescent years) are seldom deficient. Why do women find themselves in this predicament? During the reproductive years, women cycle between pregnancy, lactation, and the long periods between. Pregnancy and lactation increase demands for certain nutrients. Without special care, deficiencies will occur. During the interim periods, women lose a significant amount of blood each month. Lost cells must be replaced. Certain nutrients are necessary to make these new cells.

Women are often dieting. In limiting their calories, they limit their intake of certain essential nutrients. Also, many women are regular users of oral contraceptives that may interfere with the absorption and metabolism of certain vitamins. In addition, women are increasing their consumption of alcohol, another agent known to reduce the absorption of several vitamins and minerals. Thus, the modern American woman is taking oral contraceptives, consuming moderate amounts of alcohol, and often crash dieting. She is at particular risk for nutrient deficiencies. Finally, later in life, women undergo certain hormonal changes that constitute the menopause.

Along with the well-known manifestations of menopause are less well-known changes in a woman's body chemistry. These changes increase her needs for at least one nutrient—calcium. If you are a woman, you are naturally at greater risk for nutrient deficiencies than if you are a man. In addition, cancer of the breast and of the uterus, two very serious diseases, relate to long-term dietary patterns.

From these inferences, it might seem that women are more at risk than men for nutritionally related diseases. But for certain problems, women are; for others, men are. For example, obesity and diabetes (which can lead to atherosclerosis and heart disease), while no more frequent in men than in women, seem to be more serious in men. Which gender is more at risk is not the question.

Your Race

Simply belonging to a particular racial group can increase our risk for certain nutritionally related diseases. Our racial origins may play a part in hypertension (high blood pressure), which is much more prevalent in African-Americans than in whites. Lactose intolerance (inability to digest milk sugar, affecting older children and adults) is very severe in Asian-Americans, moderately so in African-Americans, and much less so in

Caucasians. Thus, your risk for hypertension increases if you are African-American and living in the United States. You must be particularly careful to minimize the other risks for this disease. If you are Asian-American or African-American, your risk for lactose intolerance is high. You may have to control the amount of milk and dairy products in your diet. Without dairy products, the typical American diet is low in calcium. Thus, the risk for osteoporosis increases.

We are not sure why these two conditions show racial preferences. For high blood pressure, we are not even certain that its increased incidence in African-Americans is caused entirely by genetic factors. However, it is clear that African-Americans and Asian-Americans must take race into account when determining their risk for these important conditions.

Your Family History

Many of us know the small town where our great-grandparents were born. Some of us even know our great-grandfather's occupation. How many know how old he was when he died and from what cause? As for our grandparents, few of us could say with any certainty whether Grandmother or Grandfather had high blood pressure. Even those of us who are able to trace our family back many generations, and who can reveal such details about distant relatives as their occupation, education, and religion, know very little about their health problems. Yet this knowledge could be crucial in predicting our own risks for heart attack, high blood pressure, diabetes, and other diseases.

The crucial nutritionally related diseases in which family history is important are: *atherosclerosis*, which may lead to heart attack or coronary artery disease, kidney disease, and senility; *hypertension* (high blood pressure), which can cause stroke or cerebral vascular accidents (CVA), heart failure, and kidney disease; *diabetes*, which may lead to atherosclerosis and all its complications as well as kidney failure, decreased feeling in fingers and toes (peripheral neuropathy), blindness, and weakness of the extremities; *obesity*, which is associated with atherosclerosis, hypertension, and diabetes in addition to gall bladder disease; and certain bone diseases, such as *osteoporosis*, which can cause fractures of the hip and vertebrae in later life.

While we will discuss several other important diseases for which our risks may be lowered by certain dietary modifications, those mentioned above are the most important. The more information we can gather, the better we can build our family "health tree." For living relatives, the direct approach is often the most productive. Do they have atherosclerosis? Have they ever had a heart attack or heart pains (angina)? What is their blood pressure? Did they ever have a stroke, even a mild one? Were they ever told they had heart failure? Are they short of breath when climbing two flights of stairs? Is it more difficult for them to breathe when lying flat than when propped up with two pillows? Do they take nitroglycerine or digitalis? Do they take blood pressure medication? Have they been told to limit their salt intake? Do they have diabetes? High blood sugar? Sugar in the urine? Do they take insulin or oral hypoglycemic drugs? Are they extremely overweight? Were they overweight in the past? Did the female members of the family become shorter in old age? Did any of them fracture a hip or a wrist? Were they ever told they had osteoporosis? These are the important questions. Be persistent. A family pattern may emerge that will help you determine whether you are at increased risk for one or more of the diet-related diseases.

Below is a checklist containing the most important family health information for tracing your family health tree:

> *Atherosclerosis*: heart attack, angina, blood pressure, stroke, heart failure, shortness of breath, nitroglycerine, digitalis, diuretics, told to limit salt.

Diabetes: insulin, special "diabetic" diet, numbness or loss of power in extremities, kidney disease, and blindness.

Obesity: actual weight of relatives.

Osteoporosis: shorter during old age; fractured hip or wrist.

Hypertension: high blood pressure, rise in blood pressure with age, heart attack, stroke, kidney disease.

Once you have gathered all the information available, you can see whether a pattern emerges.

Your Lifestyle

Lifestyle can be even more significant than gender, race, or family history in determining whether we are at risk for certain nutritionally related diseases. Those of us who live under constant pressure—whether real or imaginary—are at increased risk for atherosclerosis and hypertension. Smoking increases our risk for atherosclerosis. Heavy drinking and using a variety of drugs will increase our risk for certain nutrient deficiencies. Constant dieting may limit the intake of important nutrients. When carried to extremes, dieting may result in overt deficiencies. By contrast, moderate amounts of exercise not only will increase the efficiency of our heart and lungs, but may also lower our risk for atherosclerosis and its complications.

It is important that you be extremely honest in examining your lifestyle. Even if it is not possible to change your ingrained living habits, knowing your increased risk for a nutritionally related disease will help you to make informed decisions about your diet.

Your Personality

More than thirty years ago, an association was discovered between a particular set of behavioral characteristics and coronary artery disease. People who exhibited this set of characteristics were called Type A personalities. Type A behavior is a state of mental arousal characterized by a competitive, ambitious, hard-driving existence. Don't confuse this behavior pattern with simply working hard or achieving success. It more resembles an unrelenting and intensive strive toward accomplishment. Furthermore, it may be more appropriately labeled "Type H personality" because hostility or anger may be the most damaging aspect of this characteristic. There is one theory that the trait is not so harmful unless it is acted out; that if one can just brush off his anger, the body does not respond negatively to it. Type A (or "H") behavior involves a series of personality features coupled with an environment that brings those traits into a stressful existence.

Are you very hard-driving, constantly under pressure, always harried by deadlines, and does your job exacerbate these traits? Do you act out the hostilities that often accompany these traits? Since it is often difficult to perceive one's own behavioral traits, it may not be easy to answer that question objectively. Questionnaires can be used to decide whether your behavior pattern constitutes a major, moderate, or low-risk pattern. An objective assessment by your spouse or a close friend is often enough. If you fall into the relevant Type A category, then you are at risk for atherosclerosis and hypertension. If the answer is equivocal, the possibility of increased risk must be considered when you calculate your risk for hypertension and atherosclerosis. If the rest of your pattern suggests low risk, probably nothing else needs to be done. If your profile suggests that you are at increased risk for one or both of these disorders, then a change in diet and a change in behavior may make a big difference.

Cigarette Smoking

If you smoke cigarettes, you are at increased risk for emphysema (a form of chronic lung disease). But no diet is known to prevent it or lessen its severity. Cigarette smoking is only one of several major causes of atherosclerosis and coronary artery disease. Therefore, if you smoke, it is particularly important to minimize any other risks. If your diet is high in saturated fat, trans-fatty acids, and cholesterol, this also increases your risk for atherosclerosis. The two risks (smoking and increased blood-fat levels) are additive. Thus, changing your diet may put you into a lower-risk group, even if you cannot give up smoking.

Alcohol

Heavy alcohol consumption is another part of the lifestyle of many Americans that can affect our risks for nutritionally related diseases. We know that alcohol can be directly toxic to the liver and brain, and it can result in severe (even life-threatening) illnesses such as cirrhosis or dementia, but we often overlook the high-risk for certain nutritional disorders. The person who consumes three or more "hard drinks" per day over a prolonged period of time is more likely to suffer from a variety of vitamin and mineral deficiencies than the individual who drinks more moderately. Excess alcohol interferes with the body's absorption of such vitamins as folic acid, thiamin (vitamin B1), and pyridoxine (vitamin B6), and with the absorption of such minerals as zinc and magnesium. A deficiency of one or a combination of these nutrients may occur. Heavy drinkers should consume foods high in them.

Drugs

Over-the-counter drugs and prescription medications further complicate our problems. Their use has become part of the lifestyle of many Americans. Millions of us consume analgesics, tranquilizers, and pills to put us to sleep or keep us awake. Some of these drugs will increase our risk for certain nutritional deficiencies. For example, aspirin can cause gastric irritations and microscopic bleeding, which can lead to iron deficiency. The contraceptive pill can interfere with the absorption of such nutrients as folic acid and vitamin B6 (pyridoxine). Some women who have been using oral contraceptives for a long time may be at increased risk for deficiency of these two vitamins. Since alcohol interferes with the absorption of folic acid and vitamin B6, heavy drinkers who are on the pill are at double risk.

Exercise

Furthermore, our high standard of living has been accompanied by a progressive decline in physical activity. Our society has been slowly transformed from a highly active physical one to a much more sedentary type. The policeman on the beat, the firefighter, the construction worker, and the farmer all continue to lead lives full of physical activity. For most of us, life means driving to work, taking the elevator to the office, sitting in a chair most of the day, getting back in the car, driving home, and sitting in front of a TV until bedtime. This reduction in physical activity has placed us at increased risk for obesity, atherosclerosis, hypertension, and osteoporosis.

The realization that fitness can improve the quality of life and sense of well-being, and our longevity, has led to a revolution in physical fitness. Jogging, walking, bicycle riding, swimming, health clubs, aerobic dancing, have become part of the lifestyle of many of us. To the extent that we engage in increased physical activity, this reduces our risk for the diseases mentioned above.

However, exercise is not the answer to all our problems. Obesity, atherosclerosis, hypertension, and osteoporosis are each caused by a few factors acting simultaneously. Lack of exercise is just one. Usually, changes in our lifestyle must be accompanied by changes in our diet. But, don't try to do it all in one step. Begin gradually and work your way slowly into a more active lifestyle. If you already suffer from one of the above diseases, increase your exercise under professional supervision. Stick with it! Remember that you're seeking permanent changes in your lifestyle, not a short-term change such as losing five pounds before some important social function.

How do you decide whether you are too sedentary and need to increase your physical activity? Some sophisticated tests employing complicated and expensive measurements can do this very accurately. Sometimes, your doctor will order these tests. You can make a rough determination by answering a few questions. First, does your job involve a lot of physical activity, a moderate amount, or little or none? If the answer is a great deal, increasing your physical activity will probably have little effect on reducing your risk. If your answer is little or none, do you indulge in any form of regular exercise? For example, do you walk or ride a bike to work, jog daily, or play tennis three times a week? If not, you are a person of low physical activity, and your risk for the four diseases mentioned above is increased. You can lower that risk by increasing your physical activity. Many people's answers will put them in an intermediate risk level. If you are one of these, you are at somewhat increased risk and will probably benefit by increasing your physical activity. Pick a form of exercise that you enjoy. Don't jog just because your friends do. There are enough ways to increase physical activity to satisfy everyone. Get into it gradually—and stick with it!

Excessive Dieting

Calorie counting has become an integral part of life for many of us. Diet books are constantly on the best-seller list. For the most part, Americans don't diet to cure obesity or to prevent it. They diet to achieve an image equated with good health, youth, fitness, sexiness, beauty, and glamour. In other words, Americans diet primarily for cosmetic purposes. Dieting means fewer calories. Fewer calories mandate less food. Less food often means fewer nutrients, which, in certain susceptible groups, can lead to deficiencies. For example, we have seen that iron is a crucial nutrient. If you are consuming fewer than 1,200 cal per day (many diets restrict calories to even lower levels), you will be unable to fulfill your iron requirement from your food alone. Reducing your caloric intake to 1,200 or less will increase your risk for iron, zinc, vitamin B6, and folic acid deficiencies. This threat would be serious enough if calories were lowered in a way that favors the consumption of foods rich in these nutrients.

Many diets reduce calories by offering "miracle" programs that emphasize one particular food or type of food. The grapefruit diet, the pineapple diet, the diet that allows mainly meat or no meat, and the fruit diet are all so restrictive that nutrient deficiencies do occur. With its amazing resiliency, the human body is usually able to recover, but serious diseases and death may ensue.

If your life is one of constant dieting, ask yourself if you are doing it to treat or prevent obesity. If the answer is yes, then use a balanced reduction in calories that you can sustain for the rest of your life (see "Obesity"). If the answer is no, then stop dieting. If you must diet, use a low-calorie plan that provides the maximum variety of foods. Avoid crash programs that promise instant results. Even if these programs are successful, the price may be too high. As you assess your own risk, you must honestly evaluate your living habits. Do you have a Type A personality? Do you smoke, drink to excess, or use certain kinds of drugs? Is your level of physical activity low? As we discuss each disease, we shall point out which of these practices increases your risk for that affliction and how you can lower that risk by altering your habits and changing your diet.

Your Dietary Pattern

The dietary pattern we maintain is, in some ways, the most important factor contributing to our risk for nutritionally related diseases. We are not very concerned about what you ate during the past twenty-four hours or seven days. We are most concerned about your pattern or patterns over the years. Before you can make a rational decision about whether you should change your eating habits, it is important to determine the nature of the diet you now consume. Is it high in calories, fat, cholesterol, or salt? Is it low in fiber, calcium, iron, or folic acid?

In each of the following chapters, we will review dietary patterns that can lower our risk for certain diseases. When we compare these patterns with the way we eat, for most of us the differences will be great. If you are eating the types of foods that increase risks for the particular disease, changing your diet can lower that risk. Table 1 includes a list of various diseases and the types of diet that increase risks.

Table 1. **Disease Diet Relationships**

Disease	Type of diet that increases risk
Atherosclerosis	High fat
	High saturated fat
	High cholesterol
High blood pressure	High sodium
	Low calcium
	Low potassium
Cancers of the colon and breast	High fat
	Alcohol excesses
Diabetes	High calorie
Obesity	High calorie
Dental caries	High refined sugar
Osteoporosis	Low calcium
	Low magnesium
Anemia	Low iron
	Low folic acid
	Low vitamin B_{12}
Diverticulosis	Low fiber

In discussions of each disease, foods high or low in the applicable nutrient will be identified. By evaluating your long-term dietary pattern, you should be able to assess whether you are increasing your risk and whether a dietary change will be beneficial for you.

Scoring Your Risks

We have considered the major risk factors in the most important nutritionally related diseases. The importance of each risk factor varies with the specific disease. For example, race is important in high blood pressure but It is less important in osteoporosis. By contrast, gender is very important in osteoporosis and much less important in high blood pressure. Family history is important in determining risk for obesity, atherosclerosis, high blood pressure, and diabetes, and not very important in determining our risk for cancer of the colon or diverticulosis. Lifestyle is important in atherosclerosis, hypertension, and vitamin and mineral deficiencies, and of little or no importance in cancer of the breast.

We shall also see how different components of our lifestyle may be particularly important in determining our risk for certain diseases. Smoking is a major risk in atherosclerosis, a minor risk in hypertension, and not a risk in obesity. Type A personality is an important risk in atherosclerosis and hypertension, but not so important in cancer of the breast or colon. Thus, these various components will have a different weight in determining our risk for each disease.

Finally, although dietary pattern is a factor in all these diseases, your pattern may or may not be contributing to your risk for one or more of them. Your traits must be assessed separately for each disease. As you read each chapter, you will see that we have assigned a number to each risk for the disease under discussion. The numbers will vary with the disease. Below a certain score, you are at low risk. Above a certain score, you are at high risk. Between these numbers, your risk is moderate. It is also a way of rating any changes that result from your efforts to lower that risk. It is not, however, a precise set of data for calculating your chances of having any specific disease.

Risks are better defined and, therefore, will carry more weight in some cases than in others. All these considerations will be thoroughly discussed in the following chapters. Once you have estimated your risk for any of the diseases in question, you can decide whether a change in diet is appropriate for you.

Changing Your Diet

After you have determined your status and have decided to alter your diet, it is reasonable to ask: "How do I know I have reduced my risk? Have I made myself immune to atherosclerosis or hypertension or osteoporosis?" There aren't any tests that can tell you whether or not your risk has dropped from one precise level to another, and no dietary change can make any of us completely immune. Prevention of a nutritional disorder is much more difficult and complicated than prevention of an infectious disease. Every day, someone in low-risk categories dies from a heart attack. Conversely, some people in the high-risk categories live to ripe old age and die quietly in bed. By changing our diets, however, we can improve the odds. For some of us, there will be tangible evidence that the odds have changed. The levels of cholesterol and other blood lipids (fats) will change, or our blood pressure will drop slightly, or we will lose some of that excess weight.

In other cases, we may see no change. For example, if you decide to go on a low-fat, high-fiber version of the Prudent Diet to reduce your risk for certain cancers, no direct measurement can confirm whether you have accomplished your goal. We can say only that in populations who have changed their dietary patterns in a similar manner, the incidence of these cancers has dropped. We do know that people have lower incidence of cancer of the colon or of the breast if they consume a low-fat diet.

In the succeeding chapters, we will give you the best available information for making informed choices. A decision to change your diet is a personal one. Only you can decide! For each disease discussed, the amount of accessible data will differ. If you reduce the amount of total fat, saturated fat, and cholesterol in your diet, the level of cholesterol in your blood might drop between 15 and 20 percent. If this happens, we can give you a statistical evaluation of how much that affects your chances for having a heart attack.

Our ability to predict other diseases is much more limited. For example, we know that consuming adequate amounts of calcium in our younger years will offer some protection from osteoporosis and the brittle bones of later years. However, we don't know how much protection results because we have no way of monitoring the effect of the dietary change. For osteoporosis, your decision to change your diet will have to involve less quantitative data.

Another question is when to change the diet for the maximum benefit? Sometimes, the peak incidence of the disease may be forty to fifty years away. Do you have to change your diet now, or can you wait another ten or twenty years? Although there may be no precise answer, the earlier we modify our diet, the better our chances for reducing risks. The effects of an improper diet are often cumulative. The longer we continue to consume the wrong foods, the harder it will be to overcome our risks.

To those at low risk, we are not advocating complacency or a false sense of security. Even those at lowest risk for a given disease may end up suffering from that disorder. If your profile shows you in this category, your risk is lower than those of someone at higher risk but you are not guaranteed immunity. If your risk is high, your incentive for modifying your diet should be greater than average.

Atherosclerosis

If any disease can be blamed specifically on long-term nutrition and lifestyle, it is atherosclerosis (hardening of the arteries). The disease is almost unheard of in primitive societies. Yet, it is the scourge of the Western world. Eliminating it would immensely improve the quality of life for millions of Americans and add at least ten years to our average life expectancy. To some extent, atherosclerosis can be blamed on our genes. It runs in families, but genes are not as important as the way we live.

The disease develops early in life and progresses as we get older. Fatty materials, mainly in the form of cholesterol, are deposited in the lining of arteries. They form rough plaques that slowly increase in size. This process gradually reduces the opening in the artery through which blood can flow. The artery can become completely blocked, cutting off the blood supply to the tissues it normally feeds. If the coronary artery becomes blocked, the heart tissue is starved of oxygen and critical nutrients. The victim suffers a heart attack. The first apparent symptom may be sudden death. If the clogged artery services a portion of the brain, a stroke will follow.

A heart attack or a stroke is not a primary disease of the heart or brain, but a disease of the blood vessels. In addition to such drastic events such as heart attack or stroke, some insidious consequences may occur. For example, blockages in many of the smaller arteries to the brain can lead to generalized reduction in blood flow to that organ. The result is confusion, loss of memory, and incoherence.

What is the etiology of this important disease? There is no one root cause. There are many. Some we know about; others, we do not. All relate, either directly or indirectly, to lifestyle or diet. Since there is no single cause of atherosclerosis, we must consider the known risks. The major risks for developing atherosclerosis are:

Type A personality	Hypertension
Cigarette smoking	Diabetes
Hyperlipidemia	(particularly high cholesterol levels)

Any of the above features places one at risk for this disease (score five points each). If you have Type A personality, hyperlipidemia, hypertension, and diabetes, combined with cigarette smoking, you are in a very high-risk category.

There are several other features that increase our risk. If you are male, add one more point. Men seem to be slightly more at risk for atherosclerosis than women, independent of the major risks. If you have a strong family history, add two points, and, if you are obese, add two more points. Obesity increases our chances of developing hyperlipidemia, hypertension, and diabetes (these conditions can lead to atherosclerosis). Thus, an obese male with a strong family history can be in a high-risk category for atherosclerosis without having any of the major risks listed above. You should be able to determine with certainty whether you have some of these risks. It is more difficult to assign a numerical value to others.

Let us use a hypothetical example. You are male (one point), you don't smoke (zero points), your blood pressure is a normal 120/80 (zero points), and you don't have diabetes (zero points). These risks are easily scored. You are either male or female; you either smoke or don't smoke; your blood pressure is either high or normal; and you either do or do not have diabetes. The other risks are not so simple to assess. Do you have a Type A personality? Score yourself as honestly as you can. For some of you, if the answer is yes, score 5; for others, if it is no, score 0. Many of us will not be sure how to answer. Score yourself between 1 and 4, and err on the high side.

Do you have a positive family history? If several close relatives have suffered from atherosclerosis, heart attack, or stroke, or have been known to have hyperlipidemia (high blood-fat or cholesterol levels), score 2. If no relatives or only a few distant ones have had any of these problems, score 0. If your family history puts you in an intermediate category, score 1.

Are you obese? We will discuss obesity and its prevention and treatment in "Obesity". For the present, if you are 20 percent above your ideal weight, score 2; 10 percent above, score 1; if below your ideal weight, score 0 (see Table 11, pp. 68, 69).

Do you have hyperlipidemia, i.e., high blood levels of lipids or fats? The most important of these blood fats is cholesterol. The higher your blood levels of cholesterol, the greater your chances of developing atherosclerosis. The average level in the middle-aged population in the United States may be around 200 mg (milligrams) per 100 mL (milliliters), but that is not safe. Our population consumes a diet that leads to high levels of blood cholesterol. That this is our average does not mean it is normal. In certain populations who do not consume a diet such as ours, the average level is about 175 mg per 100 mL.

Since the risk for developing atherosclerosis increases at higher blood cholesterol levels (particularly levels above 200 mg per 100 mL), we should strive for levels below 200 mg. Only people who maintain these levels should be considered normal. Using a criterion of 175 mg per 100 mL as normal, most people in our society have high cholesterol levels (hyperlipidemia).

This phenomenon relates to our lifestyle and can be changed by altering our diet. Is your serum cholesterol high? Getting an answer to that question is the first step in reducing your risk for atherosclerosis. Most physicians order a blood cholesterol test as part of a routine physical. Your local hospital or outpatient clinic may offer a screening test at an annual "health fair." When you get your results, whether the level is within the "normal" range or not, consider the numerical value. If it is over 175 mg per 100 mL, give yourself a score of 1; if it is above 185, score 2; if it is 200, score 3; if 225, score 4; and if 250 or higher, score 5.

Your total cholesterol level does not tell the full story. Cholesterol in the blood is attached to protein carriers of different sizes, forming lipoproteins. Most is attached to light (low-density) lipoproteins, or LDL. The amount of cholesterol carried in this form concerns us most. High levels of total serum cholesterol almost always mean high levels of LDL cholesterol. A small amount of cholesterol is attached to another protein of much higher density called high-density lipoprotein or HDL. This form of cholesterol is desirable (good cholesterol). The higher amounts are better because this cholesterol reduces the degree of atherosclerosis. An HDL cholesterol level above 45 mg per 100 mL reduces our risk for atherosclerosis. Thus, if you know your HDL level, you can score more accurately. If it is above 45 mg, subtract one point; if between 39 to 46 mg, add zero; and if below 40 mg, add one point.

Another strong indicator of risk for heart and blood disorders is the presence of a protein in the blood that is called C-reactive protein or CRP. It is released by the liver in reaction to an inflammatory process that may be present in the blood vessels, and there are indications that it may be as important as cholesterol in predicting diseases of the heart and blood vessels. Your doctor may soon utilize this test as a routine laboratory procedure. If you know your level and it is high, add 5 to your score.

After you have added up your score, the following chart will categorize your risk:

Below 5	low risk
5-9	moderate risk

| 10-19 | high risk |
| 20 and above | very high risk |

If your score is 5 or above, you should take measures to lower it. Each of the risks should be approached separately. You can't change your sex or your family history. Changing your personality or your job may be very difficult. If you smoke, your score should provide some incentive to stop. High blood pressure must be treated by a physician and may require drugs and dietary therapy (see "Hypertension"). If you are obese, you should lose weight (see "Obesity"). Diabetes is a serious disease and must be treated by a doctor. This treatment may entail the use of insulin. Finally, if you have hyperlipidemia, specific dietary treatment is necessary.

The next step is to examine the components of your score. Focus on your hyperlipidemia score. If it is 3 or more, a low-fat diet should help lower your risk for atherosclerosis, regardless of the source of the other points. If your hyperlipidemia score is 2 or less (serum cholesterol level of under 200) and the only other risks are Type A personality or cigarette smoking, you will benefit much more by diminishing these factors than by changing your diet. If your other points are from family history, hypertension, diabetes, or obesity, you should use the low-fat diet along with any other remedy for the particular risk. The chart below shows who should use a low-fat diet:

Total score below 5—not necessary.

Total score 5 and above—hyperlipidemia score 3 and above—everyone.

Total score 5 and above—hyperlipidemia score 2 and below—remaining points from Type A personality and cigarette smoking—not necessary (if you can eliminate these risks).

Total score 5 and above—hyperlipidemia score 2 and below—remaining points from risks other than Type A personality and cigarette smoking—everyone.

Now that you have determined your risk and decided whether a low-fat diet can lower that risk, you still need to address the other factors. The major ones are additive. That is, if you are a smoker who has hyperlipidemia, you are at greater risk than from either component by itself. Either hypertension or diabetes will further elevate that risk. In this chapter, we will discuss only the low-fat diet. It has a direct impact on atherosclerosis. If you have hypertension, diabetes, or obesity, additional dietary modifications may be necessary.

The Prudent dietary guidelines for atherosclerosis are quite simple. They were developed from many experimental studies and by imitating the diets of people who have the lowest incidence of coronary artery disease. The central focus revolves around the hazards of high cholesterol. In most cases, the remedy is the same as for triglycerides—decrease your calorie intake and watch your consumption of hard (saturated) animal fats and hydrogenated vegetable oils. In a minority of cases, there is a genetic predisposition to high cholesterol. Although the genetic disorder is relatively rare, about one of five heart attack victims has it. A family history of heart attacks at an early age (in the forties) is suggestive of this form of metabolic disorder. Cholesterol levels of 300 mg per dL may alarm your doctor to consider the genetic type of hypercholesterolemia. Dietary restrictions may not be adequate. Several prescription drugs are available to treat this serious condition.

Sometimes a successful weight reduction program brings with it a lowering of blood cholesterol; sometimes it doesn't. Often someone loses unwanted pounds and simultaneously his blood cholesterol drops, only to return to its former heights shortly thereafter.

Cholesterol is a complicated substance, much more like a wax than like ordinary fat. The body requires it. It is present in the walls of all cells. Some hormones and vitamin D are made from it. The insulation around nerve sheaths in the brain is mostly cholesterol, and the gallbladder uses cholesterol in the production of bile to aid digestion and absorption of fats and fat-soluble vitamins from the small intestine. The body conserves cholesterol. It is reabsorbed from the intestine back into the bloodstream to be recycled.

Cholesterol is manufactured, in at least the required amount, by the body, regardless of the amount in the diet. A high dietary intake depresses the body synthesis of cholesterol, but not enough to cancel out the effect of the diet. A high saturated fat intake also tends to increase the amount of cholesterol circulating in the blood. When the blood has too much cholesterol—whether manufactured by the body or stimulated by a high-fat diet or from the ingestion of cholesterol itself (egg yolk is one of the chief food sources)—cholesterol settles in the walls of blood vessels. They become less elastic (hardening the arteries, causing atherosclerosis) and grow narrow so that blood flow is slowed or even stopped. If this happens in a major heart or brain artery, the result is a coronary attack or a stroke.

Some of the body's cholesterol (perhaps 25 percent) comes from our food, but most is manufactured in the liver. From there, it is transported to other organs. Our bodies try to keep the level constant. If too much is consumed, the body makes less. But this protective mechanism can be overwhelmed when we consume large quantities of cholesterol, saturated fat, and trans-fatty acids. These fats (found mainly in meat, dairy products, and hydrogenated vegetable oils) will raise the level of blood cholesterol just as will dietary cholesterol itself. By contrast, unsaturated fats in our diet obtained largely from vegetable sources, may lower blood-cholesterol levels. Exactly how these different types of fats influence the levels of blood cholesterol is not known. A good way to remember the type of fat is: saturated fats are usually solid (hard fats), whereas unsaturated fats are usually soft or liquid (oils).

Fats and oils add up to one of the main sources of energy in the American diet. They are sometimes divided into visible and invisible fats. The visible are those we add to foods: butter, shortenings, corn, peanut, and other cooking or salad oils. The invisible, those already contained in food, include: the butterfat in whole milk, the fats in eggs, fish, meats, nuts, and other things we eat.

Fat makes our food more palatable than it would otherwise be and also contributes to the "had enough" feeling. It supplies essential fatty acids, it provides transport for the fat-soluble vitamins, it offers calories in compact form, it travels around the body through the bloodstream, and it provides insulating, shock absorbing and smoothing layers under the skin and around other body tissues.

The main components of fats in food and in the body are various fatty acids. Butter, for instance, contains more than twenty-nine kinds. The differences in taste of fats depend upon which fatty acids predominate. The distribution of fatty acids also dictates the temperatures at which a fat melts, and thus determine whether fats are solid or liquid at room temperature. It makes little or no difference to the number of calories per gram; all fats and oils contain approximately 9 cal per g.

Fatty acids are chiefly carbon atoms arranged in a straight chain, with the acid part on one end. All along the carbon chain are little arms sticking out. What is on the arms determines whether the fatty acid is saturated, monounsaturated, or polyunsaturated. Saturated fatty acids have hydrogen stuck on all the little arms; they are "saturated" with it. This type is the chief component in animal (meat) fats, butter and dairy products. Such fats do not melt at room temperature. Palmitic, stearic, and myristic acids are saturated fatty acids. They raise the level of cholesterol in the blood.

Two of the arms of monounsaturated fatty acids have no hydrogen. Instead, they hold hands. So the fatty acid is not fully filled, not saturated with hydrogen. The most common monounsaturated acid is oleic. Canola, olive, and peanut oils contain this type of fatty acid predominantly. Two or more pairs of the arms of polyunsaturated acids hold no hydrogen ("poly" means "many"). The least saturated fats, they are the major types found in corn, soybean, cottonseed, and, particularly, safflower oils. Polyunsaturated fatty acids cannot be synthesized in the human body. Three of them are essential; a small amount of each must be included in the diet. Otherwise, serious skin eruptions and other disorders would occur. You can't live long on a completely fat-free diet.

In the chemically pure state, polyunsaturated fatty acids are relatively unstable. That is—they are subject to oxidation. But, in nature, other substances known as "antioxidants" accompany them and protect them from oxidation. Some of these antioxidants (vitamin E, for example) are vitamins. Beta-carotene, also an antioxidant, is a pro vitamin. It can be changed into a vitamin by enzymes in our cells. Another way to stabilize them is by hydrogenation. Hydrogenated fat is simply unsaturated fat that has had hydrogen added to it, filling up the empty arms on the carbon chain. The more fats are hydrogenated, the harder they are and the better they keep, but the more they raise the blood-cholesterol level.

"Partially-hydrogenated" means that some, but not all, of the fat has been hydrogenated just enough to make an oil act more like fat. A good example of partially hydrogenated fat is margarine, made from corn oil (or other vegetable oil). One problem with artificially hydrogenated fats is that some of the chemical bonds formed between the carbon and hydrogen atoms are not in the same geometric position as those formed in nature. These are called "trans fatty acids;" and though they may be partially unsaturated, they may raise blood cholesterol as much as if they were fully saturated. Furthermore, they lower the levels of HDL, the "good cholesterol."

Triglycerides are another name for the common form of fat. These are formed from groups of three fatty acids combined with a short molecule of glycerol (popularly known as glycerin), pretty much as the long tines of a fork are hooked together by being stuck on a short base. A better comparison would be with a three-toothed Spanish-type hair comb. Hypertriglyceridemia, "high triglycerides," is another symptom of excess fats in the blood when our metabolism of sugars is not adequate (as with a diabetic or a pre-diabetic state of health), and our body is shunting it to production of fat. Reduced caloric intake, coupled with an exercise program, will usually result in normal blood lipids (fats).

There is a lot of discussion in the nutrition literature about the beneficial effects of fish oils and other oils that are readily converted to omega-3 fatty acids in the body. "Omega" refers to the position of an unsaturated bond in the carbon chain. These fatty acids have effects on a class of hormones (eicosanoids) that affect our overall wellness, including resistance to cardiovascular disease as well as painful inflammatory disorders such as arthritis. Some of their effects are similar to those of aspirin, a well-known "blood thinner" as well as a pain reliever and anti-inflammatory agent. Fatty fish such as tuna, salmon, and halibut are good sources of these fats. Their potential benefits may justify frequent inclusion (at least twice per week) of moderate amounts of fish in your diet. Our ideas about what should constitute the "Prudent Diet" have changed since its conception, but the principles have remained the same. To dine the "Prudent" way, we limit the amount and the kinds of fat we eat. By amount, we mean that fat should contribute less than 30 percent of our total dietary calories. (The rest of the calories come from starches, sugars, and protein.) By kinds of fat, we mean that the diet should contain less saturated fat than unsaturated fat. Saturated fat should contribute no more than 10 percent of total calories. In addition, if we are at high risk for atherosclerosis, our cholesterol intake should average less than 300 mg per day. To understand these standards, let us take a closer look at foods.

All foods come from either animal or plant sources. Those from animal sources include all red meat, poultry, fish, shellfish, eggs, milk, cheese, and other products derived from these foods. Those from plant sources include fruits, vegetables, grains, beans, and nuts.

Cholesterol is present in all animal products, but not in plants. The amount of cholesterol varies among meats and other animal products. The greatest concentrations occur in eggs and organ meats (i.e., liver, kidneys, heart, and brains). Table 2 lists the approximate cholesterol content of some common foods.

Table 2. **Average Cholesterol Content of Common Foods**

Food	mg Cholesterol
1. Liver (3 oz.)	372
2. Egg (large)*	213
3. Shrimp, canned (3 oz.)**	128
4. Veal (3 oz.)	86
5. Lamb (3 oz.)	83
6. Beef (3 oz.)	80
7. Pork (3 oz.)	76
8. Lobster (3 oz.)	72
9. Chicken (½ breast, no skin)	63
10. Clams, canned (½ cup)	50
11. Chicken (1 drumstick)	39
12. Fish, fillet (3 oz.)	34-75
13. Whole Milk (8 oz.)	22
14. One percent milk (8 oz.)	9

*We have relaxed our standards somewhat by allowing up to one egg per day for those of us who are not at very high risk for atherosclerosis because eggs are otherwise packed with high nutritive value and they contain emulsifying agents that enable our digestive system to better accommodate the extra cholesterol.

**While shrimp is relatively high in cholesterol, it is so low in saturated fat that its positive effects outweigh the negative.

Shrimp does not worsen the ratio of "bad" cholesterol to "good" in the blood.

The more fat on the meat the greater the amount of cholesterol. Therefore, meat must be lean and well-trimmed. We do not recommend elimination of all "red" meats from the diet of persons who do not have other objections to them. From a nutritional point of view, red meats are still a good source of high quality protein and are rich in iron and zinc. Table 3 lists those high-fat meats and recommended lean cuts.

Table 3. **Recommended and Prohibited Meats**

Recommended	Prohibited
All fish	Cold cuts
All shellfish	Frankfurters
Veal, all cuts	Sausage
Chicken fryers & broilers*	Beef:
Rock Cornish hen*	Shell strip
Turkey (non self-basting)*	T bone steak
Beef:	Club steak
Bottom round	Sirloin
Top round	Chuck
Eye round	Rib roast
Sirloin tip	Shoulder roast
Roast filet	Porterhouse steak
Rump	Brisket

Bottom round	Short ribs
Ground round	Lamb:
Minute or cubed steak	Shanks
Lamb:	Loin lamb chops
Roast leg of lamb	Rib chops
Lamb steaks	Lamb stew
Pork:	Pork:
Lean cured ham	Loin pork chops
Lean ham steak	Roast loin of pork
	Canadian bacon
*without Skin	Bacon
	Spareribs
	Salt pork
	Ham hocks

Fruits, vegetables, grains, and grain products (such as breads, pastas, breakfast cereals, rice, etc.) and beans are virtually fat free. But if fat (such as butter or margarine) was used during preparation, you should determine how much and what kind was added.

One group of plant products that is very important in the Prudent Diet includes seeds, nuts, and the fats derived from plant sources. The most familiar products in this group are vegetable oils and margarines made from them. In choosing these foods, it is important to differentiate between kinds of fats.

Early versions of the Prudent Diet allowed liberal amounts of polyunsaturated fats because they tend to lower our blood cholesterol levels. We now know that the monounsaturated fats are more desirable than the polyunsaturated ones. The monounsaturated fats not only lower total cholesterol, they do not decrease the levels of HDL (good cholesterol). This conclusion is supported by observations that people who consume Mediterranean diets (high in olive oil) do not seem to get atherosclerosis. By restricting the amount of saturated fats in our diets, we can increase the proportion of the beneficial fats. But we do not advocate supplementing our foods with oils that provide extra calories. Adding any kind of fat to our diets may increase our risks for certain types of cancer (see "Cancer"). Restricting total calories from fat while avoiding foods high in saturated fats and trans-fatty acids is more important than the slight reduction in blood cholesterol levels that may result from adding vegetable oils or polyunsaturated margarine to our food.

The food industry has responded to public awareness of the fat and cholesterol problems with a plethora of new products, often with confusing and sometimes misleading labels. In 1990, the congress reacted with revised food labeling laws. The amount of saturated fat and the total fat content of each food we buy is now shown on every food label and new regulations will append trans-fatty acid levels. Standardization of food labels, as required by the same federal regulations, will help us evaluate the fat modified foods. (See Table 4 regarding fat levels in modified foods).

Table 4. **Fat Content of Modified Foods**

Food Claim	*Amount of Fat Allowed per Serving*
"No fat or fat free"	Less than 1/2 gram of fat.
"Loaw fat"	No more than 3 grams of fat.
"Low saturated fat"	No more than 1 gram of saturated fat.
"Low cholesterol"	No more than 20 mg of cholesterol and no more than 2 grams of saturated fat.

Some food labels also list monounsaturated fat levels.

Table 5 lists foods and their predominant kinds of fat. Remember, the harder or more solid a fat is, the more satureated it will be. The saturated are to be avoided because they increase levels of harmful cholesterol in our bodies.

Table 5. **Distribution of Fats in Common Foods**

High in Polyunsaturated Fats

Safflower oil	Soybeans
Corn Oil	Sunflower seeds
Soft margarine: made of corn oil	Sesame seeds
Walnuts	Oils made from these seeds

Moderately High in Polyunsaturated Fats

Soybean oil

Cottonseed oil

Other soft margarine

Commercial salad dressings

Mayonnaise

High in Monounsaturated Fats

Canola oil

Olive oil

Peanut oil

Olives

Peanuts and peanut butter

Avocados

Cashews

Brazil nuts

Almonds

Pecans

High in Saturated Fats

Meats high in fat: sausages, cold cuts, prime cuts, etc.

Chicken fat

Meat drippings

Lard

Hydrogenated shortenings

Coconut oil

Palm oil

Stick margarine

Coconut oil

Butter and products with dairy fat (for example: cheese, cream, whole milk, ice cream), chocolate, bakery items

High in Cholesterol

Egg yolks

Liver

Kidneys

Sweetbreads

Brains

Heart

Pate

Caviar

Dairy products

Products made with the above, for example: cakes, pies, pastries, and gravies.

To limit the total amount of fat and cholesterol in our diet, we must restrict the amount of meat we consume on a daily basis. Our meat consumption should be limited according to our total calorie allowance. If your total intake of calories is under 1,500, the maximum meat intake should be limited to four ounces per day; six ounces if your total intake exceeds 1,500 calories. This ensures a low cholesterol intake and it controls the amount of fat from foods high in saturated fats. Red meat (beef, lamb, and pork) should be limited to sixteen ounces per week. If you are at very high risk, your doctor may ask you to limit egg yolks to two per week whether eaten plain or in prepared foods. Egg whites can be eaten in unlimited quantities. Low-fat foods (such as fruits, vegetables, low-fat dairy products, grains, beans, etc.) do not need to be restricted (unless you are watching your weight).

Altogether, the amount of fat from the meat and from oils used in cooking, in salad dressings, etc. will contribute no more than 30 percent of your total calories. Use your discretion on high-sugar foods. For dessert, eat low-fat products such as gelatin, fruit ices, low-fat yogurt, angel-food cake, or homemade products containing the allowable fat. The Prudent Diet is not very different from the way people eat in those parts of the world where the incidence of heart disease is very low.

It is not necessary to replace your occasional evening of fine dining or your routine lunch hour with the monotonous brown bag. You will be surprised at the flexibility the diet offers—whether at a company cafeteria, a short-order breakfast, or a gourmet feast. However, you should always heed certain signals. For starters, look for words and phrases that describe the selection in a manner that alerts you when they are high in calories and fat so that you can avoid them.

The more simply prepared a food is, the lower in fat it will be. Spices and seasonings such as garlic, curry, bay leaves, basil, oregano, ginger, onion, and dill, and garnishes like parsley, lemon slices, or pimentos do not contribute any fat to the dish, though they can immensely enhance the flavor and appeal of a food. As a rule, poultry, fish, and seafood are the best selections. They are low in fat, and they can be prepared without addition of saturated fats and still taste delicious. Be aware that many broiled entrees may have been basted with butter or other saturated fats. Salads offer a variety of flavors and textures while still permitting utmost control over the kinds and amount of fat in the meal. It is best to ask that dressings be served "on the side" so that you can serve yourself an appropriate amount.

Here is a summary of recommended menu selections:

Table 6. Menu Selections

Appetizers—fresh fruits and vegetables as finger foods
or juices; seafood cocktail. (Avoid sour or sweet cream and
season butter or oils.)
Soups—clear consommé or broth with noodles or vegetables,
if desired. (Avoid cheese soups, cream soups, egg soups, and
onion soup; bean soups should be fat free.)
Salads—green and tossed salads; addition may inlcude
chicken tuerkey, seafood, tuna, lean roast beef, lean ham (as in a
chef's salad), clear gelatin molds; Cole slaw, potato, or Waldorf
salad—with a minimum of mayonnaise. (Avoid cheese and
creamy dressings.)
Fish—any variety prepared without fat. (Avoid tartar sauce.)
Note: We should eat at least two portions of fish per week—one
of which should be oily fish such as sardine, salmon, tuna, trout,
and mackerel—because they contribute the omega-3 fatty acids:
docosahexaenoic acid (DHA), eicosapentaenoic acid (EPA),
and alpha-linolenic acid (ALA). They reduce the risk of death from
heart attack, dangerous abnormal heart rhythm, and strokes.
"Omega-3s" are also found in some nuts (especially, English walnuts)
and vegetable oils (canola, soybean, flaxseed/linseed, olive.)
Poultry—chicken, turkey, Rock Cornish hen—prepared without fat
and with skin removed. (Avoid fried or batter dipped coatings.)
Red Meat—always lean hindquarter cuts of beef, lamb, and pork;
all cuts of veal. Cook as well done as is palatable. (Avoid prime cuts,
gravy, breaded coatings.)

Fruits—as much as you like. (Avoid cream or whipped toppings.)

Vegetables—if served plain, as much as you like.
Other—beans and peas wihtout oil or saucel walnuts and sunflower seeds.

Bread—all sandwich bread, bread sticks, hard rools; French and Italian bread,
and Syrian pita; wafers and "toasts." (Avoid biscuits,

croissants. corn. bran. blueberry muffins, and butter rolls.) Whole grain breads are preferred.

Desserts—angel food cake. gelatin desserts. frozen fruit ices. and low fat frozen dairy products. (Avoid cream and nondairy milk substitutes.)

Beverages—low fat milk products. carbonated and alcoholic beverages. fruit juices. coffee. and tea. (Avoid cream and nondairy milk substitutes.)

Extras—pickles relishes. mustard. Worcestershire sauce. catsup. steak sauce. lemon juice. vinegar. spices. and herbs.

Daytime snacks can be popcorn (unbuttered or lightly buttered). bagels. pretzels. dried and fresh fruits and vegetables. low-fat yogurt (frozen or regular). walnuts. or sunflower seeds. Of course, there are occasions when prudence takes a backseat. But as a routine. always keep the guidelines in mind when you eat or snack.

Alcoholic beverages are not prohibited in the Prudent Diet. They do not raise the blood cholesterol level. But nobody should habitually consume more than two beers. two glasses of wine. or two cocktails per day. Excessive intake of alcohol or any other high-calorie food or beverage contributes to body fat. Excess body fat does elevate the blood cholesterol level. Alcohol has nearly 80 percent as much energy per ounce as fat and nearly twice as much as the equivalent weight of protein or carbohydrate. Compare them:

Nutrient	Energy Value (cal./oz.)
Protein	140
Fat	310
Carbohydrate	130
Alcohol	240

We have good news and bad news about alcohol! There is evidence that moderate alcohol consumption will raise the level of HDL cholesterol. One martini or one or two glasses of wine can reduce our risk for atherosclerosis.

Perhaps that explains why the death rate from coronary artery disease in France is about one-fifth of that in the United States.

But heavy drinking can have serious consequences (which may explain why the death rate from cirrhosis of the liver is five times as high in France as in the United States). A little may be good, but a lot is not better. The key word with alcohol is moderation, but total abstinence may be necessary for persons (about 10 percent of Americans) at high risk for alcoholism (anyone with a strong family history for the disease or anyone who has been a "problem drinker" in the past). Also, be aware that any alcohol consumption may put women at increased risk for breast cancer and both men and women for cancer of the throat or esophagus.

The Prudent Diet is a suitable remedy for persons who may be somewhat overweight. It is low-calorie even if the portions you eat remain the same size as those you ate before. It is lower in fat. To illustrate, suppose your regular diet contained 2,800 cal and consisted of foods that contained 45 percent of the calories from fat. On the Prudent Diet, you have reduced your fat intake by 15 percent, or 420 cal, and increased your carbohydrate intake by 15 percent, or 200 cal. You have saved 220 cal per day without limiting the amount of food you eat. From another viewpoint, suppose you are of normal weight and don't need to lose. You can consume larger portions of the Prudent Diet, or you can have an extra low fat snack, or perhaps a glass or two of wine with dinner, a practice which might even reduce your risk for atherosclerosis. Thus, whether you are overweight or not, this diet has some advantages over the more traditional American diet.

Increasing Your Activity

So far we have considered the major way to reduce a high serum cholesterol level—consuming the low-total-fat, low-saturated-fat, low-trans-fatty acids, and low-cholesterol diet. Is there another means to increase our HDL-cholesterol level and, thereby, further lower our risk for atherosclerosis?

Probably the most important step we can take to raise our HDL-cholesterol level is to increase our activity. Several studies have shown that athletes, particularly those engaged in endurance sports, have higher HDL-cholesterol levels than comparable people not engaged in these sports. Some data suggest that individuals with low levels of HDL cholesterol can increase their HDL levels by engaging in such activities as walking, jogging, swimming, or bicycle riding. There is no question that cardiovascular fitness can be improved in any sedentary individual who undertakes an appropriate exercise program. Those of us who have low levels of HDL cholesterol can derive a double benefit from such a fitness program.

You may ask, "Even though my score is under five, will this kind of lifestyle change offer me insurance? Can it lower my risk for atherosclerosis even if only slightly?" There is no evidence that such insurance is of great value to anyone who is at low risk for atherosclerosis. But being at low risk for this disease should not inhibit us from making other dietary changes that might be more valuable—for example, a low-calorie diet if we are overweight, or a high-calcium diet if we are at risk for osteoporosis or brittle bones. We cannot generalize about individual cases. On the other hand, if all Americans were to emphasize low-fat, low-cholesterol foods, such a diet would become the norm rather than the exception. There is evidence that Americans are going in the right direction. The latest nutrition surveys indicate that we now consume 33 percent of our calories as fat, as opposed to 40 percent little more than a decade ago. However, Americans are now fatter than ever, primarily from lack of physical activity coupled with increased calories from snack foods. We are eating less fat, but we have become a nation of "couch potatoes"!

Hypertension

Hypertension (high blood pressure) results from narrowing of the blood vessels. Visualize a blood vessel as a flexible hose. When any liquid flows through the hose, the pressure within the hose can be increased by narrowing its inside diameter while forcing the same amount of liquid through it. The amount of blood within our system is relatively constant. Hence, if our arteries narrow either by contracting their muscular walls or as a result of some disease process, the blood pressure increases.

Our blood pressure is expressed in two values. The higher one is the systolic pressure and the lower one is the diastolic pressure. The normal value is around 120/80 when measured in the arm. Blood pressure is high when the systolic pressure reaches a level of 140 or above, or when the diastolic reaches 90 or more.

As it circulates throughout the body, the blood generates pressure within the arteries and veins. The heart initiates this pressure by forcing the blood out of its chambers, into the aorta (the main artery), and through its branches into the various tissues in the body. Blood pressure oscillates between a high and a low value, depending on whether the heart is contracting or relaxing. Contraction forces the blood into the arteries at maximum pressure. This is the systolic pressure. During the period of relaxation, while the heart is refilling with blood, the pressure within the arteries drops to a lower level. This is the diastolic pressure. Since contractions last for a short period, the arteries are exposed to the lower pressure most of the time. Thus, a high diastolic pressure is more dangerous than a high systolic pressure.

High blood pressure favors the deposition of cholesterol from the blood into the arterial wall. Hence, it is a primary cause of atherosclerosis (hardening of the arteries). In addition, high blood pressure can cause a ballooning (called an aneurysm) and a rupture of a blood vessel. This often happens in one of the smaller vessels leading to the brain, causing a cerebral hemorrhage or stroke.

Finally, prolonged hypertension can damage small vessels in the kidney, causing scarring in that organ—leading to kidney failure. Strain on the heart muscle can bring on heart failure, and damage to the small blood vessels in the back of the eye can cause other serious consequences.

There is no doubt that hypertension is a genetic disease. It is much more common in African-Americans than in whites, and it runs in families in both races. But genetics is only one part of the story. In the United States, blood pressure rises with age. Until recently, this rise was interpreted as a normal process of aging. The older a person was, the higher his blood pressure could be, and still be considered normal. In other countries, particularly among certain primitive societies such as Greenland Eskimos, Australian Aborigines, Polynesians, African Bushmen, and Native Americans, there is no rise in blood pressure with age. Moreover, high blood pressure is virtually nonexistent within these cultures. By contrast, the incidence of hypertension may be as high as 30 percent in the United States. In China and Japan, it is even higher.

While there are many cultural differences between the primitive societies mentioned above and the United States, China, or Japan, the distinction that causes high blood pressure is in the diet. There are, likewise, contrasting differences between the diets of the United States, China, and Japan. The one similarity relating to hypertension is that they are all high in salt.

A study involving a group of Samburu from northern Kenya illustrates the role of salt. Traditionally, these nomads consume a diet of meat and milk, which is low in sodium. The study followed a group of men drafted into the Kenyan army where the diet raised their sodium intake five-fold. During the second year of service, their blood pressure began to increase and continued to increase throughout their six years of service.

Knowledge of this relationship between high sodium intake and hypertension is not new. Before the advent of modern drug therapy, the only way to control high blood pressure was with a very low-salt diet. This approach is obsolete because of the restrictive nature of such a diet. Drugs to control hypertension are now safe and effective. Many of these drugs work by causing the body to eliminate more sodium through the kidneys, thus reducing the amount within the tissues and body fluids. Although the extremely low-salt diet necessary to treat hypertension is not practical in preventing the disease, moderate reduction may be an effective preventive measure in susceptible populations.

Sodium is essential for life. It is present in all cells and in all body fluids. The body must regulate the amount of sodium it contains. This regulation takes place primarily through the kidneys. When too little sodium is available, the kidney efficiently re-absorbs it, reducing the amount excreted. When too much sodium is available, the kidney filters it from the blood and passes it into the urine. Blood is filtered in the kidney through a small complex of arteries called the glomerulus. The higher the pressure in these arteries, the more efficient the filtration.

In order to filter properly, the kidney has a mechanism to raise and lower blood pressure. This involves the secretion of certain hormones, which cause the arterial walls to contract, thus increasing the pressure of the blood circulating through them. Presumably, a moderate increase in salt intake will invoke this mechanism in susceptible people. Once the arteries have been contracted for a long time, they become more fixed in that condition and will not relax as easily when salt intake is lowered. Thus, by how well the kidney regulates sodium through the hormonal response, our genes determine whether we are prone to hypertension. In some people, even mild increases in dietary sodium will evoke this response. Such people are susceptible to high blood pressure. In other people, even large amounts of dietary sodium can be handled by the kidney without any increase in blood pressures. Such people are resistant to hypertension. As the kidney gets older, its ability to filter becomes less efficient; therefore, it has to raise the blood pressure at lower and lower salt intakes. In a society such as ours, which consumes high quantities of sodium, blood pressure rises with age. By contrast, in societies where people consume small amounts of sodium, kidneys filter more efficiently, even in older people, without raising blood pressure.

A second dietary variable related to hypertension is the consistent consumption of too many calories, leading to obesity. The more overweight we are, the greater our chances for high blood pressure. This increased risk in overweight people is independent of the amount of sodium in their diet. Thus, at any given sodium intake, an obese person is more prone to hypertension than a lean individual. If you are susceptible to hypertension, stay lean if you are already thin. Lose weight if you are too heavy. The principles for losing weight or maintaining your ideal weight are discussed in "Obesity".

Animal studies have suggested that hypertension may involve low calcium intake. The American diet tends to be low in calcium, and our high-fat diet adversely affects absorption of calcium. There is already ample evidence that increasing the amount of dietary calcium may be beneficial. Prevention of hypertension may be one more important reason to improve our calcium intake. Low potassium intake, or loss of potassium due to diuretics such as excessive caffeine, is another factor in hypertension that should be considered. In some cases, particularly borderline hypertension, merely increasing the consumption of potassium rich fruits and vegetables may prevent high blood pressure. (See Table 7 for foods rich in potassium.)

Table 7. **Potassium Content of Common Foods**

Food	Size of serving	mgs per serving
Almonds	⅓ cup	345
Apple	1 medium	165
Apple juice	1 cup	250
Applesauce	½ cup	78
Artichoke	1 medium	307
Asparagus	⅔ cup	183
Avocado	½ lg.	200
Banana	1 medium	550
Beans, green	½ cup	355
Beans, lima	⅝ cup	422
Beans, baked	½ cup	416
Beef, hamburger	¼ lb.	382
Beef, live	¼ lb.	431
Beef, steak or roast	¼ lb.	309
Beer	12 oz	69
Blackberries	½ cup	173
Bred, white	1 slice	20
Bread, com	1 serving	71
Bread, whole wheat	1 slice	63
Bread, rye	1 slice	33
Broccoli, cooked	⅔ cup	390
Buttermilk	1 cup	388
Cabbage, coleslaw	½ cup	116
Cabbage, cooked	⅗ cup	163
Cake	1 slice	32
Cantaloupe	¼ medium	368
Carrots, raw	1 large	341

Food	Size of serving	mgs per serving
Cashews	½ cup	232
Celery, raw	1 med. stalk	170
Chard, cooked	³/₄ cup	321
Cheese, ched. or amer.	1 slice	23
Cheese, cottage	½ cup	72
Chicken	¼ bird	242
Clams, steamed	¼ lb.	540
Coffee	1 cup	82
Collards, cooked	½ cup	234
Cookies	2 med.	26
Corn, whole	½ cup	80
Cucumber, raw	1 medium	80
Dates	10 medium	648
Egg	1 medium	70
Figs	2 large	194
Fish, freshwater	¹/₃ lb.	384
Fish, saltwater	¹/₃ lb.	587
Grape juice	1 cup	250
Grapefruit juice	1 cup	310
Hot dog	1 average	110
Kale, cooked	¼ cup	221
Lamb	¼ lb.	246
Lettuce	3½ oz	264
Macaroni	½ cup	110
Milk, skimmed	1 cup	336
Nuts, mixed	½ cup	280
Oatmeal	½ cup	130
Orange	1 medium	300
Oysters	6 average	203
Pancakes, wheat	1 medium	45
Peach	1 medium	202
Peanut butter	3 tbs.	369
Pear	1 medium	260
Peas, green	²/₃ cup	196
Pie, fruit	1 piece	210

Food	Size of serving	mgs per serving
Pineapple	1 slice	123
Plums	2 medium2	99
Pork, ham	¼ lb.	260
Pork, roast	¼ lb.	298
Potato, baked	1 medium	755
Potato, mash.	½ cup	250
Prunes	4 medium	329
Raisins	¼ cup	271
Rice, white	1 cup	42
Rice, brown	1 cup	105
Salmon, canned	3½ oz.	361
Sardines, canned	3½ oz.	560
Soybeans, cooked	½ cup	440
Squash, cooked	½ cup	341
Strawberries	½ cup	123
Sunflower kernels	½ cup	460
Tomato juice	1 cup	556
Turkey	¼ lb.	320
Watermelon	1 wedge	600
Wine	3½ oz	145
Yogurt	1 cup	336

How do you know if you are at risk for high blood pressure?

First—Do you know what your blood pressure is? You should record it every year, preferably every six months. You don't need to see a physician for this. There are automated blood pressure instruments in many public places and many clinics will measure your blood pressure as a free service. Also, some of them sponsor annual "health fairs" where they offer free blood pressure screening tests. If your blood pressure is 120/80 or lower, it is normal. If the systolic pressure is over 140, or the diastolic pressure is over 90, you have high blood pressure and should seek medical advice. If your systolic reading is consistently between 120 and 140, or if your diastolic reading is between 85 and 90, you are at risk. Preventive measures are suggested.

Second—Are you overweight? If you are 10 percent overweight, your risk for hypertension is increased. Weight loss is suggested.

Third—Is there a family history of hypertension or a clear familial tendency toward higher blood pressure? Trace back as far as you can. Ask your relatives what they can remember. Did anyone in your family die of a stroke? If so, hypertension was probably the cause. How about heart attacks? Again, hypertension may have been involved. With this general information, a pattern may emerge. If this pattern strongly suggests that many members of your family have suffered from hypertension, you are at increased risk. If you are African-American, the pattern does not have to be a strong one. Because of the high prevalence of hypertension among African-Americans, having one or two family members with high blood pressure is enough to consider yourself at increased risk.

Fourth—What type of diet do you consume now? Are you a "saltaholic"? Do you habitually add salt when cooking? Do you use the salt shaker immediately before eating a meal? If this is your pattern, you are at increased risk even if none of the other risk aspects are evident.

Fifth—Do you live under excessive hostility and tension either at home or at work? Stress is known to raise blood pressure. The normal response to stress or fear or alarm in all animals is a rapid rise in blood pressure. When stress is constant, the blood pressure may stay elevated.

The major risk patterns for hypertension can be summarized as follows:

- A blood pressure that is creeping up being overweight.
- A family history of hypertension or a tendency to high blood pressure.
- A heavy salt habit.
- A Type A personality and excessive hostility and tension at home or at work.

By assigning a point value to each of these risk patterns, you can calculate your "hypertension score."

If your blood pressure is between 130 and 140 systolic and between 85 and 90 diastolic, score 5. If you are 10 percent above ideal weight, score 3; 20 percent or more, score 5. If you have a strong family history of hypertension, score 5; sporadic family history, score 3. If you are African-American, add three points. If you have a Type A personality that precipitates strong emotional responses, score 5; if you are unsure, score 1 to 4, depending on the likelihood (similar to the procedure you used for atherosclerosis). Finally, if you are an obvious saltaholic, score 3.

If your score is below 5, you are probably not susceptible to hypertension. However, you must remain alert to the possibility. Maintain your best body weight, continue using only moderate amounts of salt, and check your blood pressure regularly. If your score is 5 or above, you should initiate preventive measures. These measures involve changing your diet to reduce either your calories or your salt intake, or both.

A Diet for Preventing High Blood Pressure

If you are at high risk for developing hypertension, you should reduce your sodium intake. Since salt is by far the most abundant dietary source of sodium, you must begin by restricting your use of salt.

Keep the following principles in mind:

- Don't add salt at the table.
- Don't use extra salt in cooking.
- Don't eat smoked or pickled foods.
- Use processed (canned) foods with the least added salt. Avoid foods that are already high in salt.

You may not be able to accomplish these changes all at once. Some people may have acquired their taste for salt over many years. It may take months to reverse this habit. If you are at risk for hypertension, you should begin as soon as possible.

How much salt reduction is enough? Let's consider three levels of salt reduction: mild, moderate, and strict. Table 8 outlines the steps to be taken on each of these diets.

Table 8. Foods to Omit on a Sodium Restricted Diet

| Food | Level of Restriction | | |
	Mild	Moderate	Strict
Fruits	All forms are permitted (inlcuding fresh, frozen, canned, and dried).*		
Vegetables soups and vegetable juices	Omit pickled and dehydrated forms.	Limit canned to 2 servings daily.	Omit all canned and frozen if processed with salt. Omit all in Column 2.
Meats	Omit cold cuts, sausages, cured and pickled products.*		
Fish			
Poultry		Limit canned to 2 servings daily.	Omit all canned or frozen with salt.
Eggs			
Bread and grain	Omit salted crackers, pretzels, etc.*	Limit ready-to-eat and "quick products cooking" cereals, commercial breads, or baked products to 3 servings daily.	Omit all prepared with sodium.

Food	Level of Restriction		
	Mild	Moderate	Strict
Milk and dairy	Omit all cheeses and cheese spreads.*	Limit fluid milkproducts to 3 servings daily.	Omit all but low sodium products
Seasonings	Omit bouillon, dehydrated soups, and soy sauce* Limit salt to 1 tsp.	Limit salt to ¼ tsp. daily Omit catsup, mustard, commercial salad preparations, and seasoning salts.	Omit all salt, salted butter or margarine.

(*these items apply to all levels of restriction)

Strict sodium restriction is mainly for people who already have hypertension or some other medical condition requiring a very low-sodium diet. Others who should attempt to reach this kind of control are people with a hypertension score of 20 or more who are at further risk because they smoke or have high levels of serum lipids. Although there is no definitive evidence that such people need to reduce their salt intake to such low levels, clinical experience suggests that strict control of dietary sodium intake may be beneficial. If you fall into this category, it is worth a try. If you don't adhere to the strict diet, the closer you can come, the better.

For people with a score of 5 or more, moderate salt restriction is advisable. While it will require a change in eating habits, this is not as difficult as it might seem. Essentially it entails omitting dehydrated soups, bouillon, cold cuts, sausages, and other pickled or cured products, salted crackers, pretzels, cheese and cheese spreads, soy sauce, and seasonings such as catsup, mustard, commercial salad preparations, and seasoning salts. In addition, you should limit the amount of all canned vegetables, soups, and vegetable juices to two servings a week. The same is true for all canned meats, fish, poultry, and eggs. Also limit the amount of ready-to-eat quick-cooking cereals and commercial bread or baked products to three servings a day. Baking powders and sodium bicarbonate contribute a great deal of sodium to corn bread, biscuits, and other quick breads. (For home-baked products, you can substitute potassium bicarbonate, which may be obtained from your pharmacist.) Finally, limit the amount of milk and milk products to three servings per day, and use no more than one-fourth teaspoon of salt per day in seasoning all foods.

To begin your moderate salt restriction, take careful stock of what you are eating. It is helpful to record everything you eat for a week. Examine your record. Where does it differ from the desired pattern of moderate salt restriction? Are you adding more than one-fourth teaspoon of salt to your food? If so, cut back, even if you have to do it gradually. Are you eating too many canned goods? This is a common source of excessive sodium intake. Many food processors add large amounts of salt to their products. A few years ago, your only alternative was to avoid eating canned goods by using frozen or fresh produce. Today, another alternative is becoming more and more practical—the use of canned products that contain no added salt. Read the label! When given a choice of two brands of vegetables or soup, choose the one without added salt. Manufacturers are becoming more aware of the high salt content of our food and are learning that it is good business to have a low-salt alternative. By choosing wisely, we can maintain our usual food pattern and still gain considerable protection against high blood pressure.

Besides the precautions noted above, it is useful to know which foods are naturally high or low in sodium. Table 9 lists vegetables that are high in sodium, and Table 10 lists foods permitted at any level of restriction.

Table 9. **Vegetables Naturally High in Sodium**

Artichokes	Celery flakes	Mustard greens
Beet greens	Chard	Parsley flakes
Carrots	Dandelion greens	Spinach
Celery	Kale	Whole hominy
		White turnips

Table 10. **Foods with Insignificant Amounts of Sodium**

Grains	Wheat, oats, rye, rice, barley, and their products (e.g., pasta, yeast breads, flours, uncooked cereals)
Vegetables All those not in Table 8 or canned, frozen salt free	
Fruits	All fresh canned fruits and juices
Meats	All fresh or frozen/canned without salt beef, lamb, pork, veal, poultry, fish, shellfish, and game meats
Eggs	All fresh
Fats	All vegetable oils and shortenings, lard, and unsalted butter and margarine Condiments Vinegar, all spices, mustard powder, flavorings (without added salt)
Sweeteners Sugar, honey, syrup, jellies, molasses Beverages	Alcoholic beverages, coffee, teas, soft drinks

An adult diet balanced in the essential nutrients includes at least the following daily servings:

Dairy foods (milk, yogurt, unsalted cheese)	2
Protein foods (meats, poultry, fish, eggs, beans)	2
Fruits	4
Vegetables	3
Breads, cereals, pastas, and rice	6

With meals prepared at home, limit salt to one-fourth teaspoon per day and select the appropriate foods in Tables 9 and 10. The following meal suggestions apply to a moderate sodium restriction:

Breakfast
Juice or grapefruit
Egg, egg whites or unsalted cottage cheese, whole wheat toast
Unsalted butter or margarine
Cooked cereal (prepared without salt), milk (whole or skim), tea, or coffee

A Brown Bag Lunch
Sliced chicken, lettuce, tomato, alfalfa sprouts on whole wheat bread
Raisins and nuts (unsalted)
Apple
Canned fruit juice, coffee, tea, or milk

A Short Order Lunch
Hamburger on whole wheat bun with lettuce and tomato, tossed salad
Vinegar and/or oil (not salad dressing), soda or flavored milk, fruit gelatin

A Dieter's Lunch
Unsalted wafers or sandwich bread
Hearty tossed salad (with everything except diced cheese and assorted canned vegetables such as those served at salad

bars) with vinegar and/or oil (as above)
Melon half with unsalted cottage cheese
Fruit juice, coffee, tea, skim milk (limit use of sodium based
artificial sweeteners to 2 packets per day)

Evening Meal
Broiled codfish
Broccoli with lemon sauce
Saffron rice (homemade without salt), Dinner roll
Unsalted butter or margarine, tossed salad
Fruit compote
Coffee, tea, or milk

Enhance the variety of your menu at home by making your own mayonnaise and salad dressing. For entertaining, try some of the following items:

Dips
Using yogurt as a base, stir in curry powder or black pepper, dill and black pepper, onion and garlic powder (not garlic salt).

Dippers
Cherry tomatoes
Cold diced cooked white potatoes, fresh bean sprouts
Sliced green peppers, sliced carrots, zucchini slices, sliced celery, etc.
Wafers, unsalted crackers, bite-sized sandwich bread, pita bread
Gourmet favorites, such as stuffed mushrooms, pastry puffs, escargots (snails), steamed seafood, meat balls and aspics should be prepared without salt.

Experiment with such spices as coriander, cumin, fennel, ginger, and others you have never tried. For fancy occasions, convert your favorite recipes to salt-free versions.

For dining out, patronize restaurants that cook to order and prepare fresh vegetables. You will have more control over the amount of sodium in your food. Asian-American restaurants use soy sauce, monosodium glutamate, and other pickled items. Their meals are inescapably high in sodium. Seafood and steak houses may be good choices if you can ensure that salt is left out during preparation of your food. Salads and baked potatoes, which usually accompany entrees, are safe if you forgo most dressings and sauces. Fast-food chains and other establishments that serve deep-fried foods usually add a lot of salt to their products. Here again, a boiled or broiled version of the same food is a better choice.

A mild sodium-restricted diet simply omits pickled and dehydrated vegetables, cold cuts, sausages, and cured or pickled meat and fish products; salted crackers, pretzels, and other snacks; cheese and cheese spreads; bouillon, dehydrated soups, and soy sauce. It limits any additional salt to one teaspoon. Such a regimen is suggested even if you have only one risk. Thus, anyone with a strong family history of hypertension, or who is obese, should use this diet. In addition, if you have independent risks for atherosclerosis such as high serum lipids, or if you are a cigarette smoker, you should use this diet even if your hypertension score is below 5.

For those with scores below 5 and no risks for atherosclerosis, the American diet is probably still too high in salt. Although there is no real evidence that any dietary change is necessary for this group, if you are an excessive salt user, you cook with a lot of salt, and salt your food before tasting it, it would be prudent to use the salt shaker more sparingly. Since we do not know all the causes of high blood pressure, you may be prone to this disease even without any of the known risks. A high salt intake can only worsen your chance. Although modifying your diet is very important, if your total hypertension score is too high, you should also pay attention to other life practices that may contribute to your risk.

Personality is very important. If you have a Type A profile, complicated by environmental stress and nagging anger, try to modify your behavior. Rest, meditation, and exercise are valuable tension relievers. People relax in different ways. Find the way that works for you and that can be applied regularly. This is particularly true if you have any of the other risks for high blood pressure. Watching your diet while continuing to live in a pressure cooker isn't enough. High blood pressure is the silent killer! You don't feel it. Uncontrolled, it can attack with little warning. For yourself, and in consideration of your family, take all the necessary steps to prevent this disease!

Obesity

There are two primary reasons why obesity is a major health problem in the United States. First, it increases a person's risk for some of the most serious diseases that afflict our society. Second, it can impair our quality of life, even without any of these diseases. Obesity is risky because of what it does and because of what it leads to. In this chapter, we will discuss prevention and treatment of this disorder. Proper diet is a cornerstone of both. But before we discuss either prevention or treatment, it is very important that we understand what obesity is, how it develops, and why it is dangerous.

Obesity is not simply being overweight. An obese individual is a person whose body contains too much fat. The 280-pound linebacker for the Dallas Cowboys is not obese; nor is the gold medalist in the women's Olympic shot-put competition; nor is the well-conditioned heavyweight boxer. These people may be overweight, but their excess weight is in the form of muscle tissue. For most of us, overweight means too much fat.

The simplest way of judging whether you have an excess of fat in your body is to examine your weight relative to height. Are you too heavy for your height and body build? Table 11, adapted from Metropolitan Life Insurance data, shows the ideal body weights for both men and women of a given height and body build. This table was constructed from actuarial data. Although we cannot say that these are necessarily the best numbers for you, they serve as a good general guide.

As any population begins to exceed ideal weight, the lifespan of that population starts to decrease. If you weigh 10 percent above your ideal weight, you are bordering on obesity. A figure of 20 percent above your ideal weight means definite obesity. If your weight is between those ranges, you are in the caution zone. If you are obese, you are at risk of shortening your lifespan.

If you are not sure that your overweight means too much fat, there are sophisticated ways of determining the amount of fat in your body. One of these methods employs skin calipers to measure the thickness of the fat layer on your arms or back. The skin-caliper is useful in differentiating the very muscular individual from the person who is equally overweight because of too much fat tissue. This method is also valuable in following the course of weight gain in infants and children. It can pick up small deviations that may be early warning signals for impending obesity. However, for most of us, special techniques like these are not necessary. Ten to twenty percent above ideal weight means danger. More than twenty percent means obesity—too much fat in our body.

Table 11. The Metropolitan Height & Weight Table

Women

Height		Small Frame	Medium Frame	Large Frame
ft.	in.			
4	10	102-111	109-121	118-131
4	11	103-113	111-123	120-134
5	0	104-115	113-126	122-137
5	1	106-118	115-129	125-140
5	2	108-121	118-132	128-143
5	3	111-124	121-135	131-147

5	4	114-127	124-138	134-15
5	5	117-130	127-141	137-155
5	6	120-133	130-144	140-159
5	7	123-136	133-147	143-163
5	8	126-139	136-150	146-167
5	9	129-142	139-153	149-170
5	10	132-145	142-156	152-173
5	11	135-148	145-159	155-176
6	0	138-151	148-162	158-179

Men

Height		Small Frame	Medium Frame	Large Frame
ft.	*in.*			
5	2	128-134	131-141	138-150
5	3	130-136	133-143	140-153
5	4	132-138	135-145	142-156
5	5	134-140	137-148	144-160
5	6	136-142	139-151	146-164
5	7	138-145	142-154	149-168
5	8	140-148	145-157	152-172
5	9	142-151	148-160	155-176
5	10	144-151	151-163	158-180
5	11	146-157	154-166	161-184
6	0	149-160	157-170	164-188
6	1	152-164	160-174	168-192
6	2	155-158	164-174	172-197
6	3	158-172	167-182	176-202
6	4	162-176	171-187	181-207

Although obesity simply means too much body fat, the nature of that obesity may vary, depending on how that fat is stored in our bodies. Like any other tissue, fat or adipose tissue is composed of hundreds of millions of cells (adipocytes or fat cells), each of which contains a droplet of fat within its walls. When the body burns more fat, the droplets shrink. When the body needs to store more fat, the droplets swell. In some obese persons, fat cells are swollen to three or four times their normal size. Thus, one way to become obese is to expand our fat cells. A second way in which the body can deposit excess fat is by creating more fat cells. If you are obese, your body contains too much fat. This fat may be packaged in different ways. You may have a normal number of fat cells, each swollen with an excess of fat and, therefore, too large. You may have too many fat cells, each containing a normal amount of fat and hence of normal size. Or you may be obese as a result of an excess number of fat cells, each of which is too large.

It is important that we understand the differences between these types of obesity. The nature of the obesity may determine the success or failure of treatment. Weight reduction is accomplished by shrinkage in fat cell size and not by a reduction of fat cell number. If you have excess fat cells, you will always have too many fat cells, no matter how much dieting you do. For example, let us suppose a person has twice as many fat cells as normal and that each cell contains just the right amount of fat. Such a person would be quite obese. His or her body would contain twice as much total fat as it should. For that individual to achieve normal weight, half of the fat from each cell would have to be burned. Thus, the fat cells would shrink to half their normal size. The fat tissue of this person, who has painfully dieted down to ideal weight, would appear more abnormal than when he or she was obese. There would be too many fat cells which are now too small as well. The body somehow senses this double abnormality and struggles to rectify it by filling "depleted" fat cells with more fat. For this reason, it is very difficult for a person whose obesity is due to too many fat cells (hyperplastic obesity) to lose weight. It is even more difficult for that individual to maintain the weight loss.

By contrast, let us examine the obese individual who has a normal number of fat cells, each containing twice as much fat as it should. The fat cells shrink as this person loses weight. When ideal weight is attained, the fat cells return to their normal size. This person's weight is normal. He or she has fat tissue composed of a normal number of normal-sized fat cells. This condition, with normal fat cells, is therefore much easier to maintain. Since the most dangerous form of obesity is characterized by an increased number of fat cells, it is fair to ask how this happens.

Most tissues of the body increase their cell number only during the early phases of their growing period (from fetal life through early childhood). Adipose tissue also adds new cells early in life. The period during which this can occur extends from before birth to the end of adolescence. Thus, the person who first became obese as an adult will simply have enlarged the size of already existing fat cells. By contrast, obesity beginning any time during childhood incorporates an increased number of those cells. This is why childhood obesity is particularly serious. It almost invariably leads to adult obesity, usually the kind that is very intractable. The causes of childhood obesity are very similar to those of adult obesity. The consequences, however, may be quite different.

Fat is deposited when the energy from the food we eat is greater than the energy expended to keep our body functioning at rest and during exercise. It seems simple enough. Energy in equals energy out plus fat. The person who is fat consumes more energy than he expends. For years, however, people have interpreted this to mean that the obese person consumes more food or exercises less than the lean person. This may be true for a few obese people but, for the vast majority, it is not. They simply do not eat more than lean people, and while they may exercise less, many will have exercise patterns similar to those of their lean counterparts but still gain weight or remain obese. Some basic experiments dramatized this paradox.

Some obese volunteers spent several weeks in specially constructed rooms in which the amount of energy expended by all forms of exercise could be measured. One obese female patient gained weight. Yet, she was given the same number of calories necessary for a lean woman to maintain her weight, and she burned the same number of calories by physical exercise. To reduce, she needed to lower her caloric intake to levels below that necessary for the leaner woman to lose weight. Even more impressive was that a person weighing 250 lbs, but whose ideal weight was 150 lbs, first reduced to that weight and then stayed in the type of room described above. In an adjoining room was a woman who was always at her ideal weight of 150 lbs. Both women received the same number of calories daily. Both did the same daily exercises and measurements showed that both expended the same amount of energy doing the exercises. Yet, over the course of several weeks, the formerly obese woman gained significant weight; whereas, the woman who had been lean all her life remained the same.

Why obese and lean people respond differently is now understood. Most of the energy in our food is expended to keep our complex body machinery running. Energy is used in every heartbeat, in every breath we take, in the contraction of our stomachs, in the functioning of our kidneys, etc. It is also used to maintain our body temperature at 98.6°F. The amount of energy necessary for all these functions varies from person to person. Some people are much more efficient than others. When food is scarce, the people who use energy most efficiently have an advantage. Their bodies run smoothly on fewer calories. They will survive longer periods of famine than their neighbors will. Thus, as the human race evolved in a world constantly plagued by food shortages, the more efficient calorie converters were favored to survive by the process of natural selection.

Obesity is not a punishment for gluttony but a "reward" for efficiency. The abundance of food in modern Western societies is a disadvantage for the efficient calorie converter. At any given level of intake, such an individual requires fewer calories to run his metabolic processes, and he rapidly develops a calorie surplus that his body converts to fat. The obese individual handles calories more efficiently than the lean one who can eat seemingly unlimited calories and not gain weight. With our abundance, inefficiency is rewarded.

One observation that has provoked a great deal of speculation is the existence of a thermogenic organ known as brown fat. This organ converts food energy into heat energy. It is very pronounced in hibernating animals, which explains why they can stay warm without any physical activity and without shivering in the cold. In rodents, brown fat can increase energy expenditure by as much as 200 percent. It is not as pronounced in humans. Yet, our 2 oz of brown fat can increase our energy expenditure by nearly 25 percent. This explains why babies can stay warm without putting on clothes, lighting fires, or shivering. We lose most of our brown fat at around thirty years of age. Is it a coincidence that this is when we start putting on our "middle-age spread"? Do some people retain their 2 oz of brown fat longer than others? We don't have the answers.

There are three ways to lose weight: reduce the number of calories to such an extent that even an efficient metabolism is starved; change the metabolic rate to become less efficient; or increase the amount of physical exercise to burn off the excess fat. In practice, only the first and last alternatives are available. There are no good methods for making our bodies waste calories. Certain drugs do this either temporarily or permanently, but they have serious side effects. Various diets have been advocated to waste calories, or change the metabolic rate, but some of these diets may be dangerous. If you try one of the unbalanced regimes, consider yourself a "human guinea pig." There are some studies on low carbohydrate diets, for example, that show promise for quick weight loss, but the long-term consequences are not known. Until we devise a safe method for altering an obese person's metabolism, the only way to lose weight is to consume fewer calories, exercise more, or (preferably) both. Neither of these options is easy for obese people. Some will have to consume fewer than 1,500 cal per day to keep from gaining weight, even if they exercise quite vigorously every day. It is not surprising that most reducing diets fail to achieve and maintain ideal weight.

The Causes of Obesity

Like most nutritionally related diseases, obesity has several causes. There is a genetic component, which we are just beginning to understand. Other components are related to lifestyle. The person with a genetic predisposition to obesity becomes obese because of his or her way of life.

Obesity runs in families. If one parent is obese, the chances of a child being obese are about 30 percent. The chances increase to over 60 percent if both parents are obese. These statistics alone, however, do not prove that obesity is in any way a genetic disease. Obese parents may simply tend to overfeed their children. In fact, a study published several years ago in an attempt to "disprove" the genetic theory of obesity suggested a prediction that not only would obese parents have obese children, but that the family dog, too, would be obese.

Accurate studies have revealed more directly the importance of genetics in obesity. For example, identical twins raised in different foster homes tended to conform to the same body type regardless of whether the foster parents were obese. Thus, if one twin was fat, the other was fat. If one was lean, the other also was lean. The genetic similarity between identical twins was so close that it overrode all the contributions of the children's different environments. By contrast, as the genetic similarity became less close (fraternal twins or siblings), the environmental effect was more noticeable. The children began to assume the body type of the rest of the family in which they were raised. From these observations, we can deduce that two factors contribute to the high incidence of obesity in children of obese parents. One is the child's genetic background. The other is the environment in which the child grows up.

Animal studies suggest the nature of one type of genetic abnormality. Several strains of laboratory rats and mice are genetically obese. In some of these strains, the type of obesity resembles that in humans. The animals formed too many fat cells early in life. Later, the fat cells swelled. Careful evaluations showed that beginning at about two weeks of age, the rate of replication of fat cells is faster than normal. Thus, genetically obese animals lay down more fat cells because the fat cells replicate themselves too quickly. However, this is not the only reason these animals wind up with an enormous excess of fat cells. In normal rats, fat cells stop dividing by one month of age. In genetically obese animals, fat-cell division continues until they are at least six months of age. The genetic abnormality lies in both the speed at which the fat cells divide and the length of time they continue to divide.

If we can draw an analogy to humans, it means that division of fat cells continues beyond adolescence in genetically susceptible persons. This has enormous implications for both prevention and treatment. Until recently, we believed that if we could prevent obesity in childhood, we would be able to eliminate the kind of obesity in which fat-cell numbers increased. We now know that this may not be true in all genetically prone people. In such people, preventing the creation of too many fat cells may require special precautions through middle adult life. Another aspect of this phenomenon involves the differences between men and women. It appears that women may increase their number of fat cells during pregnancy. With multiple pregnancies, this can result in cumulative growth in fat cell numbers.

While cellular abnormality may be the genetic weakness in some obese people, the genetic factor is probably quite different in most of us. As we have seen, some people are more efficient in the way they handle calories. They inherited this increased efficiency from their parents and it puts them at increased risk for obesity. The more efficient we are, the higher our risk.

The number of calories that constitutes an excess varies from person to person. Thus, our risk for obesity depends on our metabolic efficiency and how many calories we consume. Our efficiency, as far as we know, is genetically determined. By contrast, the calories we consume are largely a function of our lifestyle, and therefore under our own control.

If we agree that the amount of fat we gain depends on the number of calories we consume minus the number of calories we expend on metabolic processes and on physical exercise, then the way we can reduce that fat is to reduce the calories we ingest, or increase the amount of our exercise (or both). This means that we must alter our lifestyle—sometimes radically!

The number of calories a person consumes depends on the amount and the kinds of food he or she eats. However, the quantity and quality of our diets are influenced by a great number of additional factors—appetite, culture, religion, ethnicity, social customs, and many others. Therefore, while it is easy to agree that calorie control is the cornerstone of any program to prevent or treat obesity, limiting the number of calories we consume may be very difficult.

Let us begin with appetite. Some people appear to be hungry all the time. Others consume tiny amounts of food and have to force themselves to do that. Appetite is controlled by a center in our brains called the hypothalamus. That center is divided into two areas, one that stimulates appetite and another that inhibits it. In addition, when one of these areas is turned on, it turns the other off. Thus, a control mechanism within our brains can make us eat more or less. In animals, destroying the appetite-stimulating area of the hypothalamus will cause the animal to starve itself to death in the presence of an abundance of food. By contrast, destroying the appetite-inhibiting area causes the animal to eat enormous amounts of food and rapidly become obese. There are people with tumors of the hypothalamus that have affected their appetite regulation so that they have become morbidly obese. Their obesity is cured when the tumors are removed.

A network of nerve connections from other parts of the brain influences both the appetite-stimulating and appetite-inhibiting areas of the hypothalamus. These nerves can be activated by "cues" from outside the body (external cues) or from inside the body (internal cues). In other words, our appetite can be stimulated or inhibited by what we see, what we smell, or what we taste (all external cues). It can also be aroused by contractions in our gastrointestinal tract or even by the thought of a delicious meal (both internal cues).

There is a natural substance (ghrelin) that carries messages between the brain and the digestive system. Secreted by specialized cells in the stomach and the upper part of the small intestine, it acts on the brain. Ghrelin levels in the blood spike before meals and drop afterward. People given ghrelin injections felt voraciously hungry and, when turned loose at a buffet, ate 30 percent more than they normally would.

Dieters who lose weight and then try to keep it off make more ghrelin than they did before dieting, as if their bodies are fighting to regain the lost fat. By contrast, very obese people who have an operation called gastric bypass to lose weight wind up with relatively little ghrelin, which may help explain why their appetites decrease markedly after the surgery.

Leptin, an appetite suppressant made by fat cells and once thought to have great promise as a treatment for obesity, has turned out to be a disappointment because most overweight people are resistant to its effects.

Because it occurs outside the brain, ghrelin may be a relatively easy target for scientists looking for ways to manipulate weight.

Indeed, you may think that we already have a "safe" medication for obesity, and it is true that some of the worst hazards of "diet pills" have been reduced or eliminated with the introduction of some drugs now available by prescription. These prescription drugs act much like amphetamines but are not nearly so addictive, and they do not seem to have as much danger of the severe mind-altering effects of amphetamines. But they introduced a new hazard (pulmonary hypertension) which does not threaten everybody who takes them but is often fatal to those who are afflicted with this drug-induced disorder. Also, the drugs do not "cure" obesity. People who take them usually gain the weight back when they discontinue the drugs, and even if drugs do succeed in eliminating the need for "reducing" diets, our need for nutritional balance in what we eat will still be there.

If we could control our hypothalamus, we would have a powerful weapon for combating obesity. We are beginning to understand how this complex area of the brain works. However, we have not reached the stage where we can safely alter hypothalamic function in obese people. We do know that the function of the hypothalamus, and, hence, control of appetite, differs between obese and lean people. A dramatic example comes from a series of studies in which obese and lean subjects received all their food in liquid form. The supply of this liquid was kept in a refrigerator that had a drinking tube protruding through one of its walls. Whenever the person was hungry, he or she drank as much as desired. The amount consumed was registered electronically in another room.

After a few days, each person reached a constant caloric intake. Not surprisingly, the obese subjects did not consume very many more calories than the lean subjects did. After a few days at this intake level, the calorie content of the liquid diet was cut in half while its taste and consistency remained the same. The subjects were unaware of the change. Lean subjects almost immediately began to consume almost twice as much of the liquid diet. By contrast, obese participants continued to consume roughly the same quantity as before. In a lean subject, the number of calories being offered was somehow communicated to the hypothalamus, which by regulating the appetite centers was able to control the amount of food intake. For an obese individual, there seemed to be another kind of control. Either this type of feeding regimen did not influence the hypothalamus or the volume of liquid was governing the food intake.

Another series of studies was devised to differentiate between these two possibilities. Lean and obese subjects were given access to unlimited quantities of food in a smorgasbord fashion. Again, over a few days, both lean and obese subjects reached a constant intake. In this experiment, however, the obese individuals did tend to take in more food than the lean ones—but not enough to account for the obesity. Then a sugar substitute was incorporated into the foods to reduce their caloric content. Again, the subjects were unaware of the change. The lean subjects, as before, increased their food intake enough to reach the caloric level they had previously been consuming. The obese subjects changed their eating patterns very little. In addition, since a great variety of foods was available and all the subjects had free choice, markedly different volumes were consumed by subjects in both groups.

There was no relationship between the amount of food consumed and the change in appetite that occurred when the caloric content changed. Again, the lean individuals were responding to an internal cue sent to the brain in response to the number of calories in the diet. By contrast, the obese subjects were not responding either to the caloric content of the food or to the volume consumed. Experiments such as these have led us to believe that the food intake of obese individuals is regulated more by external cues than by internal cues. Or, simply, lean individuals eat when they are hungry. Obese individuals are more likely to eat out of habit—when they are bored, when they are nervous, when they watch television, and so forth. The eating pattern of an obese individual, then, is much more sensitive to certain lifestyle components not usually associated with diet. It is not yet clear which came first, the obesity or the altered response of the hypothalamus. Do obese people respond more to external cues because they are obese? Or do people who respond more to external cues tend to become obese?

One external cue that we have assumed for years to be much more sensitive in obese people is their preference for sweet-tasting foods. Obese individuals were said to have a "sweet tooth," and this sweet tooth was thought to be largely responsible for their obesity. Controlled studies show that neither of these statements is valid. Obese adults given a series of liquid solutions of increasing sweetness preferred the less sweet solutions. Their lean counterparts did not. This preference persisted even after weight reduction. In obese adolescents, the results were somewhat different. They also preferred less sweet solutions, but after weight reduction, their preference was the same as in the lean subjects. Thus, obese individuals, if anything, have less of a sweet tooth than lean people. Even after losing weight, they show no increased preference for sweet foods.

Other data suggest that obese subjects do prefer fat in their diets. This preference may persist after weight reduction. Since fat contains more than twice as many calories per gram as either carbohydrates or protein, this suggestion could be very important. Reducing diets low in fat may be particularly difficult for obese people to maintain. Since low fat is a cornerstone of most sensible reducing diets, and since Americans consume a high-fat diet, which also increases their risk for certain other serious diseases, the challenge may be in determining how to reduce the fat in an obese person's diet without destroying his or her incentive to continue that diet.

One approach that has had perhaps more success than any other in achieving lasting weight reduction has been behavior modification. This method uses the premise that by altering our behavior, we can minimize our exposure to the external cues that stimulate our appetite center. As important as appetite is, it alone does not control the number of calories we consume. People do not eat simply because they are hungry. They also eat and drink for social reasons. Almost no social occasion is observed without some kind of food or beverage. These are often very high in calories.

Even more important is the kind of foods consumed at regular meals. This will vary with a person's ethnic background, family customs, and many other factors. Italians eat quite differently from the Japanese. And, even after several generations in the United States, many ethnic differences remain. Religious practices such as keeping kosher or eating no meat carry with them certain obvious nutritional implications. Often the kind of foods eaten will determine the number of calories consumed. Seventh Day Adventists are almost always on a low-calorie diet. Eastern European Jews often eat more fat and, hence, have a higher calorie diet than do Asian-Americans. Therefore, any weight reduction program must take into account that person's eating habits. There is no sense in trying a diet that consists of foods that you will not be able to incorporate into your way of life. Even if you can stay on such a diet long enough to lose some weight, you will gain it back as soon as you resume your previous eating habits.

Physical exercise will affect our weight in two ways. First, exercise burns calories directly. Second, exercise, in some manner, causes the body to consume more energy than can be accounted for by the amount of physical work. Whether certain exercises cause the body to become less "efficient" in handling calories is still unclear. We do believe that this is an important mechanism by which exercise aids in weight reduction.

A pound of body fat contains about 3,500 cal. To lose one pound of fat, you must burn 3,500 cal more than you eat. If you burn 500 cal more a day than you eat, you will lose one pound of fat a week. Thus, if you normally burn 1,700 cal a day and you stick to a 1,200-cal-per-day diet, you can theoretically expect to lose a pound of fat each week. When you begin a weight reduction diet, you may at first lose weight somewhat faster, primarily because of loss of water.

Alternatively, you may continue to eat the same number of cal (1,700 cal in the example given above) and burn 500 cal more a day by increasing your exercise. Or, better yet, you may lose weight by combining both exercise and reduced caloric intake. To determine how you can lose one pound per week, first decide what is your ideal weight (from Table 11, for example), estimate your activity level, and then subtract 500 cal from the corresponding calorie level in Table 12.

Table 12: **Ideal Caloric Level Based on Desirable Weight, Activity Level, sod Sex**

Desirable Weight	Sex	Activity Level				
		Very Sedentary	Sedentary	Active	Moderately Active	Super Active
90	M	1170	1260	1350	1440	1530
	F	1053	1134	1215	1296	1377
95	M	1235	1330	1425	1520	1615
	F	1111	1197	1282	1368	1453
100	M	1300	1400	1500	1600	1700
	F	1170	1260	1350	1440	1530
105	M	1365	1470	1575	1680	1785
	F	1228	1323	1417	1512	1606
110	M	1430	1540	1650	1760	1870
	F	1287	1386	1485	1584	1683
115	M	1495	1610	1725	1840	1955
	F	1345	1449	1552	1656	1759
120	M	1560	1680	1800	1920	2040
	F	1404	1512	1620	1728	1836
125	M	1625	1750	1875	2000	2125
	F	1462	1575	1687	1800	1912
130	M	1690	1820	1950	2080	2210
	F	1521	1638	1755	1872	1989
135	M	1755	1890	2025	2160	2295
	F	1579	1701	1822	1944	2065
140	M	1820	1960	2100	2240	2380
	F	1638	1764	1890	2016	2142
145	M	1885	2030	2175	2320	2465
	F	1696	1827	1957	2088	2218

150	M	1950	2100	2250	2400	2550
	F	1755	1890	2025	2160	2295
155	M	2015	2170	2325	2480	2635
	F	1813	1953	2092	2232	2371
160	M	2080	2240	2400	2560	2720
	F	1872	2016	2160	2304	2448
165	M	2145	2310	2475	2640	2805
	F	1930	2079	2227	2376	2524
170	M	2210	2380	2550	2720	2890
	F	1989	2142	2295	2448	2601
175	M	2275	2450	2625	2800	2975
	F	2047	2205	2362	2520	2677
180	M	2340	2520	2700	2880	3060
	F	2106	2268	2430	2592	2754
185	M	2405	2590	2775	2960	3145
	F	2164	2331	2497	2664	2830
190	M	2470	2660	2850	3040	3230
	F	2223	2394	2565	2736	2907

Activity levels are defined as follows:

- *Very Sedentary:* Limited activity, confined to a few rooms or a house. Slow walking, no running. Most major activities involve sitting.

- *Sedentary:* Activities involve mostly walking or some sporadic slow running at a jogging speed of approximately ten minutes per mile. Recreational activities include bowling, fishing, target shooting, horseback riding, motor boating, snowmobiling, or other similar activities. Less than ten minutes of continuous running (faster than a jog) per week.

- *Moderately Active:* Activities include golf (eighteen holes), doubles tennis, sailing, pleasure swimming or skating, aerobic dancing, Jazzercise, downhill skiing, or other similar activities. Between ten and twenty minutes of continuous running at least three times per week.

- *Active:* More than twenty minutes of sustained activity such as jogging, swimming, competitive tennis, or cross-country skiing more than three times per week, or more than forty-five minutes of recreational tennis, paddle ball, or other activities at least three times per week.

- *Super Active:* At least one and a half hour of vigorous activity (training for competitive athletics, full-court basketball, mountain climbing, weight training, football, wrestling, or other similar activity) four days per week or more than two and a half hours of recreational activity four or more times per week.

To summarize, obesity occurs when the body is taking in more energy than it is expending. This condition can occur in anyone consuming enough calories. In most obese individuals, however, it occurs at caloric intakes that are not greater than the caloric intakes of lean individuals. The obese person may handle calories more efficiently. Hence, at the same caloric intake as a lean person, he or she will have an excess that becomes fat! To treat obesity, we must reduce the number of calories consumed or increase the amount of physical exercise (or both). As yet, we are unable to alter the body's metabolism safely to make it a less efficient calorie converter.

Thus, the treatment of obesity does not really get at the core of the problem. In order to reduce caloric intake we must decrease an appetite that may be perfectly normal. This is not an easy task. We must try to alter the pattern of food intake and the kind of foods eaten; a system that may be deeply rooted in religion, ethnicity, and family background. Finally, we can increase the amount of exercise. This approach is an excellent one in the prevention of obesity but of limited use in its treatment.

Is it any wonder that more people are cured of even the most malignant type of cancer than are permanently cured of obesity? What happens then to those people not cured of obesity? Is it worth the effort a person must go through? Is our society too concerned about being overweight? Is the billion-dollar-a-year diet industry producing any effect on our health?

The Consequences of Obesity

In order to answer these questions, let us examine the health consequences of obesity:

1. Obesity increases our chances for developing three of the major risk factors for atherosclerosis: high blood pressure, high blood levels of cholesterol, and diabetes. In addition, obesity directly increases our risk for gallbladder disease and for certain forms of cancer. Thus, obesity can lead to premature death—directly and indirectly.

2. Obesity by itself can cause health liabilities such as shortness of breath, sleep apnea, increased risk for any surgical procedure, and a greater propensity for certain kinds of accidents.

3. Obesity will result in major restrictions on a person's living habits and interfere with the quality of life. The obese individual is a member of an oppressed minority. He or she is often viewed by society as deformed through his or her own gluttony.

It is ironic that the third problem, which in many ways is the most serious an obese person faces, is not his or her fault but that of the society in which he or she lives. In Polynesia, if you are obese, you are worth your weight in gold. In the United States, at best, society pities you. As we shall see, the health risks attributed to overweight, while real, are minimal for most people.

If only those people who are truly obese and at increased risk for major health problems were to undertake serious weight reduction schemes, a billion-dollar diet industry would shrink to nothing and book publishers would be in financial trouble. Let us therefore examine obesity as a major health risk.

We have already defined obesity as 20 percent above our ideal weight. In this section, we are not discussing the person who is 5, 10, 15, or even 20 lbs overweight. If you should weigh 150 lbs, you are obese at 180 lbs. If you should weigh 180 lbs, you are obese if you weigh 216 lbs.

There is no evidence that people who are overweight but not obese are at any significantly increased risk for any of the major diseases listed above. Your ideal weight is the weight that offers you the greatest longevity. Statistically, the risk curve rises sharply only after we are well into the obesity range. For practical purposes, then, you should be concerned about overweight potentially shortening your life when you approach the obesity range. If you are 10 to 20 percent above ideal weight, you are in a caution zone. If you are in this zone, you do not necessarily need to lose weight. It is much more important that you don't gain any more weight. A person who is 10 percent above ideal weight and has been that way for ten years may need only to keep careful watch on his or her weight. By contrast, a normal person whose weight begins to creep up slowly but steadily and approaches the 10 percent mark should begin an active program to stop any further weight gain.

Once we have reached the obesity range, our risk for the abnormalities and diseases listed above increases. But the risk does not increase linearly the heavier we get. At most, there is a small increase in risk until we are moderately to severely obese. The number of pounds we can sustain before this sharp increase occurs will vary from person to person and with the abnormality or disease in question. Thus, we may have to be forty pounds overweight before our risk for high blood cholesterol has increased significantly, and perhaps thirty pounds for high blood pressure or diabetes. If you are at the lower end of the spectrum, though technically obese, your risk may not increase very much. We do not mean to say that if you are mildly obese don't worry about it. What we are saying has very practical value in weight reduction. The most important objective of any weight reduction program should be to lower our risk for the diseases we have discussed. It is much more important for us to lose enough weight to change our risk category than it is to reach an "ideal" weight.

One major reason that most reducing programs fail is because we set inappropriate goals. For the man whose ideal weight is 180 but who weighs 240, a loss of twenty-five pounds may reduce his risk markedly even though it won't change his physical image very much. Most important is that a loss of twenty-five pounds may be attainable and sustainable. If he attempts to lose forty or fifty pounds, he will most likely fail and wind up frustrated.

Atherosclerosis, hypertension, and diabetes are the three major killer diseases to which obesity makes a significant contribution. (Obesity also increases the risk slightly for a few rare cancers.) As we have seen in the chapters "Atherosclerosis" and "Hypertension," atherosclerosis and hypertension both involve multiple risk factors. We shall see in the chapter "Diabetes" that the same holds true for diabetes. The nature of obesity's contribution to the risks for these major diseases is still not entirely clear. The distribution of excessive body fat is also significant. In general, people with excessive fat below the waistline (pear shaped) are at lower risk than those with excessive fat above the waist (apple shaped). Sex hormones play an important role in distribution of body fat, and men more often exhibit large abdomens while women accumulate fat in the hips and thighs.

Careful analysis of available data has led some experts to believe that obesity is important only if we already have a genetic predisposition to the diseases and only if we are severely obese. If you fall into this category, you are at high risk and should make every effort to lower your weight sufficiently to reduce that risk. If you do not fall into this category and are not very obese, while there is no room for complacency, weight reduction may be less of an emergency.

Many of us are above our ideal weight, but not all of us in that category are obese. Before considering a crash diet, assess your personal condition. Are you obese? If so, how obese? Do you have a positive family history for atherosclerosis, high blood pressure, or diabetes? Are you in the danger zone? Only after you have answered these questions honestly can you decide whether weight reduction will improve your health and how much adjustment is necessary in your particular case.

Preventing Obesity

Perhaps with no other disease is the old adage "an ounce of prevention is worth a pound of cure" as true as with obesity. It is, therefore, well worth the trouble to assess our risk for becoming obese and, if we are in danger, to do something about it. As we have seen, there is a strong genetic component to obesity. Therefore, family history is important. If your family health tree shows obesity, your own tendency to become overweight increases. Even if there is no history of obesity in your family, a careful examination of the rest of your propensities is still important. Since obesity is particularly hazardous when coupled with a genetic inclination for high cholesterol levels, high blood pressure, or diabetes, a history of any of these conditions in our family background makes obesity more dangerous. While a positive family history for any or all these abnormalities may not increase our risk, conversely, if we do become obese, our risk for heart attack or stroke will increase.

If you were obese as a child, you are at increased risk of being obese as an adult. You must consider yourself at risk even if your weight is normal. Beyond your own history and your family background, consider your lifestyle. Are you becoming more sedentary because of your age, your job, or just because of a new way of life? Are you a compulsive eater whose appetite is triggered by external cues, especially during periods of tension? Have you increased your consumption of alcohol, a major source of hidden calories? If the answer to any of these questions is yes, you are at increased risk. Finally, if you are a woman and have children, did you gain a little weight permanently after each pregnancy? Do premenstrual tensions result in your eating more? If the answer is yes, your risk increases. To get a numerical rating of your risks for obesity, evaluate

- *first*, your present weight: if you are 10 to 20 percent above ideal weight, you are in the danger zone, and you should score 5;
- *second*, your family history on a scale of 1 to 5: if your family health tree is abundant with obese relatives, score 3; if your father or mother was obese, score 4; if both parents were obese, score 5;
- *third*, your own history: if you were truly obese as a child, score 5; if you have always had a problem controlling your weight, score 3; and
- *fourth*, your lifestyle: if you are a compulsive eater, score 2 to 5, depending on how much tension you are under and how much food you consume during periods of tension. If you are a moderately heavy drinker, add 2. If you live a moderately sedentary life, score 2; if you do almost no exercise, score 4. If you are a woman and have been getting heavier with each pregnancy, add 2.

A score of 5 or more places us at risk for obesity. As our score increases, our risk rises, but anyone scoring 5 or above should take measures to prevent obesity. If you suffer from atherosclerosis, or have high blood-cholesterol levels or high blood pressure or diabetes, you should start preventive measures, even if you are of normal weight. It is also good advice to use preventive measures even if you do not suffer from those diseases but do have a strong family history for one or more of them. Again, your risk for obesity may not be high, but the potential for becoming obese is greater.

There is no specific number of calories that must be consumed to prevent obesity. The right number for you may be too much for your friend even though you are both of the same age, gender, and body build. You have to find your own level. Begin by checking your weight several times a week. If it is stable and you are not in the danger zone, check it once a week. Note the amount of food you take in and estimate your average daily caloric intake. As long as it remains stable, no other measures are necessary. If your weight begins to increase, even by one or two pounds, recalculate your caloric intake. If your intake has gone up, cut back to where it was before. This may be difficult if your eating pattern has changed. It may require some modifications. By using some simple measures, you may nip a potentially serious problem in the bud.

If you are in the danger zone (10 to 20 percent above ideal weight) and your weight is stable, you need to lose some pounds, but you have plenty of time in which to do it. You can decrease the number of calories you consume, increase the amount of physical activity you perform, or both. Don't go on a crash program; you will just bounce back after you stop. Most Americans on crash diets at any given time are either in the caution zone, or are even less overweight. Only a few are obese. Remember that you are not at increased health risk. You should lose some weight to prevent yourself from becoming obese later in life when there is a tendency to gain more weight. If you take your time making a few changes in your diet and your lifestyle and aim for any weight loss that you can comfortably sustain, you are more likely to succeed in losing those pounds.

Certainly, you will have to reduce the number of calories you take in. The best way to do this is to identify the sources of calories in your diet that contain the lowest nutrient value. The principle we wish to convey is not to go on any special diet, but rather to modify the one you are on now to reduce the number of calories in it without affecting the amount of nutrients it contains. If your diet has been poorly balanced to start, it may still be poorly balanced and probably should be changed. The time to change it is after you have reached the proper caloric level and sustained that level for several months. The less radical the changes as you begin to limit your calories, the better.

What contributes the unwanted calories in our diets depends on our individual habits. For some of us, it may be beer or other alcoholic beverages; for others, refined sugar or chocolates; for others, fat; and for many, all three. There are some general rules to help us decide what foods or beverages to eliminate or reduce in quantity. Fat has twice the number of calories per gram as sugar. Thus, eliminating a given quantity of fat reduces our calories twice as much as eliminating the same amount of sugar. Suppose you consume 2,500 cal per day from the following foods: whole milk, toast and butter, coffee (three cups a day) with two teaspoons of sugar, tuna fish or chicken salad sandwich, steak, home-fried potatoes, vegetables, salads, and cheesecake or apple pie—a standard American diet. In addition, you have one martini before dinner and a glass or two of wine with dinner.

You want to reduce your intake to 2,200 cal. What are your options? First, identify those sources of calories that have little or no nutrient value:

- *Alcohol*—cutting out the martini will save calories.
- *Sugar*—eliminating the sugar from your coffee or substituting a non-caloric sweetener saves calories.
- *Fat*—carefully trimming your meat and having a baked potato may save calories (if you don't add butter or sour cream to the potato).
- *Combined fat and sugar*—replacing the cheesecake or apple pie with a piece of fruit can reduce your caloric intake by more than 100 cal.

The number of ways in which we can eliminate 300 cal from our diet and still keep the nutrient values the same is almost infinite. Just be aware of what you are eating and initiate the kind of changes that are easiest for you. Your main goal is to reach the caloric level that will begin to bring about weight reduction.

Be sure to incorporate balance into your menus. To attain rigid control of you calorie count, use the exchange lists explained in "Diabetes." Start with the normal number of calories you eat in a day and then divide by 30. If you normally eat 1,200 cal a day, you should limit your fat intake to 40 g of fat. For 1,500 cal, it is 50 g; for 1,800 cal, 60 g; for 2,000 cal, 66 g; and for 2,500 cal, 83 g. By staying within these guidelines, you will be able to keep to the limit of 30 percent of calories from fat. Do not try to reduce your fat calories to less than 30 percent without professional help. Some fat in our diets is important for its satiety value, for flavor enhancement, and as a media for some of the essential nutrients. Excessive use of "fat free" products is a potential hazard to your health.

Sometimes the number of calories we consume can begin to creep up because of a change in our lifestyle. For example, a job promotion could make it necessary to entertain clients at lunch once or twice a week. Likewise, eating in the company cafeteria instead of the executive dining room can increase our caloric intake enough to result in a slow weight gain. Be alert to this possibility. If you do begin to gain, cut your calories back to the previous level. This doesn't mean you have to give up your new lifestyle. It means you have to adapt it to the number of calories that maintain your own weight at a healthy level. Maybe ordering differently at lunch is the answer, or perhaps modifying your dinner, or both. Choose whatever methods work best for you. Once your caloric intake is at its previous level and you have shed the extra pound or two, maintain this pattern of eating while continuing to weigh yourself several times a week. Usually, you will have stabilized at your previous weight and will have averted a potentially serious weight problem.

Changes in lifestyle often occur so subtly that they go unnoticed for a long time. Sometimes these changes are accompanied by significant weight gain. The gradual shift from the active exercise pattern of high school and college to the less active pattern of a young man or woman entering the workforce can often result in a weight gain. Increasing our alcohol intake, giving up smoking, traveling more often for business or pleasure, all may be accompanied increased caloric intake and gradual increases in our weight. In today's hectic pace of life, the American people are not getting enough sleep, and that changes our eating habits. We tend to eat more for comfort or to wind down after a stressful day. If you are at risk for obesity, you should be always on the alert for these changes. Anticipate them and adjust your calorie intake accordingly.

Finally, certain activities are usually accompanied by eating. Who can go to the movies without eating some popcorn? A baseball game is not complete without a hot dog or soft drink. Part of going to the theater is the coffee and pastry we have after the show. All these activities enrich our lives. To suggest giving them up is neither necessary nor practical. If they occur only occasionally, don't worry. If they form a regular and frequent part of your life, then the calories you consume at these events must be considered as part of your daily calorie intake. It is important for us to be aware of what we are eating. We can change the pattern in a way that preserves the social event and at the same time eliminates unwanted calories.

Perhaps watching television is the most significant sedentary activity contributing to obesity. For many of us, it is also a time for unconscious eating. Finally, at least half the commercials are for food or beverages. Analyze your television viewing time. Are you a beer and pretzels football game spectator? Do you nibble on candy or crackers throughout your favorite program? For several evenings, write down everything that you eat as you watch. Then calculate the calories: how many? 500? 750? Find a way to bring that number down. Put the peanuts on the top shelf of the closet. Substitute fruit for pretzels and juice or sugar free iced tea for beer. You don't need a prescribed plan to tell you how to reduce your television calories. You only need to be aware that you are consuming calories as you watch. You need to know how many you are consuming, and you need determination to alter the pattern and reduce your caloric intake. There is no single best way. If one method fails, try another. Use any method that works for you, but control the amount and kind of food. Keep the number of calories to a level that sustains your weight and prevents it from creeping up.

Between the ages of twenty-five and fifty, Americans do not increase their food intake to any great extent. Yet, we all tend to gain weight. Do you eat more now than when you were twenty-five? If anything, you probably eat less. This gain is due partly to changes in our metabolism, but, mainly, it results from a steady decline in physical activity in the normal course of the day. Many opportunities can easily go unnoticed. Simply walking a few miles a day or taking the stairs instead of the elevator can make a big difference. The key is regularity. We should make exercise part of our regular daily habits. We need to introduce more activity into each routine. This may be the greatest challenge any of us face in our struggle to prevent obesity.

Regular physical activity will increase both our caloric expenditure and our physical fitness. Some of us jog or walk briskly every day. Some people play tennis, others work out in gyms, but whatever activity it is, it should be done on a regular basis. It must become an integral part of our lifestyle. Therefore, it is essential that we enjoy it. Don't run because everyone else does. If running bores you, you'll never sustain it. Besides, running may be too hard on your joints. Even Dr. Cooper, the "father of aerobic exercise," now feels that he overdid himself in his early years of zest. If you like to dance, do it regularly. Take a daily walk to the post office, the supermarket, or a friend's house. Ride a bicycle; swim, if you have access to a pool. Any of these activities will consume calories. The best one is not the one that consumes the most calories but the one you can make a part of your daily routine. Whatever you do, your bathroom scale will measure your success. But the scales alone won't tell the full story of your exercise program. Because muscle tissue is denser than adipose tissue, you can gain weight while losing fat. This is particularly true of "bodybuilding" exercise. You can theoretically lose two inches in your beltline while gaining twenty pounds on the scales. You are simply changing fat to muscle.

Two major incentives must be kept in mind in treating obesity:

1. You wish to reduce your body weight to a range that lowers your risk for the complications of obesity.
2. You wish to start preventive measures against atherosclerosis, high blood pressure, diabetes, and other disorders that are more common in obese people.

Unfortunately, true obesity is an affliction that will most likely plague you the rest of your life. Most obese people have tried many plans, lost and regained hundreds of pounds with little permanent success in controlling their weight. Therefore, while it is important that you lose weight, it is equally important that you accept the possibility that you may always be obese. Try to protect yourself from its complications.

Just as there is no perfectly safe and effective pill for obesity, there is no such thing as the "perfect diet" which will take off thirty pounds in three weeks. Such a diet does not exist! For an obese person to lose significant weight and to keep it off means a lifetime of hard work. However, we can give you some tips that might help lessen the burden of constantly watching your diet. Remember that you may not be an overeater. Instead, you may be an under-user of calories. This means that, for you to lose weight, you may have to reduce your number of calories to a level below that which a non-obese individual would have to consume. The number of calories we can take in while still losing weight will vary from person to person. For some obese subjects, 2,000 per day will achieve weight loss; for others, 1,500; for some, 1,200 or even less. Find your level and construct your own diet by eliminating fat, sugar, and alcohol, and by using foods whose caloric value totals the necessary number of calories per day. If you find that you must consume 1,500 cal or less to begin a slow but steady weight loss, take a multivitamin and mineral supplement. Any brand that gives you the Recommended Daily Intake of B vitamins, vitamin C, iron, zinc, and calcium is right.

Continue at this caloric level until you stop losing weight. This plateau will often occur after two to three weeks. Your initial weight loss is partly water, and the resulting tissue dehydration is correcting itself. You are still losing fat tissue, but the scale isn't showing it because you are replacing water. Be patient! In another week, after you rehydrate, you will begin to lose weight again. After a few weeks, you may reach another plateau. Your metabolism is fighting you by increasing its efficiency. This is time to fight back. Reduce your caloric intake by another 100 to 200 cal. Your weight will begin to decrease again.

The procedure we have outlined does not take two weeks, or two months. It takes much longer: six months, nine months, or twelve months, depending on how obese you are and also on your metabolism. Remember that your primary goal is not to achieve ideal weight but one that will minimize the risks of obesity. Any weight that is below the danger zone is excellent. Even if this results in you remaining within the danger zone, you are much better off than you were before.

Here is an example: Suppose you weigh 250 lbs and your ideal weight is 180 lbs; 110 percent of your ideal weight would be 198 lbs, so at 216 lbs you are obese. Thus, to reach ideal weight, you must lose seventy pounds and maintain that weight loss. To be below the danger zone, you have to lose fifty-two lbs and maintain that weight. To be no longer obese, you will have to lose 34 lbs. Thus, you need to lose half as much weight to be no longer obese than to achieve your ideal weight. However, by losing those thirty-four pounds, you may reduce your risk for the complications of obesity by 40 percent or more. The next 36 lbs will only reduce your risk by an additional 15 to 20 percent. Certainly, it would be best for you to achieve and maintain your ideal weight, but experience has taught us that this goal is almost unattainable. Therefore, you should set a goal you can achieve and which eliminates the major portion of your risk.

Maintain that weight until it becomes your new stable level. Then if you wish to take off more and can succeed, you will have reduced your risk a little more and obtained important cosmetic and psychological effects to boot. If you fail and return to your new baseline, you will still be at much lower risk than when you started. Keeping your weight stable with the least amount of caloric restriction possible is easier if you are active. Therefore, when you reach your desired goal, begin a moderate exercise routine that can be incorporated along with your new eating habits. Exercise will not only help you keep your new weight, but may directly reduce your risk for atherosclerosis and hypertension and their dreaded complications—heart attack or stroke.

The best way for any of us to minimize the risks of obesity is to lose sufficient weight that we are no longer obese. Unfortunately, even if they set proper goals, many obese people will not, or cannot permanently reduce their weight. These people are at increased risk for several diseases including high blood pressure and atherosclerosis, which can be influenced by diet. If you are obese and have not been able to reduce your weight, you should be constantly alert for these diseases. Your blood pressure should be taken at least twice a year, and your serum lipids should be analyzed with the same frequency. If you have a serum cholesterol above 200, you should alter your diet as set forth in "Atherosclerosis." If you are a male with a family history of atherosclerosis and you are obese, you should consume a low-fat diet even if you have no other risks for atherosclerosis. If you are a female with marked obesity (30 percent or more above ideal weight) with a positive family history for atherosclerosis, you should similarly modify your diet.

As for hypertension, obesity itself is reason enough to reduce the amount of salt in our diet (see "Hypertension"). If you are African-American or have a family history of high blood pressure, you must be even more careful about your salt intake.

Beyond these dietary changes, it is important to have your blood pressure carefully monitored. It may go up even if you modify your salt intake. Today, very effective drug therapy exists for hypertension (high blood pressure). The key is to begin early. This can be done only if you are aware that your blood pressure is high. If you are obese, you are more at risk for hypertension, and therefore must take special pains to start controlling this disease as early as possible.

Once you have achieved you goal in weight reduction (whether by "sensible dieting," "crash dieting," or with a "miracle drug"), place more emphasis on healthy eating patterns for you and your family, i.e., your maintenance program. The following guidelines will help you maintain proper balance in your daily menu plans:

Eat 6 to 11 servings per day of whole grain, enriched breads, cereals and other grain products. One serving equals 1 slice of bread; 1/2 hamburger bun; 1/2 English bun; a small roll, biscuit, or muffin; 3 to 4 small crackers; 2 large crackers; 1/2 cup cooked cereal, rice or pasta; 1 ounce of ready-to-eat cereal.

Eat 2 to 4 servings per day of fruits (citrus, melon, berries, and other fruits). One serving equals a whole fruit such as a medium apple, banana, or orange; 1/2 grapefruit; a wedge of melon; 3/4 cup of juice; 1/2 cup of berries, 1/2 cup of cooked or canned fruit, 1/4 cup dried fruit.

Eat 3 to 5 servings per day of vegetables (dark green leafy, deep yellow, dried beans and peas, or legumes, starchy, and other vegetables.) Include a wide variety by eating from all five vegetable subgroups (dark green, bright yellow, legumes, starchy vegetables, and other vegetables), but make sure to use dark green leafy vegetables and dried beans and peas several times a week. One serving equals 1/2 cup of cooked vegetables; 1/2 cup of

FRONTIERS OF NUTRITION

chopped raw vegetables; or 1 cup of leafy raw vegetables such as lettuce or spinach.

Eat 2 to 3 servings per day of meat, poultry, fish, or vegetarian alternates such as eggs, dried beans and peas, nuts and seeds. Try to limit this to about 5 to 7 oz of cooked lean meat, poultry, or fish each day. One ounce of meat equals 1 egg; 1/2 cup cooked beans; 2 tablespoons of peanut butter.

Eat 2 servings per day of milk, cheese, and yogurt. Try to stick to the low-fat or no-fat varieties. Women who are pregnant or breast-feeding, as well as teenagers, should get 3 servings per day. Pregnant or breast-feeding teenagers should increase this to 4. 1 serving equals 1 cup of milk; 8 oz of yogurt; 1-1/2 oz of natural cheese; 2 oz of processed cheese.

Fats, oils, sweets, and alcoholic beverages should be consumed sparingly.

If 3 to 5 servings of vegetables and 6 to 11 servings of "grains" seems like a lot to you, remind yourself that these are not the serving sizes that you are accustomed to. You can include multiple servings of one or two foods. When you have "seconds," (or if you eaten 2 slices of bread, instead of one) that doubles the number of servings in the pertinent food category. However, "Variety is the spice of life!" Eat as many different foods as you can. Limit the meat items, milk fat, and other fatty foods.

▶ 99

Diabetes

D iabetes is one of the most serious and common diseases in modern society, and the incidence of the disorder continues to climb. It can be viewed as two separate diseases. One form (Type 1), usually affecting younger people—even young children— is attributable to absolute deficiency of insulin (a hormone produced by the pancreas). The mechanism within the pancreas that normally manufactures insulin becomes badly damaged and can no longer produce the hormone. This type of diabetes, often called juvenile-onset diabetes, is very severe and must be treated with insulin. Juvenile-onset diabetes is rare, and, while diet is a mainstay in its treatment, we cannot prevent its occurrence through dietary modification.

The second form of diabetes (Type 2) is known as maturity-onset or adult-onset diabetes. This type of diabetes is much more common than the first—and, according to the National Institute of Digestive and Kidney Diseases, its prevalence has increased almost 50 percent in the past twelve years. It also results from a deficiency of insulin, but this deficiency is a relative one. The pancreas is perfectly capable of manufacturing the hormone. It often manufactures more insulin than before onset of the disorder, but the body needs more hormones to function properly. Certain changes occur within the tissues, increasing their requirement for insulin. The pancreas responds by making more. First, it increases production of insulin. Finally, it works at maximum capacity. If the requirement continues to increase, the pancreas simply cannot manufacture enough insulin. The patient becomes insulin-deficient, and the symptoms of diabetes appear. Sometimes, if this chemical imbalance is not relieved, the overworked pancreas will burn itself out, becoming unable to manufacture insulin. A relative deficiency can then become an absolute deficiency. In certain people, the risk of acquiring the disease may be lowered by dietary modification.

In this chapter, we shall discuss dietary modifications that can lower our risk for adult-onset diabetes and principles for dietary management of the disease when it is already present. Anyone with either type of diabetes must be under a doctor's care. The dietary principles outlined here will make it easier to understand why your doctor prescribes a particular type of diet.

Juvenile-onset diabetes has a very definite genetic component. The genes involved have been identified so that it is possible to predict (with certain specialized tests) which individuals are at risk. However, making this prediction offers little advantage to the person who has the genes that put him at risk for the disease. Only a small number of this population will develop diabetes, and nothing can be done either to identify or to protect them. Presently, we believe that some people with the genetic predisposition are susceptible to what appears to be a viral infection.

Whatever the case, the insulin-producing cells within the pancreas are selectively destroyed. Before the availability of insulin, all patients with true juvenile-onset diabetes died within a short time. Today, with the availability of insulin, most can live a relatively normal life. However, such patients become susceptible to the same long-term complications of diabetes as those who develop the adult form of the disease. Since the dietary modifications designed to prevent or decrease the severity of these complications are similar, both types of diabetes will be discussed.

There are no dietary controls to prevent juvenile-onset diabetes. There is no relationship to the number of calories consumed; the amount of carbohydrate, either complex or simple; or the amount of fat in the diet. Disregard any suggestion that you got diabetes because you were too fat (most juvenile-onset diabetics are thin), or that you ate too much candy, or ice cream, or sugar. Nothing you did caused juvenile-onset diabetes.

Maturity-onset diabetes typically begins after the age of fifty and it too runs in families, but dietary modification may lower the risk. First, we must understand how this relative insulin deficiency develops. Then we can attempt to alter the pattern of development.

The pancreas lies buried in the abdomen behind the liver and intestines. Insulin producing cells (beta cells) are present in small clumps, or islands, interspersed between the ducts of the pancreas. These islands called islets of Langerhans (after the man who discovered them) have a characteristic appearance under the microscope. The insulin manufactured in the beta cells is secreted directly into the bloodstream and carried to all the tissues of the body. Protruding from the cells of these tissues are specific appendage-like molecular structures into which the insulin molecules fit and are thereby bound to the cell surface. These appendages, called receptors, are specific for insulin. Usually, there are more receptors than insulin to fill them. As the demand goes up, more insulin is produced. It immediately becomes fixed to a receptor and is rapidly taken into the cell. If the receptors are not working right, the pancreas will have to produce more insulin for the same amount to get into the cells.

Once inside the cell, insulin facilitates the passage of glucose, the body's main energy source, from the blood into the tissues. In the tissues, glucose is either used as fuel or stored as glycogen (a complex carbohydrate similar to starch). Excess calories, beyond the quantity used immediately and that needed to load the tissues with a twenty-four hour or so glycogen reserve, are stored as fat.

The body needs more insulin than when caloric intake is lower. Thus, to build up or maintain fat stores, an obese person requires more of the hormone than a lean individual. The beta cells have to work harder as the body's need for insulin increases. If they can meet that need, the body will function normally. If they cannot, there is an insulin deficiency. The symptoms of diabetes will appear. In some people, the added need for insulin does not stress the beta cells. They simply make more. In others, the cells cannot make it fast enough. Which type of person we are depends on our genetic makeup.

Maturity Onset Diabetes

Maturity-onset diabetes is a genetic disease that manifests itself when the body requirement for insulin is not satisfied. Under normal circumstances, a person who is at risk for the disease because he or she is carrying "diabetic genes" is likely to develop it at age sixty-five or seventy, or even older.

Excessive strain on the pancreatic beta cells may cause symptoms to appear when that person is in the fifties or even younger. People who are genetically prone to the disease will develop it much sooner and much more seriously if they consume excess calories. Calories can come from a variety of sources, and some of these sources are more risky than others.

The level of blood glucose signals the pancreatic beta cells to make more or less insulin. As the glucose level increases, more insulin is produced. As glucose decreases, less insulin is made. As glucose gets into the cells, the amount in the blood will fall. Thus, another function of insulin is to regulate the level of blood sugar. The level of blood sugar is also sensitive to diet, particularly to the type and the amount of carbohydrate we consume. Complex carbohydrates must be converted to simple forms before they are absorbed from the intestines into the body. Thus, complex carbohydrates release sugar into the blood slowly. Refined sugar (sucrose) is very quickly split by intestinal enzymes into its two simple sugars, glucose, and fructose. These sugars are absorbed into the bloodstream very rapidly. Hence, consumption of sucrose will raise blood sugar more quickly than the consumption of complex carbohydrates.

It has been postulated that a diet high in refined sugar will put an added strain on the beta cells and that, over a long time, such a diet will induce diabetes in susceptible men or women. Several studies have been cited to support this hypothesis. None of these studies were scientifically sound. Yet, there may be an association between high intake of refined sugar and diabetes. People who consume large amounts of sugar also consume excess calories. We have already seen that too many calories can increase a susceptible individual's risk for diabetes. To the extent that consuming large amounts of sucrose increases our caloric intake, it is a risk for maturity-onset diabetes. Beyond its caloric content, there does not seem to be anything special about sugar that increases the risk.

The best way to lower our chances of getting maturity-onset diabetes is by reducing our intake of fat. A low-fat diet will necessarily be high in carbohydrate. A low-carbohydrate diet is high in fat. Therefore, it would be very difficult to construct a diet low in both these components. If both calories and the amount of carbohydrate independently increased our risk for diabetes, then dietary prevention and treatment would be very complicated. Fortunately, this is not the case. Calories are important, but the portion of the diet consisting of complex carbohydrate is not causative in diabetes.

A diet high in complex carbohydrate may be especially beneficial in treating diabetes. Large amounts of refined sugar must be avoided because such a diet will provide low bulk and a tantalizing source of excess calories. However, severe restriction of refined sugar is not advocated as a preventive measure for maturity-onset diabetes.

Who Is a Risk?

Anyone with a family history of diabetes is at risk for developing the disease. The stronger the family history, the greater the risk. Also important in determining the influence of the genetic component is the time of life when diabetes appeared in those members of your family who developed it. The earlier the onset of their disease, the more you are at risk. But a family tree totally free of diabetes is not absolute assurance for a lack of genetic risk. Life expectancy has increased dramatically in recent decades, and since diabetes may appear late in life, susceptible members of your family may not have lived long enough to show it, or it may not have been diagnosed. As many as half of those who have the disease are not aware of it.

If you belong to an ethnic group in which the risk for diabetes is high, you are at risk. Among these high-risk groups are Ashkenazi Jews, African-Americans, and Native Americans. If you fit in to one of these groups, you should examine your family tree very carefully. If information about certain close relatives is unavailable, you should assume yourself at increased risk. The dietary modifications to reduce this risk are simple and safe. They are also useful in protecting against other diseases (atherosclerosis, hypertension, and obesity). It is better to err on the safe side.

If you are a woman and have children, did you have high blood sugar during pregnancy? If so, you are at risk for diabetes. Pregnancy puts an added strain on the pancreatic beta cells. Because your own growing tissues and those of your developing fetus require increased amounts of energy, and because you must deposit fat in your own body for use during lactation, your body requires more insulin. If the beta cells are not able to keep up with these extra demands, insulin production will be insufficient and blood sugar will rise. If your blood sugar goes too high, you may require treatment during pregnancy. You have what we call gestational diabetes. Even if it disappears after delivery (it usually does.), this is a warning sign that you are at risk for developing maturity-onset diabetes later in life. If you fall into this category, you must be considered at risk.

If you have ever had a glucose tolerance test, you should know if it was normal. A glucose tolerance test consists of having a person drink a fixed amount of glucose (100 g) in water and then doing blood-sugar determinations periodically for the next four to six hours. This test indicates the ability of the pancreatic islets to produce insulin. As the blood sugar rises from the initial loading dose, the beta cells respond by releasing insulin. This promptly results in a lowering of the blood sugar, which, in turn, signals the beta cells to cut back insulin production. If a person has a "tendency to diabetes," the beta cells respond sluggishly and the blood sugar rises initially to levels above normal. In addition, once the blood sugar is lowered by the release of insulin and returns to normal, the sluggish beta cells continue to release insulin beyond the necessary time. The result is that the blood sugar drops below normal before it returns to its proper range. This high one-hour blood-sugar level followed by a low three- or four-hour blood-sugar level is the characteristic diabetic or pre-diabetic pattern sometimes called "metabolic disorder."

While not as definitive as a glucose tolerance test, fasting blood sugar levels are valuable in detecting pre-diabetes. Fasting blood sugar tests are easily done, inexpensive, and require—at most—the discomfort of a pricked finger. Anyone with a moderate risk for diabetes should have this test as part of an annual physical examination. In preparation for the test, you need to go without food for twelve hours before the blood is drawn. Refrain from food (water is allowed) after midnight on the day before the test and delay breakfast until after your morning visit to the clinic. A high fasting glucose test will alert your doctor to order more specific tests for a definitive diagnosis.

Certain medications, the most important of which are the cortisone-like drugs, independently raise blood-sugar levels and thereby invoke an insulin-releasing response in the pancreatic beta cells. A sluggish response by these cells will result in a "diabetic-like" syndrome, often called cortisone-induced diabetes. If you respond in this manner, you are at increased risk for developing maturity-onset diabetes. Any person who takes cortisone or its derivatives, particularly for a chronic illness such as asthma or arthritis, should have a glucose tolerance test, or at least a fasting blood sugar test, while under the influence of the drug. If a diabetic pattern emerges, it is a warning to take whatever steps possible to lower your risk.

Finally, are you obese? The question of obesity as an independent risk for diabetes has not been settled. There is a strong association between obesity and maturity-onset diabetes. Both diseases have a solid genetic component. Hence, it is possible that people who are genetically prone to diabetes are also genetically prone to obesity. However, some studies suggest that the relationship of diabetes to obesity is more than this type of genetic linking. First, obesity puts a specific strain on the pancreatic islet cells. Second, in some obese patients who develop diabetes, weight reduction alone can control the disease. Third, in populations where diabetes was once rare, the disease has become much more common as that population has become heavier. These data strongly suggest that in people who are at risk for diabetes, obesity will significantly increase that risk. It is much less clear whether obesity per se increases a person's risk for diabetes. We do know, however, that people without any other known risks for diabetes are more likely to develop the disease if they are obese than if they are lean. While this does not prove that obesity is an independent risk for diabetes, it suggests that we treat it as if it were. Since we already know that obesity should be prevented for many different reasons, we will include it as a risk for diabetes. Until more information is available, this is the most prudent course.

What about the lean individual with a sweet tooth? The person who consumes large amounts of refined sugar and does not gain weight? We all know and envy people like these. Are they increasing their risk for maturity-onset diabetes? If they have no other risks, they are probably not. If they are already at risk, we are not certain. There are theoretical reasons that consumption of large amounts of refined sugar might increase the stress on an already susceptible pancreas. However, there is no data suggesting that this happens. Thus, we will assume that a person who has an increased risk for diabetes will not increase that risk by consuming moderate amounts of refined sugar. As for the true "sugar-holic," even though the evidence may not support any belief, we feel that the possibility of additionally increasing our risk is sufficiently strong that we recommend such persons reduce the amount of refined sugar in their diet.

Since diabetes is genetic in origin, it will be more prevalent in some demographic groups than in others. African-Americans, Native Americans, and Jews of European extraction are among those who have a high incidence of the disease. However, diabetes can and does occur in almost every ethnic group. Therefore, you are not completely safe even if you belong to a low-risk population.

Your family history is more important. Question your living relatives about their health and that of their ancestors. Spread the branches as far as feasible. If your relatives are not sure, try to piece together as much information as possible. Even if only one close relative is known to have had diabetes, your risk increases. How much depends on how prevalent this disease is in your family health tree.

If only one or two distant relatives have had diabetes, score 3. If a few close relatives or many more distant relatives are diabetics, score 5. In addition, if you belong to a high-risk ethnic population, add 2. If you have had persistently high blood sugar levels or an abnormal glucose tolerance test during pregnancy, score 5. If your fasting blood sugar was elevated occasionally during pregnancy, score 3. If you have had one or more very large babies (nine pounds or more), score 2. (This is because infants of mothers with diabetes or a tendency toward it are often large.)

If your glucose tolerance test results in a diabetic-like curve or a higher-than-normal half-hour or one-hour blood sugar (even if the values were not high enough to diagnose diabetes), this significantly increases your risk for developing the disease, so score 5. If your fasting blood sugar was high on several occasions, you should get a glucose tolerance test. If that test is abnormal, score 5. However, even if it is normal, you must still consider yourself at increased risk. If you show repeated high fasting blood sugar levels, score 3.

Adrenal steroids are used in the treatment of a large number of chronic diseases and are often taken for long periods of time. As we have seen, these drugs independently raise blood sugar, and insulin production is stimulated by these high levels. Thus, the beta cells of any patient consuming these drugs will be under constant stress. If you have a tendency toward diabetes, your beta cells may not respond perfectly and your blood sugar may be somewhat elevated. Any patient with steroid-induced high blood sugars should have a glucose tolerance test while on steroids. If a diabetic-like curve appears, score 5. If not, we still cannot be complacent—score 3.

If you are truly obese, that is 20 percent or more over your ideal weight, you must consider yourself at high risk for diabetes, even if you have no other risks. Therefore, we are assigning a risk factor of 5 to this condition. If you are overweight but not clearly obese (105 to 120 percent of your ideal weight), score 3. Suppose you are not obese but are at high risk for becoming obese (see the previous chapter), score 2. Being moderately overweight or being at risk for obesity without any other risk does not require dietary modifications. By contrast, a strong family history of gestational diabetes, an abnormal glucose tolerance test, or true obesity all place you in a high-risk category.

Add up your scores from all of the above risk factors (maximum 38 points). Any score of 5 or more warrants attention. You should attempt to lower your risk for diabetes.

Our dietary strategy will pursue two objectives simultaneously—*first*, to prevent (or at least delay) the onset of diabetes, and—*second*, to prevent (or at least minimize) its complications if the disease does occur. The first objective is best achieved by controlling calories; the second by controlling fat. Let us explain the reasons behind this approach.

As we have seen, the one major risk that you can do something about is obesity. Thus, if you are obese, it is important that you lose weight. If you are overweight (but not obese) and your total score is over 5, you should reduce to as close to your ideal weight as possible. If you are at risk for obesity and your total score is over 5, it is important that you do not become obese. You must pay particular attention to your weight.

In the chapter "Obesity," we outlined the safest and most effective way to lose weight and to keep weight off. The same methods should be employed to lower our risk for diabetes. Since refined sugar is a food of very low nutrient density, large amounts of it should not be consumed on any reducing diet. This is especially true if a major reason for controlling your weight is to lower your risk for diabetes. If you are a true sugarholic, you may be putting an unnecessary strain on your beta cells, and you are surely consuming calories in an inefficient manner. Thus, while you do not need to avoid all sugar, you should cut back sufficiently to allow the rest of your low-calorie diet to provide all the essential nutrients you require.

In our society, a major principle of any reducing diet is lowering the consumption of fat. Fat is the most concentrated source of calories. Therefore, we get the maximum caloric benefit per serving if the food we eliminate from our diet is high in fat. In a weight control program, it is even more important to minimize our risk for diabetes by restricting the amount of fat in our diet.

One of the major complications of diabetes is atherosclerosis. This disease may lead to heart attack and stroke. A diabetic person is automatically at high risk for atherosclerosis (see "Atherosclerosis").

Similarly, someone at high risk for diabetes is potentially at high risk for atherosclerosis. Since many people at risk will develop diabetes, even if they control their weight, it is important to adhere to a low-fat diet as early as possible. If you are destined to become diabetic, the earlier you begin to control your serum lipids, the better. A low-fat diet (particularly a low-saturated-fat diet) is the best way to do this. "Atherosclerosis" outlines such a diet. It is by nature low in calories. Hence, if you are not obese, you may not need to control your caloric intake any further.

If you are obese, use this approach, combined with the principles outlined above. Avoid empty calories such as alcohol and refined sugar. Consume foods of high nutrient density. Eat plenty of roughage (fiber), and increase your level of exercise. To construct your diet, refer to "Atherosclerosis." If you are at high risk, diabetes is a constant threat. Thus, the program you will embark on is not a short-term reducing diet to drop five or ten pounds quickly. It is a lifelong eating pattern and must be approached as such. Quick results are not important. A sustained reduction in weight and lowering of your serum lipids will give you maximum benefit.

Dietary Treatment of Diabetes

If you already have diabetes, controlling your diet will be a major part of your treatment. If juvenile-onset diabetes is the problem, you will need insulin. By contrast, maturity-onset diabetes may not require insulin injections. Oral medications may be sufficient. Sometimes, particularly if you are obese and the disease is mild, slight weight reduction may be enough to control the disease. The balanced low-calorie approach remains best for weight reduction and control of diabetes. It is most likely to produce long-term results. Longterm results are essential. It may be more dangerous to lose weight and gain it back several times than to remain obese. Such "seesawing" may put even more stress on the beta cells of your pancreas than being obese. It is imperative that you limit your fat along with your calories.

If you are already diabetic, you are automatically at risk for atherosclerosis. Therefore, a low-total-fat, low-saturated-fat (with restriction of trans-fatty acids), low-cholesterol diet is necessary. If you have diabetes, regardless of the type, and need treatment with insulin, the foundation of your eating pattern similarly will be the low-calorie, low-fat diet. This diet will almost certainly be high in carbohydrates. Contrary to what you may have heard, a high-carbohydrate diet is preferable for anyone with diabetes. Some interesting statistics highlight this fact.

Historically, in this country, most people with diabetes were treated with a low-carbohydrate diet (which was high in protein and in fat). In Japan, diabetes was treated with the standard Japanese diet (high-carbohydrate). The mortality rate from the most serious complication of diabetes, atherosclerosis, was much higher in the United States than in Japan. The same disease, the same type of insulin treatment—the only difference was the type of diet used. The high-carbohydrate diet gave the lower mortality rates. Today, we follow the principle that insulin controls the disease. Diet lowers the risk of certain major complications.

Keeping our blood sugar within a narrow range may have a beneficial effect on some of the other complications of diabetes. Besides atherosclerosis and its accompanying heart disease and stroke, which are known as macrovascular complications (or diseases of the large blood vessels), the most serious are microvascular complications (diseases of the small blood vessels). These complications are serious because the small blood vessels most often involved are those in the kidney and in the retina of the eye. Severe kidney disease and blindness are dreaded complications of diabetes. Recent evidence suggests that the more stable our dietary control, the lower the incidence of microvascular complications. A strict diet may lower our risk not only for atherosclerosis, but for kidney and eye disease as well.

Although the basic program for any diabetic includes a high-carbohydrate, low-fat diet, the nature of the carbohydrate consumed may be very important. If you are on insulin, you will be taking one or more injections during the day. The type of insulin prescribed by your physician may vary. Some are long-acting; others are short-acting. You may be taking either type or, more often, a combination of them. The insulin is adjusted to reach a peak concentration in your blood when your blood sugar reaches the highest level. In addition, it is given in a dose designed to bring that blood sugar back to normal without producing hypoglycemia (low blood sugar). Thus, whereas your own beta cells normally react to your blood sugar level, this does not happen when the cells do not function properly. Your doctor must anticipate your blood sugar level when prescribing insulin for you.

By following two additional dietary rules, you can make your doctor's job easier, and hence bring your diabetes under better control. The first is consistency. You must try to consume the same number of calories at the same times each day. This does not mean that every day you must eat the same number of calories at every meal and every snack exactly on schedule. It means that you and your physician will design an eating pattern that is consistent with your needs and your lifestyle. You will tailor the time and dose of your insulin accordingly.

This pattern may be more difficult to follow on weekends than on weekdays. It may be different when you are on vacation, and it may change on days when you are very active. For example, during the week, you may consume 25 percent of your calories at breakfast, 20 percent at lunch, 30 percent at dinner, and split the remaining 25 percent between two snacks, one in mid-morning and one in mid-evening. By contrast, on weekends you may consume 40 percent of your calories at brunch, 40 percent at dinner, and the remaining 20 percent as snacks. The timing of your insulin dose may be different, but either pattern can be dealt with effectively. After a while, with your doctor's approval, you may be able to alter your anticipated eating and activity schedule. This approach is not as restrictive as it may seem. Most people establish routine patterns in the way they eat. They vary them very little. The standard pattern of breakfast, coffee break, lunch, dinner, and evening snack applies to millions of Americans.

A second rule concerns the nature of the carbohydrates we consume. Carbohydrates come in two forms: simple sugars, consisting of a single molecule (monosaccharides) or two molecules bonded together (disaccharides); or complex carbohydrates (polysaccharides), consisting of many simple sugars joined as a chain or a series of branches. The simple sugars are rapidly absorbed from the intestines and reach the bloodstream very quickly. Therefore, our blood glucose level will increase sharply when we consume a large quantity of simple sugars.

Table 13 outlines the nutrient content of the typical American diet, and compares it with the ideal diet for a person with diabetes.

Table 13. **Composition of the Diabetic Diet**

	Typical American Diet	*Recommended Diabetic Diet*
Carbohydrate	40% (high in simple sugars)	55%-60% (high in complex carbohydrates; e.g., starches and vegetables)
Fat	40% (high in saturated fat)	20%-30% (1:1:1 ratio of polyunsaturated to monounsaturated to saturated fat)
Protein	20%	12%
Fiber	low	high

Let us summarize the most important nutritional guidelines for a person with diabetes:

- *Calories* should be aimed at achieving ideal weight. (In the juvenile diabetic, this often means gaining weight; in the maturity-onset diabetic, this usually means losing weight.)
- *Fat* should be limited to 20 to 30 percent of the total calories consumed.
- *Saturated fat* may supply 10 percent of the total calories; and vegetable fat (polyunsaturated and monounsaturated) can provide another 10 to 20 percent.
- *Protein* should contribute 12 to 15 percent of all calories.
- *Simple sugars* should be restricted to 10 to 15 percent of all calories consumed, and only a small amount should come from refined sugars.
- The remainder of the calories (about 40 to 50 percent) should come from *complex carbohydrates* (starch).
- *Dietary fiber* should be increased by ingesting raw vegetables and whole-grain and bran cereals (or bread).

Our last recommendation is based on several studies that showed that adding 20 g of crude fiber to the diets of diabetic patients reduced their blood-sugar levels and the amount of insulin necessary to maintain good control of the disease. There are several possible explanations for these results. The one with the most support is that fiber delays the absorption of simple sugars from the gastrointestinal tract. For example, dietary fiber might delay emptying of the stomach, thereby slowing entrance of the meal into the small intestine where absorption takes place. Alternatively, dietary fiber may affect the cells that are responsible for breaking down and absorbing simple sugars and might help slow glucose absorption.

Whatever the exact mechanism, the result of a high fiber meal is a slower and more sustained release of glucose from the gastrointestinal tract into the bloodstream. This is very desirable because it will prevent the wide swings in blood sugar that occur when simple sugars are ingested without any fiber. In addition, it often reduces the amount of insulin necessary to control blood sugar.

From a practical standpoint, a person with diabetes should consume sugars in a form as close to the natural state as possible. For example, an apple is better than applesauce or apple juice. Furthermore, a diabetic person should increase the fiber content of his or her regular diet. We can add fiber in the form of bran or raw vegetables. Another form of fiber often overlooked is pectin, a soluble fiber from apples and citrus fruits. A powdered form is available in the canning section of your grocery store for making jellies and jams. A tablespoonful of it added to iced tea, for example, gives a fruity flavor, and it will significantly increase your fiber intake.

Although the importance of fiber in the diet of the diabetic patient has become more and more firmly established, the issue of the rate of release of simple sugars from foods is not settled. There were some surprising results when we compared the speeds with which different foods raise the blood-sugar levels. With a system that lists foods in their "glucose equivalents," glucose is assigned the number 100 and other foods are compared with it. Foods can then be related to each other as a percentage of the rate of absorption of glucose. This number is called the glycemic index. The more rapid the absorption, the higher the glycemic index. The lower the number, the more slowly the food raises the blood sugar. Table 14 shows the glycemic indexes for some common foods. Notice that certain foods previously thought to affect the blood sugar very slowly have a higher glycemic index than refined sugar (sucrose). Carrots, potatoes, and certain breads and cereals fall into this category. We seldom eat these foods in isolation (except as snacks), but as part of a meal in which they are mixed with fats, protein, and fiber.

Table 14. Glycemic Indexes of Common Carbohydrate Foods

Grain, Cereal Products:	(%)		(%)
		Potato (instant	80
		Potato (new)	70
Bread (white)	69	Potato (sweet)	48
Bread (whole grain)	72	Rutabaga*	72
Buckwheat	51	Yams	51
Millet	71	*Dried and Canned Legumes:*	
Pastry	59		
Rice (brown)	66	Beans (canned, baked)	40
Rice (white)	72	Beans (butter)	36
Spaghetti (whole-wheat)	42	Beans (green)	31
Spaghetti (white)	50	Beans (kidney)	29
Spaghetti (white)	50	Beans (soya)	15
Sponge cake	46	Beans (canned soya)	14
Sweet corn	59	Peas (blackeye)	33
Breakfast Cereals:		Peas (chick)	36
All-Bran	51	Peas (green)	47
Corn flakes	80	Lentils	29
Granola	66		
Oatmeal	49	*Fruits:*	
Shredded Wheat	67	Apples (Golden Delicious)	39
Cookies, Crackers:		Bananas	62
Digestive	59	Orange juice	46
Oatmeal	54	Oranges	40
Water	63	Raisins	64
		Sugars:	
Fresh Legumes:		Fructose	20
Broad beans*	79	Glucose	100
Frozen peas	51	Maltose	105
		Sucrose	59

Root Vegetables:			
Beets*	64	Dairy Products:	
Carrots*	92	Ice cream	36
Parsnips*	97	Milk (skim)	32
		Milk (whole)	34
		Yogurt	36
Miscellaneous:			
Sausages	28	Mars bar	68
Fish sticks	38	Tomato soup	38
Peanuts*	13	Honey	87
Potato chips	51		

*Only 25 g carbohydrate portion given

These components will attenuate the rate of absorption of the carbohydrates. When consumed alone, as in snacks, the glycemic index may be significant in how fast the sugars get into your bloodstream.

Finally, besides the composition of the diet, the frequency of meals is very important, particularly in the juvenile-onset diabetic and in patients with the most severe symptoms of maturity-onset diabetes. As we have seen, wide swings in the level of blood sugar should be avoided. Your physician will probably prescribe a combination of long-acting and short-acting insulin. Spacing your meals will help by producing a lower, but more sustained, elevation of blood sugar throughout the day. The person with juvenile-onset diabetes or severe insulin-dependent maturity-onset diabetes should consume five or even six meals per day. A good routine would be: breakfast, a mid-morning snack, lunch, a late afternoon snack, dinner, and an evening snack shortly before retiring.

The diet to lower our risk for diabetes depends on whether we are overweight. For anyone who is obese, the diet discussed in "Obesity" should be followed. There is no difference between weight-reduction diets for a person at risk for diabetes and for a person who is not. However, the urgency for starting weight reduction may be considerably greater if you are obese and also at high risk for diabetes. If you are obese, do not procrastinate!

If you are at risk for diabetes (whether you are overweight or not), you should use the Prudent Diet (low-total-fat, low-saturated-fat, low-trans-fatty acids, low-cholesterol) outlined in "Atherosclerosis." It is a low-cost insurance policy that should be instigated by anyone at risk for diabetes. In addition, if one of your risk factors is obesity or a tendency toward it, you should adhere to necessary calorie control as outlined in "Obesity." The diabetic individual should lower the amount of refined sugar in his or her diet, introduce day-to-day consistency, and utilize proper meal spacing. All these can be accomplished with plenty of variety in our food choices.

There is evidence that some individuals with latent diabetes are low in "glucose tolerance factor," an organic complex which includes chromium (much like vitamin B12 contains cobalt and hemoglobin contains iron) and assists insulin in getting sugar into the cells. These individuals may be helped temporarily with organic complexes containing chromium. The form of the element in most nutritional supplements, chromium picolinate, is relatively nontoxic, but high doses could be harmful. The best way to get trace minerals (in the right form) is by consuming plenty of fruits and vegetables. Chromium deficiency is not widespread. The metal is found in water (however, some of the metal in water may be toxic due to contamination from industrial waste. Chromium is poisonous in the chemical form used in chromium plating of automobile parts, for example.), beverages, and practically everything we eat. There is no scientific proof that chromium supplements will help us lose weight, build muscle, or lower our cholesterol levels. However, there is evidence that chromium supplements (or, preferably, foods and beverages rich in chromium) may improve glucose tolerance in persons who have Type 2 diabetes or are borderline diabetics.

To start calculating your diabetic diet, find your ideal body weight in the table on page 68. Because most food calculations use the metric system, convert your ideal body weight from pounds to kilograms by dividing the number by 2.2. Now, use the chart below (or the chart on page 82 of "Obesity") to calculate your energy need per day for each kilogram of ideal body weight, depending on your body weight and your level of physical activity.

Table 15. **Calorie Expenditure for Wt. and Activity**
(Calories per kilogram)

	Sedentary	Moderately active	Extremely active
Overweight	20-25	30	35
Normal	30	35	40
Underweight	35	40	45-50

Let us assume your ideal weight is 160 lbs. Dividing this figure by 2.2 gives about 73 kg. If you are obese and lead a sedentary life, multiply your ideal weight (73 kg) by 20; 1,460 cal per day is what you should consume. If you are overweight but not obese, multiply your ideal weight (73 kg) by 25; you are allowed 1,765 cal per day.

By contrast, if you are a very active person whose ideal weight is 73 kg and who is not overweight, multiply 73 by 40. You should consume almost 3,000 cal per day. As a final example, let us take a tall, somewhat underweight young juvenile diabetic who should weigh 160 lbs (73 kg) and who takes part in competitive athletics. Such an individual might require 73 times 50, or 3,650 cal per day.

Having determined the number of calories you require, you are now ready to allocate those calories between protein, carbohydrates, and fat.

Proteins—proteins (plural because there are more than one) are the most complex substances known to man. One scientist has called them "the noblest pieces of architecture invented by nature." Proteins, which can be likened to words and sentences, are made up of twenty amino acids, many used more than once, comparable to the twenty-six letters of varying combinations of our alphabet. And from these twenty amino acids, millions of different proteins can be manufactured.

Each type of cell in every animal, vegetable, and microbe contains its own particular kind of proteins; thousands of them. Indeed, proteins are the primary, basic components of life (hence their name, which comes from a Greek word meaning "of first rank"). Some proteins, such as the protein in bones, are part of the carpentry that keeps us erect. Some glue our cells together. Some (enzymes) act as chemical engineers whose job is to help put other substances together or take them apart, while others (antibodies) protect us from disease as part of our immune mechanism.

Little by little, we have discovered the structure of proteins, the arrangement of those building stones called amino acids. Some of these (the "essential" amino acids) have to be provided in the diet because the body cannot make them, while others (the "nonessential" amino acids) under the right conditions can be synthesized in the body. For a century, we've known that all proteins are not equivalent. For example, gelatin is a source of proteins, but you couldn't live on it as your only source because the proteins in it are incomplete. Incomplete proteins are somewhat, or completely, lacking in certain essential amino acids. In general, animal proteins (eggs, milk, meat, and fish) are complete proteins, while vegetable proteins are often incomplete. This means animal proteins contain the twenty amino acids that make up protein in about the same proportions we need to make body protein. Vegetable proteins have amino acids in less favorable proportions.

A mixture of animal and vegetable proteins adds up to better nutrition than do vegetable proteins alone. In fact, a mixture of vegetable proteins—say rice and peas—together with a relatively small amount of animal protein (as in a Chinese meal) may be as good as animal protein, considerably less expensive, and lower in fat than a huge steak!

In one sense, protein builds muscles. Protein is second only to water as a main constituent of body structures, particularly muscles but also tendons, skin, and other tissues. We need protein to develop muscles and keep them healthy. But muscle "building" or firming and strengthening doesn't come from eating an unusually large amount of protein. Muscle building takes exercise. And exercise does not significantly increase the need for protein over and above what your body requires if you lead a sedentary life.

Proteins from the foods we consume are broken into fragments by stomach acids and enzymes, and they are broken down even further (into single amino acids) in the intestine. After absorption from the intestines into the bloodstream, they're reassembled into human proteins. The body can even make some of its own amino acids out of other amino acids. These are the "nonessential" amino acids—so called not because they aren't essential to life, but because it isn't essential to eat these specific amino acids to get them. So long as you eat enough protein, generally, your body can manufacture them. Eight of the amino acids are essential; they must come from food because the body can't make them from other substances.

We need some kind of protein more than others. We can still use our analogy with printing: in the English language, the most frequently used letter is *e*, the next is *t*. So you need more of these letters to write something in English than you need *g*'s or *x*'s. Thus, proteins that contain the right proportion of amino acids necessary for life and health have greater "biological value."

The value of breast milk is high—close to a perfect 100. Whole egg protein is a close second—about 94—while cow's milk ranks 85, and meat and fish are fourth on the list, ranging from 76 to 86. Rice (surprisingly) ranks a fairly good—80. Lesser values are found in potatoes, soybeans, grains, peas, and beans.

You already know that meat ranks a little lower than some other proteins in value. But there's more to it than that. For one thing, about 60 percent of the calories in untrimmed meat come from fat; hence, you may have to eat a lot of calories and a lot of saturated fats to get the proteins from beef. Not only that, a mixture of proteins is often better than a single one—or several single ones—taken one at a time. Wheat, for example, is low in the amino acid lysine. But milk does contain it more liberally. So—believe it or not—ordinary white bread made of wheat and skim milk powder is a fairly good source of protein with good biological value. Chinese meals show how well proteins supplement each other. Rice is low in four essential amino acids, but beans supply two of these, and the other two are in beef, pork, poultry or fish, the usual components of Chinese dinners.

Convincing studies have shown that an ounce a day of pure protein of good quality is minimally sufficient for the average adult woman. A man, being bigger, needs somewhat more. Children, adolescents, and pregnant and nursing women need considerably more. A number of experiments have shown that habitual strenuous exercise does not increase protein requirements, in spite of almost universal belief to the contrary among coaches, athletes, and the public.

We don't know the advantages, if any, of going far above the minimum protein necessary for life or optimal growth. In the adult, we have seen that an ounce or so of a good protein daily will maintain the average man or woman in good health. To ensure a safety margin, the usual recommendation is about 2 oz. Actually, many American men eat between three and 4 oz of protein every day, three to four times as much as is required, and almost twice the recommended intake, which already has a margin of safety.

While both low-protein and high-protein diets have had their proponents, the evidence in favor of or against either position are scant. The long-term differences between high- and low-protein diets are especially hard to evaluate. High-protein diets are usually based on meat and are high in saturated fats (beef, unless it is very lean, may have up to three times as many calories from fat as from protein). Very low-protein diets are often poor from other viewpoints; for instance, they are low in certain vitamins and minerals.

The legumes (dry beans, lima beans, peas, and peanuts) are relatively high in protein of fairly high biological value. Cereal proteins have low biological values, but when they are combined with milk or cheese, their biological values increase. The essential factors missing in cereal proteins are abundant in milk proteins.

Most vegetarians include dairy products and eggs (high quality, "complete" animal proteins) in their diets. So they are not vegetarians in a strict sense, but "ovo-lacto" vegetarians. When no animal protein is consumed, there is danger of vitamin B12 deficiency. Much caution is needed when there are growing children in your family. They need lots of complete (high biological value) protein to build enzymes and hormones, muscles, and other tissues for growth.

Making a rough estimate of your protein intake is fairly simple. An ounce (28.4 g) of relatively lean meat or an ounce of fish, poultry, or cheese contains, on the average, 7 g of protein, as does one egg. Fattier meats, of course, provide less. An 8-oz glass of milk provides 8 g. A serving from the bread and cereal group contains about 2 g, and a cup of dried peas or beans is about 14 g or about twice the amount in an ounce of meat.

So, if you eat 6 oz of meat-group foods (which adds up to 42 g of protein), 2 cups of milk (16 g), and 4 servings from the bread and cereal group (8 g), you have easily met your protein requirement for the day. Cereal proteins, which are not as complete as others, are enhanced by combining them with animal proteins. Eating dry cereal with milk is a classic example of how cereal protein is improved in a natural combination of foods. Protein is one of the nutrients listed in grams per serving right on the label under the guidelines for nutritional labeling of foods.

A more generous allowance for an adult and the most frequently quoted rule of thumb is 1 g per kg of your ideal weight, no matter what you weigh. Thus, all the people described above would have the same protein requirement—73 g (for the person whose ideal weight is 160 lbs). This represents roughly 300 cal.

The obese, sedentary individual will therefore be taking in 20 percent of his calories as protein. This amount is somewhat high, but is acceptable in the absence of kidney or liver disease. Other individuals should have no problems with this amount of protein. Three hundred calories represents about 18 percent of 1,800 cal, 10 percent of 3,000 cal, and about 8 percent of 3,600 cal. Use the 12 percent rule for the latter two. (12 percent of 3,000 is 360, and 12 percent of 3,650 is 438).

Carbohydrates—are made of carbon and of hydrogen and oxygen in the proportion seen in water, hence their name. They are major sources of energy for most of the world's people. They are assembled in green plants by the light from the sun working on carbon dioxide and water. They come to us as starches and sugars for nourishment and as cellulose for roughage (fiber). The starches figure prominently in such foods as potatoes, cereals, and breads. Ordinary table sugar, white or brown, is sucrose, which is made of fructose and glucose—two "simple" sugars. Glucose (known also as dextrose or blood sugar) deserves emphasis. It can be synthesized by the body from other carbohydrates and also from protein. Glucose is the only true "brain food." It is overwhelmingly the main fuel for the brain (perhaps the only one under normal circumstances). Under resting conditions (sleeping), the brain uses 50 percent of the total energy consumed by the body. When blood glucose is very low, the brain can use ketones (from breakdown of amino acids) for energy. The level of our blood glucose must be neither too low (hypoglycemic) or too high (hyperglycemic).

The body stores some glucose in the liver and the muscles as glycogen, a complex carbohydrate similar to starch; enough for quick energy needed in the next twelve to twenty-four hours. The remainder of that not needed for immediate energy production is converted to fat.

Carbohydrates should account for 55 to 60 percent of total calories—at least 825 cal for the obese and sedentary person (ideal weight 73 kg), 990 cal for the overweight sedentary person, 1,650 cal for the active, not obese person, and 1,980 cal for the young, active, underweight diabetic. Remember that 10 percent, or less, of total calories should come from simple sugar and only a small amount of this should be refined sugar. Thus, the first person is allowed 150 cal from these carbohydrates, the second 180 cal, the third 300 cal, and the fourth 365 cal. More specifically, the obese sedentary person can consume 625 cal as complex carbohydrate and 150 cal as simple sugar (total 825). The overweight sedentary person can consume 810 cal as complex carbohydrate and 180 as simple sugar (total 990). The normal-weight, very active person can consume 1,350 cal as complex carbohydrate and 300 as simple sugar (total 1,650), and the underweight diabetic athlete can take in 1,615 cal as complex carbohydrate and 365 as simple sugar (total 1,980).

Fats—the rest of your calories will come from fat. See "Atherosclerosis" for a discussion of fats. In the case of the first person discussed above, 1,500 (total) minus 300 (protein) and 825 (carbohydrate), or 375 cal will come from fat. One-hundred-fifty cal (10 percent of total energy) of this can be saturated fat. The second person could take in slightly more fat calories, 510; the third, about 990 cal; and the fourth, about 1,182 cal. (Remember that protein and carbohydrate yield 4 cal per g, whereas fat yields 9 cal per g.) Thus, even the young underweight athlete will be consuming only about 130 g (about 4.7 oz) of fat. To construct your own diet, you need to know the composition of all the foods you consume. However, it is not practical for a diabetic to calculate his or her allowances from scratch. Therefore, "exchange lists," which group foods of similar composition, have been devised. By knowing the number of calories you require and employing these lists, you can arrange a diet that meets all the criteria outlined above.

Using the exchange lists in Table 16, you can convert your diet requirements into food servings, and distribute these among meals and snacks without going through all the calculations. The foods in the exchange lists are grouped according to their nutrient similarities: vegetables; fruits and juices; and starchy foods (breads, cereals, and beans) are together as are meat, fish, and poultry; milk products; and fats. Within each list, foods are shown in specific quantities or units. An "exchange" means a serving of a food within a list can be exchanged for another one within the same list. On the fruit list, you can exchange ten cherries for 1/2 cup of orange juice. On the meat list, you can substitute 1 oz of lean beef for 1 oz of fish or skinned poultry, or for two teaspoons of peanut butter. Or you can make two or more exchanges. For example, ten cherries and one-half cup of orange juice equal one large apple (each equals one-half apple, or one small apple). Three meat exchanges would equal 3 oz of lean meat, or three small lobster tails, or 3/4 of a cup of tuna fish or salmon, or two eggs and 1/2 oz of hard cheese. To accommodate individual preferences, the possible combinations allow many choices.

Table 16. **Exchange Lists**

List 1. *Free Foods*

Bouillon	Mustard	Endive		
Clear broth	Pickle, sour	Escarole		
Coffee		Pickle, dill—	Lettuce (all	
Sparkling water		unsweetened	kinds)	
Tea			Parsley	Radishes
Gelatin,	Chicory	Vinegar		
(unsweetened)	Chinese	Watercress		
Lemon, lime		cabbage	Watercress	

List 2. *Vegetable Exchanges*
One exchange (½ cup cooked or 1 cup raw) of vegetables contains about 5 grams of carbohydrate, 2 grams of protein, and 25 kcal.

All leafy greens	Cauliflower	Sauerkraut	
Asparagus	Celery	Summer squash	
Bean sprouts	Cucumbers	Tomatoes—1 cup	
Beans (green or wax)	Eggplant	(raw or ½ cup)	
Broccoli	Mushrooms	Tomato or vegetable	
Beets	Okra	juice—6 oz.	
Brussels sprouts	Onions	Catsup (2 tbs.)	
Cabbage (all kinds)	Peppers (red or green)		
Carrots	Rutabaga		

List 3. *Fruit Exchanges*

One exchange of fruit contains 15 grams of carbohydrate and 60 kcal.

FRUITS:

Apple—1 small
Applesauce—½ cup
Apricots, fresh—4
Apricots, dried—7 halves
Bananas—½ (9" fruit)
Fruit cocktail, canned—¾ cup
Figs, dried—2 small
Grapefruit—½ med.
Grapes—15
Honeydew—⅛ med.
Mango—½ med.
Nectarine—1 med.
Orange—1 med.

Blueberries—¾ cup
Cantaloupe—⅓ med. (5" diam.)
Cherries—12 large
Dates—2 ½ med.
Papaya—½ med.
Peach—1 med.
Pear—1 small
Pineapple—¾ cup
Prunes, dried—3
Raisins—2 tbs.
Strawberries—1¼ cup
Tangerine—1 large
Watermelon—1¼ cup, cubed

JUICES:

Apple, pineapple—½ cup
Grapefruit, orange—½ cup
Grape, prune—⅓ cup

List 4. *Starch/Bread Exchanges* (cooked servings).

One exchange of starch contains 15 grams of carbohydrate, 3 grams of protein, and 80 kcal.

BREADS:

Any loaf—1 slice
Bagel—½
Dinner roll—1 (2" diam.)
English muffin—½

Bun, hamburger or hot dog—½
Cornbread (1½")—1 cube
Tortilla (6 "diam.)—1

VEGETABLES:

Beans or peas (plain), cooked—½ cup
Corn—⅓ cup or ½ med. ear
Parsnips—⅔ cup
Pumpkin—¾ cup

Potatoes, White—1 small or ½ cup
Potatoes, sweet or yams—¼ cup
Winter squash—½ cup

DESSERTS:

Fat free sherbet—4 oz

Angel cake (1½" square)—1

CRACKERS:

Graham (2½" square)—2
Matzoh (4" x 6")
Melba toast—4
Oyster (½ cup) 20

Pretzels—8 rings
RyKrisp—3
Saltines—5

CEREALS:

Bran—5 tbs.

Dry flakes—²/₃ cup

Dry puffed—1½ cups

Hot cereal—½ cup

Pasta—½ cup

Rice—½ cup

Wheat germ—2 tbs.

List 5. *Meat Exchanges* (cooked weight)

One exchange of meat contains 7 grams of protein, 5 grams of fat, and 75 kcal. (Based on med. fat meat—For higher fat content of meat, count one fat exchange (list 7) for each 5 grams of additional fat.

Beef, dried, chipped—1 oz.	Beef, lamb, pork, veal (lean)—1 oz.	Cottage cheese, uncreamed—¼ cup
Poultry without skin—1 oz.	Tuna, packed in water—¼ cup	Egg—1 med.
Fish—1 oz.	Salmon, pink,	Hard cheese—½ oz.
Lobster Tail—1 (small)	canned—¼ cup	Peanut butter—2 tsp.
		Oysters, clams, shrimp—5 med.

List 6. *Milk Exchanges*

One exchange of milk contains 12 grams of carbohydrate, 8 grams of protein, and 90 kcal.

Buttermilk, fat free—1 cup   Skim milk—1 cup   1% fat milk—7 oz.

Yogurt, plain, made with nonfat milk—³/₄ cup

List 7. *Fat Exchanges*

One exchange of fat contains 5 grams of fat and 45 kcal.

Avocado (4" diam.)—⅛	French dressing—1 tbs.	Olives—5 small
Bacon, crisp—1 slice	Roquefort dressing—2 tsp	Peanuts—10
Butter, margarine—1 tsp	Thousand Island	Oil—1 tsp.
Dressing—2 tsp	Walnuts—6 small	Mayonnaise—1tsp

The same exchange lists are used regardless of how many calories you will be consuming. Table 17 lists the number of items from each exchange list permitted daily for persons taking in 1,000, 1,200, 1,500, and 1,800 cal (most adult-onset diabetics). If you need more calories, simply double the items in the appropriate column. For example, if you require 2,000 cal, double the 1,000-cal list; if 3,000, double the 1,500-cal list, and so forth. When Table 17 is used, the protein intake at all calorie levels will be adequate. Vitamin and mineral supplementation should not be necessary if selections are made from a variety of foods, except that iron should be given to women on 1,000 or 1,200 cal. Let us now construct a daily menu for a person on a 1,500-cal diet. By using similar menus that fit the overall number of exchanges listed in Table 17, you can devise an endless variety and remain within the limitations set forth in this chapter. This system takes into account your individual food preferences, and when spaced according to your doctor's orders, it will allow the use of the minimum amount of insulin necessary to control your diabetes. As a practical matter, some of your meals such as soups, stews, and pizzas, you may include prepared foods composed of combinations of the exchange groups.

We have included a list of commercial meals, frozen entrees, snacks, etc. in "Appendix A" (page 245). Alcoholic beverages (alcohol is counted as fat) are listed in "Appendix B" (page 255).

These lists are included for your perusal to evaluate your personal food choices, not to recommend any commercial products, and because manufacturers occasionally change the composition and packaging of their products, the values presented here may not exactly represent products currently on the market.

Table 17. **Number of Exchange Portions Allowed Daily for Various Calorie Levels**

Food Exchange Group	1000	1200	1500	1800
List 1-Free Foods		.....Unlimited.....		
List 2-Vegetable Portions	2	2	3	3
List 3-Fruit Portions	3	4	5	5
List 4-Starch Portions	3	4	6	9
List 5-Protein Portions	4	4	4	5
List 6-Milk Portions	2	2	2	2
List 7-Fat Portions	1	2	4	4

Since diabetes is often accompanied by other medical problems that require special diets, the basic diet may have to be further modified. Salt restriction may be necessary if you have heart or kidney disease. Some people with kidney or liver problems may need to lower their protein intake. For most diabetic people, however, the basic diet offers calorie control, low fat, high complex carbohydrate, and low simple sugar. If used wisely, it can provide ample amounts of fiber and plenty of variety.

It may be difficult at first to use these lists, but in the long run, it will be worth your patience to stick with it. While this plan may be somewhat more restrictive than some, it can be used not only for the person who already has diabetes but also by anyone who wishes to lose weight or lower his or her risk for atherosclerosis. A sample seven-day menu is presented in Table 18. You can easily revise it for your own taste by exchanging your choice for each item from the appropriate food list. It offers a viable alternative to people at risk for obesity or atherosclerosis. It is not very different from the plans used in the chapters that discuss those diseases. It does not control your salt intake. If you are at risk for high blood pressure, it must be adjusted in the same way as any other diet (see "Hypertension"). A person who has a combined high risk for diabetes and high blood pressure can modify this diet to lower its salt content and still get all the necessary nutrients.

Table 18. **A Sample Basic Menu Schedule**

Day 1
Morning

List 4 = 1 starch	½ cup cooked oatmeal
List 4 = 1 starch	1 slice raisin toast sprinkled with cinnamon-sugar
List 3 = 1 fruit	½ cup orange juice
List 6 = 1 milk	1 cup 2% milk
List 7 = 1 fat	

Noon

List 5 = 2 protein	¼ recipe tuna and pasta salad:
List 4 = 2 starch	1 can tuna in spring water, 4 cups cooked shell pasta
List 2 = 2 vegetable	2 cups tender-crisp chunks of carrots and zucchini, chopped scallions
List 7 = 2 fat	2 tablespoons reduced-calorie mayonnaise
List 3 = 2 fruit	2 medium tangerines
List 1 -- free --	1 glass ice tea

Evening

List 4 = 2 starch	2 sl. of 10-inch thin-crust cheese pizza
List 5 = 2 protein	Lettuce salad with 1 cup tomato wedges, cucumber slices, mushrooms and scallions
List 2 = 1 vegetable	
List 7 = 1 fat	2 tbs. red-wine vinegar/Canola oil dressing
List 6 = 1 milk	1 cup 2% milk
List 7 = 1 fat	

Snack

List 3 = 2 fruit	1 cup cubed cantaloupe with squeeze of lemon

Day 2
Morning

Egg and muffin sandwich:

List 5 = 1 protein	1 poached egg and sliced tomato on
List 4 = 2 starch	1 English muffin
List 3 = 1 fruit	½ cup orange juice
List 1 -- free --	1 cup coffee

Noon

List 2 = 1 vegetable	1 cup cream of broccoli soup (made with 2% milk)
List 4 = 2 starch	

List 6 = ½ milk
List 7 = 2 fat   1 ounce reduced-fat cheddar cheese
List 4 = ½ starch   2 bread sticks
List 2 = 1 vegetable   6 cherry tomatoes
List 3 = 1 fruit   1 small pear
List 6 = ½ milk   ½ cup 2% milk
List 7 = ½ fat

Evening

List 5 = 3 protein   3 ounce broiled halibut steak marinated in
                              juice of 2 lemon and 2 lime, chopped
List 7 = 1 fat   garlic, and shallots
List 4 = 1 starch   ½ cup packaged rice mix (made without
   .   margarine)
List 2 = 1 vegetable   ½ cup steamed beets sprinkled with fresh
                              chives
List 4 = 1 starch   1 slice crusty whole wheat bread
List 3 = 1 fruit   ½ cup fresh fruit salad
List 6 = 1milk   1 cup 2% milk
List 7 = 1 fat

Snack

List 4 = 1 starch   3 cups microwave popcorn (light)
List 7 = 1 fat
List 3 = 2 fruit   1 large apple
List 1 -- free --   Sparkling water

Day 3
Morning

List 4 = 2 starch   2 frozen blueberry waffles
List 7 = 1 fat
List 1 -- free --   1 tablespoon reduced-calorie syrup
List 3 = 1 fruit   1 kiwi
List 6 = 1 milk   1 cup 2% milk
List 7 = 1 fat

Noon

List 5 = 2 protein   2 ounces lean roast beef,
List 2 = 1 vegetable   Dijon mustard, sweet onion,
List 4 = 2 starch   lettuce and tomato on onion roll
List 3 = 2 fruit   1 banana
List 1 -- free --   Sparkling water

Evening

List 5 = 3 protein   3 oz. ginger-chicken (stir-fried with chopped

List 7 = 1 fat	garlic and ginger root in 1 teaspoon sesame oil
List 2 = 2 vegetable	1 cup snow peas, fresh mushrooms and red peppers
List 4 = 1 starch	½ cup brown rice
List 3 = 1 fruit	½ cup mandarin oranges
List 6 = 1milk	1 cup 2% milk
List 7 = 1 fat	

Snack

List 4 = 1 starch	5 oyster crackers (1 oz.)
List 3 = 1 fruit	4 oz. orange juice

Day 4
Morning

List 4 = 2 starch	1 bagel
List 7 = 1 fat	1 tablespoon cream cheese
List 3 = 2 fruit	1¼ cup low-calorie cranberry juice cocktail

Noon

List 4 = 1 starch	½ cup cooked spaghetti topped with
List 2 = 2 vegetable	¼ cup meatless spaghetti sauce
List 5 = 2 protein	2 tablespoons Parmesan cheese
List 4 = 1 starch	1 piece garlic bread
List 7 = 1 fat	1 teaspoon margarine
List 3 = 2 fruit	1 cup fruit cocktail

Evening

List 5 = 2 protein	2 ounces lean ham
List 4 = 1 starch	½ cup packaged au gratin potato mix (made with skim milk)
List 2 = 2 vegetable	Spinach salad with 1 cup shredded
List 1 -- free --	carrots, tomato wedges, sweet
List 7 = 1 fat	onion and white wine-wine vinegar with tarragon/canola
List 3 = 1 fruit	1 small pear
List 6 = 1 milk	1 cup 2% milk
List 7 = 1 fat	

Snack

List 4 = 1 starch	2 graham crackers
List 6 = 1 milk	1 cup 2% milk
List 7 = 1 fat	

Day 5
Morning

List 4 = 1 starch	½ cup bran flakes cereal
List 4 = 1 starch	1 slice whole-wheat toast
List 1 -- free --	1 teaspoon low-sugar spread able fruit
List 6 = 1 milk	1 cup 2% milk
List 7 = 1 fat	

Noon

List 2 = 1 vegetable	1 cup vegetable soup
List 4 = 2 starch	2 slices crisp bread
List 5 = 2 protein	2 ounces reduced-fat Swiss cheese
List 3 = 2 fruit	1 large apple
List 6 = 1 milk	1 cup 2% milk
List 7 = 1 fat	

Evening

List 5 = 2 protein	1 cup Broccoli Seafood Linguine
List 4 = 1 starch	
List 2 = 1 vegetable	Cucumber salad with herb-flavored
List 7 = 2 fat	vinegar/canola oil dressing
List 3 = 1 fruit	2 plums
List 1 -- free --	1 glass ice tea

Snack

List 4 = 1 starch	5 gingersnaps
List 3 = 2 fruit	1 cup orange juice

Day 6
Morning

List 6 = 1 milk	1 cup plain non-fat yogurt mixed
List 3 = 1 fruit	with ½-cup chunky applesauce
List 4 = 1 starch	1 English muffin
List 1 -- free --	1 teaspoon low-sugar spreadable fruit
List 3 = 1 fruit	½ cup orange juice

Noon

List 5 = 1 protein	1 ounce sliced turkey breast
	1 tablespoon reduced calorie mayonnaise,
List 7 = 1 fat	sliced tomato and alfalfa sprouts on
List 4 = 2 starch	2 slices dark rye bread
List 3 = 1 fruit	2 tablespoons whole cranberry sauce
List 2 = 1 vegetable	½ cup green pepper sticks
List 1 -- free --	1 glass iced tea

Evening

List 5 = 3 protein	3 ounces broiled top round steak
List 7 = 2 fat	with fresh mushrooms sautéed in
	Worcestershire sauce and
	1 tablespoon olive oil
List 2 = 1 vegetable	1 4-inch frozen corn on-the-cob
List 2 = 1 vegetable	½ cup baby carrots
List 4 = 2 starch	2 slices French bread (toasted)
List 6 = 1 milk	1 cup 2% milk
List 7 = 1 fat	

Snack

List 4 = 1 starch	12 pretzel sticks
List 3 = 2 fruit	1 large apple
List 1 -- free --	Sparkling water

Day 7

Morning

List 3 = 1 fruit	½ small grapefruit
List 5 = 1 protein	1 large poached egg
List 4 = 1 starch	1 slice whole wheat bread
List 6 = 1 milk	1 cup 2% milk
List 7 = 1 fat	

Noon

List 5 = 1 protein	2 slices fat-free cheese, lettuce,
List 1 -- free --	pickles, lemon juice, vinegar
List 4 = 2 starch	2 slices bread
List 7 = 2 fat	2 tsp. mayonnaise
List 2 = 1 vegetable	3 slices tomato
List 3 = 1 fruit	½ cup diced pineapple
List 6 = 1 milk	1 cup 2% milk
List 7 = 1 fat	

Snack

List 3 = 2 fruit	1 large apple

Evening

List 5 = 2 protein	2 oz. chicken (no skin), lettuce, radishes, soy
	sauce, vinegar
List 2 = 2 vegetable	½ cup string beans
	½ cup cauliflower
List 4 = 1 starch	1 slice bread
List 3 = 1 fruit	1 medium orange
List 1 -- free --	Sparkling water

Snack

List 4 = 1 starch   ½ cup low-fat ice cream
List 7 = 2 fat
List 4 = 1 starch   1½ in. square sponge cake

*This basic menu has 1,500 calories—about 55 percent from carbohydrate, 20 to 25 percent from protein and less than 30 percent from fat. If you need more than 1,500 calories, use this guide:

1,600 calories—add servings: 1 starch (list 4)
1,700 calories—add servings: 2 starch, 1 protein (List 5)
1,800 calories—add servings: 3 starch, 1 protein,
1,900 calories—add servings: 3 starch, 1 protein,
    1 fruit (list 3),1 vegetable (List 2),1 fat (List 7)
2,000 calories—add servings: 3 starch, 2 protein,
    1 fat, 2 fruit, 1 vegetable.

Once you have diabetes, you will have it for the rest of your life. Therefore, it is important to have a regimen that will offer you the most options. Develop your own plan (with whatever professional help you need)—and stick with it! You will reap many benefits.

Cancer

Cancer will soon overtake heart disease as the leading cause of premature deaths in the United States, and there is a strong linkage between the kinds of food we eat and the incidence of specific types of the disease. It has been estimated that 50 percent of all cancers in women and 30 percent in men are associated with environmental factors. Food supply is one of the most important causes. Concern has been mounting that food additives of various kinds may be contributing to the rising incidence of certain types of malignancies. In addition, there is evidence that substances "contaminating" our food supply, such as pesticide residues or industrial wastes, are increasing our risks for certain cancers.

These data, important as they are, should not detract from linkage between the kinds of food we eat and the increasing incidence of specific types of cancer. This problem defies regulation and cannot be blamed on any product or any manufacturer. The evidence comes both from studies of large human populations and from experiments on animals. The best data relate to two very common types of cancer—those of the breast and colon.

Cancer of the breast is a leading cause of death in the United States. The incidence of breast cancer is much lower in other parts of the world. If we list countries in the order of incidence of breast cancer, we can make an important generalization. The more highly developed the country, the higher the incidence of breast cancer. More careful scrutiny of the data gives us certain clues about which aspects of "modern living" contribute to this problem. Certain westernized countries—for example, Japan—do not show this high incidence of breast cancer.

By contrast, when Japanese people migrate to California and adopt the Western eating pattern, their children have the same incidence of this cancer as other Californians. If, on the other hand, they continue to eat as their parents did in Japan, few have cancer of the breast. Therefore, some element in our Western diet contributes to the high incidence of the disease. The strongest correlation appears to be with the amount of fat in the diet. The more fat the population of a particular country consumes, the higher the incidence of breast cancer, regardless of how developed a country is. The United States, with its high-fat diet, ranks high; but certain countries that consume more fat, such as Finland, rank even higher.

How does this high consumption of fat contribute to breast cancer? We know that hormones play an important role. The disease appears predominately in women. Animal studies suggest that a diet high in fat will result in an imbalance of female hormones. It is postulated that this hormone imbalance in some way promotes the occurrence of cancer of the breast. Women may alter their hormonal balance by consuming a high-fat diet, becoming more susceptible to breast cancer.

Colon cancer: cancer of the large intestine is very common in the United States, and its incidence is increasing. Like cancer of the breast, it occurs more often in developed countries. Certain migrating populations have an incidence of this cancer that more closely matches that of their adopted country. This increase is noticeable as soon as they change their eating patterns to resemble those of the native population. The best correlation of cancer of the colon is with dietary fat. The more fat consumed, the higher the incidence of the disease. People such as Seventh

Day Adventists, who consume little fat, show a low incidence of colon cancer.

Sex hormones play little or no role in the development of colon cancer; it happens with equal frequency in men and women. How then does this disease originate? Animal experiments suggest that a high-fat diet changes the normal bacterial makeup in the large intestine to favor the survival of bacteria that can easily transform fat into other products. One or more products of this bacterial transformation may act as a carcinogen (cancer-producing agent) or may promote the activity of carcinogens already in the large intestine. For example, certain substances normally secreted in the bile are known to be carcinogens. A high-fat diet may indirectly increase the carcinogenic activity of these substances.

The low-fiber content of the American diet may intensify the problem. Fiber is the carbohydrate portion of our food that is not digested and absorbed by our bodies. It is derived from plant sources, such as the bran of certain grains and from the skin and fleshy portion of fruits and vegetables. Dietary fiber draws water into it. Hence, as the fiber passes through the gastrointestinal tract, it softens the stool. The softer the stool, the faster it moves through the colon and the less time it is in contact with the intestinal wall. Thus, if the diet is high in fiber, the length of time the wall of the colon is exposed to cancer-inducing components in the stool will decrease. This is the theoretical mechanism by which a high-fiber diet provides some protection against colon cancer.

*Cancer of the uterus:*Another of the most common forms of cancer in women affects the uterus. This form of cancer is slightly more frequent in obese than in lean women. This is particularly true in those who have been obese since childhood. In one study, uterine cancer was one and a half times as frequent in women who suffered from obesity since adolescence as in women who were not obese. (The adolescent form of obesity often leads to an intractable form of adult obesity.)

There is some evidence that cancer of the ovaries and of the prostate may also be directly related to dietary fat intake. Cancer of the stomach, while affected by diet, is probably not related to fat. This cancer is much more prevalent in Japan than in the United States, and its incidence decreases when Japanese people migrate to California or Hawaii. However, the incidence of stomach cancer in Japan is decreasing. This may be due to their increased use of refrigeration as opposed to salting to preserve foods. The use of food additives such as BHA and BHT (antioxidant preservatives) in processed foods is another explanation for decreases in the incidence of stomach cancer.

Certain other factors are implicated for cancer of the breast, which occurs almost exclusively in women. It is most common among Caucasian women, less common among African-American women, and least common among Asian-American women. (The risk in men is so small that the male population can be excluded from our discussion.)

Any woman who wants to determine her risk for breast cancer should examine her family history as completely as possible. A strong family history increases a woman's risk for the disease. The closer your relationship to the member of your family tree who has or had breast cancer, the higher your risk. If your mother had breast cancer, your chances of developing it are statistically greater than if your great-aunt or a cousin had the disease. If the disease appears regularly in your family, your risk is greater than if it appears sporadically.

Regardless of other risk factors, women of high socioeconomic status have a slightly higher incidence than women of lower social or economic status. The reason for this is not certain. We feel that it is due to higher amounts of fat consumed by the higher-status women. Single women are at greater risk than married women. This may be because they are much less likely to have completed a pregnancy. The more times a woman has become pregnant and carried to term, the lower her risk for cancer of the breast. While some reduction in risk is associated with each subsequent pregnancy, the greatest difference is between women who have never carried a pregnancy to term and those who have completed at least one pregnancy. The younger a woman is when she completes her first pregnancy, the lower her risk for breast cancer. Most of the difference occurs in women who are over thirty-five at the time they complete their first pregnancy. Though significant, the increase in risk is very small.

Women who reached puberty (menarche) late are at lower risk than those who underwent an early puberty. The trend toward earlier puberty in girls in Western countries may be associated with the increasing incidence of breast cancer. This trend may relate to our "better" diet. Some epidemiological studies suggest that, to the extent that this "better" diet is higher in fat, it may be contributing to the increased incidence of breast cancer. Japanese girls attain puberty later than American girls. The average caloric intake of the Japanese diet is about 1,000 cal less than ours. The primary difference is in the amount of fat consumed. Some studies suggest that the heavier a girl is, the earlier her menstrual periods will occur. As Japanese girls in higher socioeconomic classes have adopted Western lifestyles and a Western diet, their average weight has increased, their dietary fat consumption has gone up, their menstrual periods have begun earlier, and their incidence of breast cancer has risen. Thus, the increased risk imparted by the early onset of menstruation may be indirect. The direct cause may be an increase in the fat content of the diet.

The later the occurrence of menopause and the longer a woman's reproductive life, the higher her risk of developing cancer of the breast. Thus, women who have shorter reproductive lives because of late onset of menarche, early menopause, or both, are at lower risk than women who have long reproductive lives.

The risks for cancer of the uterus are not as well defined as those for cancer of the breast. One risk seems to be obesity, especially a history of it during adolescence, but the increase is small and may be indirect. Obesity is associated with early menarche, and this combination of features may contribute to the incidence. Late menopause or the use of estrogens to prevent the discomforts associated with menopause also increases the risk somewhat. This is a major concern, but, as we shall see in the chapter on osteoporosis, the use of progesterone together with estrogen substantially reduces and may even eliminate the threat.

No general aspect of cancer of the colon separates people at high and low risk. However, one specific factor, the existence of polyps, under certain conditions, predisposes us to colon cancer. Polyps are non-cancerous growths that may occur within the intestine. If present, polyps should be treated by a physician.

Tests are now available to identify individuals in high-risk families who carry specific genes for cancer of the breast. However, while this form of cancer has the best-defined risk, it is not possible, at this stage of our knowledge, to separate all individuals who are at high risk from those at low or moderate risk. If you have several of the factors mentioned above, your risk is substantial. Cancer of the breast is serious enough that all women should consider dietary modification, especially if they are affected by one or more risk factor. Neither cancer of the colon nor uterine cancer can be quantitated. We can only recommend dietary changes based on the statistical chances of developing certain cancers. Someday, we may identify everyone at risk for particular cancers and be able to recommend specific dietary changes for them.

Since the dietary modifications are similar to those needed to reduce the risk of breast cancer, a low-fat, high-fiber diet is the best protection from the diet-related cancers that occur in this country. There is already enough evidence to encourage prudence in the amount of fat we eat. We estimate that most Americans consume an average of 12 g of fiber daily, compared with 20 to 30 g recommended by the American Cancer Society. Fiber-rich foods are fruits, vegetables, peas, beans, nuts, and grains. These foods are also sources of complex carbohydrates (starches) and, except for nuts, are very low in fat.

On the other hand, whole milk and whole milk products are high in fat and virtually fiber-free. Ideally, fat, whether visible (as in meat) or invisible (as in cheese), should contribute no more than 25 percent of the day's total calories. If you eat 2,000 cal a day, no more than 500 should come from fat, and that amount is equal to 55 g of fat. To keep within that amount, fried foods and spreads are limited and low-fat protein foods are encouraged (see Table 19).

Table 19. **Fat Content of Some Protein Foods**
(in Servings Providing 10 Grams of Protein)

Food	Amount	Grams Fat
Skim milk	9 oz.	0.1
Uncreamed cottage cheese	½ oz.	0.17
Cooked shrimp	1½ oz.	0.5
Cooked rice and beans	½ cup	0.7
Chicken (no skin)	1½ oz.	1.5
Pink salmon (canned)	1¾ oz.	3.0
Haddock	1¾ oz.	3.3
Veal (trimmed)	1½ oz.	4.5
Low-fat yogurt	10 oz.	5.0
Hamburger (lean)	1½ oz.	5.0
Hamburger (regular)	1½ oz.	8.5
Eggs (large)	1½ oz.	10.0
Ham	1½ oz.	10.0
American cheese	1½ oz.	13.5

The recommended changes require simple adjustments. Eat more vegetables—the more raw, the better—and whole grain products. Eat the skin on your boiled or baked potato, consider raisins or almonds as alternatives to candy bars, and avoid fried foods in favor of fresh fruits and salads. Consider a slice or two of "fat free" cheese on whole wheat bread for breakfast or with an apple for your evening snack. It will contribute calcium to your diet without the hazards of the saturated fats in regular dairy products.

Table 20. **High- and Low-Fiber Menus**

Low-Fiber/High-Fat   *High-Fiber/Low-Fat*
                    Breakfast
8 oz. orange juice   1 orange
1 slice white bread   1 slice whole wheat bread
1 tsp. butter   1 tbs. apple butter
6 oz. whole milk   1 cup 40% bran flakes
½ cup canned peaches   6 oz. skim milk
1 cup corn flakes   1 tbs. almonds and
                                  1 tbs. raisins

                    Lunch
3 oz. roast beef   3 oz. turkey (white meat)
1½ tbs. mayonnaise   on whole wheat bread
20 French fries   mustard and lettuce
6 oz. instant onion soup   tossed salad with lemon juice
Cola   1 cup vegetable soup
Gelatin dessert and topping   8 oz. apricot nectar
                                  1 medium apple

                    Snack
Snack pie   ½ cup dried fruit- and-nut mix
Coffee and cream   6 oz. vegetable juice
                    Dinner
4 oz. fried chicken   4 oz. broiled fish
½ cup macaroni and cheese   1 cup gumbo (corn, tomatoes, okra)
¼ cup Cole slaw   1 cup brown rice
½ cup buttered peas   1 cup fresh relish (radishes, celery,
2 dinner rolls   green pepper, carrot curls)
2 tsp. margarine   1 slice Banana Bran Bread
¾ cup frozen yogurt   ¼ cantaloupe wedge
                    Snack
10 potato chips   1½ cups popcorn
12 oz. carbonated beverage   (plain, air popped)
                                  12 oz. apple juice

                    Total
120 grams fat   45 grams fat

Tables 20 and 21 will help you select some of your favorite foods to increase the fiber content of your diet.

Table 21. **Dietary Fiber Content of Some Foods**

Food	Measure	Fiber(g)			
Almonds	½ cup	3.2	Lettuce, romaine	2 leaves	0.4
Apple, unpeeled	1 small	2.8	Macaroni, cooked	½ cup	1.1
Asparagus, cooked	½ cup	1.8	Mushrooms	10 small	0.8
Bananas	1 small	2.2	Noodles, cooked	½ cup	1.7
Beans, green, cooked	½ cup	1.2	Oatmeal, cooked	½ cup	2.9
Beam, white, cooked	½ cup	5.0	Orange	1 med.	0.9
Bran, wheat	2 tsp.	3.3	Orange juice	½ cup	0.1
Bread, white or French	2 slices	1.2	Peanuts, roasted	½ cup	5.8
Bread, whole wheat	2 slices	3.0	Peas, green, cooked	½ cup	4.3
Broccoli, cooked	½ cup	2.4	Popcorn	3 cups	3.0
Bulgur wheat, dry	1 oz.	5.2	Potatoes, baked	1 med.	1.8
Cabbage, cooked	½ cup	1.8	Potatoes, mashed	½ cup	1.2
Cabbage, shred, raw	½ cup	0.7	Prunes, dried	3 med.	1.7
Carrots, cooked	½ cup	1.8	Rice, brn, cooked	½ cup	2.4

A diet high in fiber and low in fat pleases people all over the world. People who live in the exotic islands of the Pacific eat a variety of fish, fruits, and vegetables. Herdsmen in parts of Europe and Russia drink low-fat cultured milk and eat whole grain breads with fresh fruits and vegetables. Compare the total fat and fiber in the above menus (Table 20) and get hints from them.

There are numerous claims that large doses of certain vitamins or minerals will protect us against cancer. Some of these claims are based on theoretical considerations with little or no data to support them. Others do not even have a theoretical reason for being used. Yet, the practice of taking vitamin C or E or the mineral selenium to prevent cancer has become widespread. Vitamin E has been shown to offer some protection against certain cancers in animals. No studies in humans have confirmed this effect. The data we have in human populations do not show any protective effect for vitamin C. While high doses of vitamin C have not shown serious toxic effects, there has not been enough experience with these doses for long enough periods of time (over many years) to be sure.

While selenium may have some effect against cancer in humans, there has been no experience with long-term administration of high doses of the element. Such a practice could be dangerous. Like fluoride and other trace elements necessary for life in trace amounts but toxic in larger doses, the range between the amount that is optimum and the dosage at which this micronutrient becomes toxic is very narrow.

Experimental data with vitamin A coupled with some human studies showing that populations with a high incidence of vitamin A deficiency also have a high incidence of certain cancers has led to recommendations that an abundant amount of vitamin A be included in our diet. Potent supplements of vitamin A have been shown to have a protective effect against some types of cancers, but the product is very toxic in high doses. The structure of vitamin A has been altered in the laboratory so that its toxicity is reduced while its cancer-preventing properties are preserved. Several such "analogs" of vitamin A are being tested in populations at very high risk for certain cancers—for example, people with bladder papillomas (a pre-cancerous condition) or asbestos workers, who are at very high risk for lung cancer. However, even in the animal experiments, these analogs, like vitamin A itself, are effective only as preventive measures. They are not a cure for cancer. Beta-carotene, the form of vitamin A in plants, is considered to be non-toxic. One study indicated that supplements of beta-carotene increased the incidence of lung cancer in heavy smokers (but not in non-smokers). We believe that was a valid finding and not a chance occurrence or a statistical fluke. One plausible explanation is that the beta-carotene provides more protection for cancer cells (or precancerous cells) than for normal tissue—in contrast to the selective lethal effects of toxic drugs on cancer cells.

Cruciferous vegetables (the cabbage family) such as Brussels sprouts and broccoli are particularly noteworthy for their content of phytochemicals (substances of plant origin) which aid in prevention of some forms of cancer, and tomato-based products (rich in lycopene) seem to lower men's risk for prostate cancer. In practice, this means eating carrots, squash, and other yellow/orange vegetables in addition to the green ones such as Brussels sprouts, spinach, collards, turnip greens, and broccoli, and the red ones such as tomatoes and red peppers. These vegetables also contribute fiber to our diets and they are low in fat. Culinary artists displayed colorful vegetables on our dinner plates long before we knew about their protective values. Now, they even include edible flowers. While this is no sure way of preventing cancer, it is a reasonable step to take.

Lest we go overboard with any single food, it is important to reconsider the old adage, "You can get too much of a good thing." Cabbage and other cruciferous foods, if eaten in large quantities, every day, can cause goiter. We can present a long list of beneficial phytochemicals in familiar foods, but we can also present a long list of toxins that, if consumed in large enough quantity, can make you sick. Don't go overboard with any single food. Variety in our daily menus breaks monotony, and it also averts excesses of foods that are protective in reasonable amounts but toxic when carried to extreme.

A number of substances, some of them found in foods, have been promoted as cancer cures. Some of these claims have been made by sincere people; others, by out-and-out phonies. In either case, this is a serious problem. Cancer patients may forgo proven methods of treatment to try some unproved remedy. This practice is costing lives that may have been saved (while draining the victim's family of its hard-earned savings). Many cancers can be cured if proper therapeutic measures are initiated during the early stages of the disease. Great progress has been made in identifying phytochemicals (taxol, for example) which are useful in treatment of cancer and other diseases, but the products are pharmaceuticals (not nutrients). A better known example is aspirin. It is a natural product, long known for its palliative properties as an extract from willow tree bark before it was synthesized in the laboratory. "Curative" products are often labeled as food supplements to avoid the rigid test standards of the Food and Drug Administration. These products are not on the market for their nutritive content and should not be classified as foods. There is no known nutrient that will cure cancer.

Anemia

Our bloodstream carries oxygen from our lungs to every cell in our body, and it carries carbon dioxide back to the lungs for release into the air. It transports the nutrients used for fuel and those necessary for the growth and repair of tissues. In addition, it carries the waste products of tissue metabolism to be excreted by the kidney. Furthermore, our blood is a reservoir of cells to fight infection either by carrying immune substances or by engulfing invading organisms. For these functions, the blood has evolved into a very special tissue containing several constituent parts, each of which is highly adapted.

There are two types of cells in the bloodstream: red cells and white cells. The white cells protect us against infection. The red cells (erythrocytes) carry oxygen and carbon dioxide. They give the blood its color. Either quantitative or qualitative changes in these cells will cause anemia.

An erythrocyte is a very special cell highly adapted for its job as a carrier of oxygen and carbon dioxide. In its mature form, the cell circulates through the blood as a small sphere filled with hemoglobin. Hemoglobin is a large molecule made of two kinds of subunits: heme, a small iron-containing ring-like structure; and globin, a large chain-like protein molecule. The hemoglobin carries both the oxygen and the carbon dioxide. The more hemoglobin, the more seats available on the oxygen-carrying train; the less hemoglobin, the fewer seats. When the amount of it drops below a certain level, the person is anemic. Simply stated, anemia means having too little hemoglobin.

To carry out its special functions, the red cell sacrifices certain properties that are present in all other cells. During its development, it loses its nucleus (the part of all cells that is responsible for maintaining many of the cell's life processes). Consequently, the red cell has a much shorter life than any other cells. Its average lifespan is 120 days. About 8 percent of our red cells die every day and must be replaced.

These cells are replaced in the bone marrow, where cells that contain nuclei divide rapidly and constantly increase in number. Some of these cells undergo a maturation process during which they will synthesize hemoglobin and lose their nuclei. They become mature erythrocytes, which are released into the bloodstream to replace those that were lost. The bone marrow constantly produces new cells and releases them to the blood as they are needed.

Because red cells are constantly lost and replaced, it is easy to understand how anemia can develop. If they are lost faster than they can be replaced, the amount of hemoglobin circulating in the blood will drop. We will become anemic. Such an imbalance between the rate of cell loss and the rate of replacement can occur either because the cells are withdrawn from the bloodstream too rapidly or because they are released from the bone marrow too slowly.

Both of these situations happen, and either has important nutritional implications. Perhaps the most obvious loss of red cells (and the hemoglobin they contain) occurs when we bleed. When the bleeding is mild, the bone marrow is able to compensate by speeding up the production of red cells and rapidly releasing them into the bloodstream. This will prevent the hemoglobin levels from falling. When the bleeding is severe, even if the bone marrow is working at capacity, it is unable to replace the lost cells fast enough. Anemia will ensue. Therefore, whether we become anemic following blood loss depends on how well our bone marrow can supply new erythrocytes. This ability to respond depends, in part, on our nutritional status.

As we have seen, new red cells are constantly manufactured in the bone marrow. The immature red cells must divide rapidly, and new hemoglobin must be synthesized within the maturing cells. Both of these processes depend on the availability of certain nutrients. Three nutrients essential for cell division are: folic acid, vitamin B12, and zinc. Iron is crucial for the synthesis of hemoglobin. A deficiency in folic acid, vitamin B12, or zinc will cause a reduced rate of cell division within the bone marrow and result in the production of fewer red cells. A deficiency of iron will result in a reduced synthesis of hemoglobin within the maturing red cell. Thus, the most common forms of nutritional anemia are caused by inadequate supplies of iron, folic acid, vitamin B12, and zinc to the bone marrow. Our diet is the ultimate source of these nutrients.

Iron is so important to the body that specific mechanisms have evolved for its conservation. Iron is an integral part of hemoglobin, and most of the iron in our bodies is present in this form. Every type of cell contains small amounts as part of the enzyme systems necessary for cell respiration. Finally, iron is present in muscle cells in a molecule known as myoglobin, which is important in voluntary muscle function. It is also stored in the liver, spleen, intestines, and to some extent in other organs.

Almost all the iron from tissues, including that released by dying red cells, is carried in the blood to storage sites for withdrawal when needed. Thus, under normal conditions when no blood is lost from the body, very little is excreted; almost all is revitalized. Even an injury to the tissues, such as in a bruise, releases iron that the body can reuse.

Dietary iron requirements for an adult male are small. Therefore, deficiency of this element in adult males is rare. When it does occur, it usually signals bleeding from an unseen site. This is a serious symptom that requires immediate medical attention. By contrast, iron deficiency is quite common in both sexes during the human growth period and is usually due to inadequate intake. The volume of blood must grow. Hence, red cells are constantly added over and above those that are lost. More hemoglobin is synthesized, and more iron is required. An infant's blood volume can double during the first year of life. The one-year-old has twice the number of total red cells and, hence, twice as much body iron as the newborn. If an adequate supply is not available, iron deficiency and (possibly) anemia will occur. Adolescence is another period of very rapid growth when the total number of red cells must increase and iron deficiency may develop.

During her reproductive life, the adult woman is also at risk for iron deficiency. She regularly loses blood through menstruation. Again, if her intake of dietary iron is inadequate to meet the demands imposed by this constant iron loss, she will develop an iron deficiency and, eventually, the anemia that accompanies this condition. Anemia is the last stage of iron deficiency. It occurs only after the iron stores within the body have been exhausted. For this reason, even a mild anemia due to iron deficiency should not be ignored. It means all our stores have been exhausted and we are not consuming enough iron to keep our hemoglobin level high enough for optimal body function.

A woman is particularly at risk for iron deficiency during pregnancy. Her blood volume expands; hence, more red cells must be manufactured to meet this expansion. In addition, the fetus is growing and developing. Part of that growth is the establishment and rapid expansion of its own blood supply. This requires iron, which must come from the mother—either from her diet or from her iron stores. The more pregnancies a woman has undergone, the greater her risk for iron deficiency, both during later pregnancies and between them. Pregnancy places such a demand on iron requirements that supplements are routinely prescribed for pregnant women.

Iron deficiency is a progressive that begins with a slow depletion of iron stores and proceeds to mild, then moderate, and, finally, severe anemia. The rate at which anemia develops depends partly on the existing level of stores and on the difference between the amount of iron lost and the amount in the diet. Let us suppose that a woman has iron stores of 1,000 mg, she consumes 10 mg per day of usable iron, and she loses 15 mg per day (this includes menstrual losses prorated on a daily basis). She is losing 5 mg per day more than she is absorbing. In two hundred days, her entire reserves will be used up. Anemia will begin to develop. Even a loss of 1 mg per day more than her body absorbs will result in a depletion of her entire iron reserves in less than three years. If she donates blood, has an accident that involves blood loss, or suffers a nosebleed, these losses must be factored into the equation. For a woman to prevent iron deficiency, she must absorb as much iron as she is using. If her reserves are low, then she needs to restore them by absorbing more than she is using, i.e., by being in a state of positive iron balance.

Iron is supplied by variety of foods. Therefore, it is reasonable to ask why anyone should be in negative iron balance. There are two reasons. First, the body will absorb only a small fraction of the iron in our food. How much depends on a number of factors: the kind of food, the other components of the diet, and the state of our iron reserves. Second, the lifestyle of "modern" American women reduces the amount of iron in their diets.

Iron is absorbed by an active process. First, it is converted by hydrochloric acid in the stomach into a form that can be absorbed. When it reaches the small intestine, it is carried into the surface cells by ferritin (a specialized protein). This binds the iron and pulls it into the cells of the intestinal wall, where it is either deposited as storage iron or released into the bloodstream. While in the bloodstream, the iron is bound to transferrin, another carrier protein, which circulates in the plasma. The amount of iron absorbed depends on the nature of the iron-containing food, the other components of our diet, and the state of our iron reserves. The state of our iron reserves is the most important factor determining how much iron we will absorb. When our reserves are low, absorption is high. When they are high, absorption is lower.

Iron in our food has two forms: heme iron, from hemoglobin, and nonheme iron. Heme iron occurs primarily in meat, fish, and egg yolks. Nonheme iron is found in plant sources. About 15 to 20 percent of the heme iron in our diet will be absorbed. By contrast, we absorb only about 5 percent of nonheme iron. Only about 10 percent of dietary iron in the mixed American diet is used. For any individual, however, the amount of absorption will vary. If you are a vegetarian, you will absorb less than 10 percent; if you eat much meat, more than 10 percent.

Regardless of the source of dietary iron, its absorption is influenced by other components of the diet. Vitamin C consumed at the same meal will increase iron absorption. Thus, the orange juice we drink at breakfast will increase the iron we absorb from eggs or fortified cereal. By contrast, certain components of cereal grains known as phytates interfere with iron absorption. This is not a problem in the usual American diet because our major grain sources (wheat, corn, and rice) are not rich in phytates. The phytate they contain in their original state is almost entirely removed in processing. In some countries, such as Egypt and other Middle Eastern countries, staple grains are high in phytates, and the absorption of iron and other minerals can be diminished.

The nature of the signal by which our bodies regulate iron absorption is not known. Depending on how much is already present, somehow, a signal is sent to the cells lining the small intestine to hold back or speed up the process. This internal system affords a very important protection against both deficiency and overload. When iron is abundant, the body will absorb only what it needs. Unfortunately, for a variety of reasons, iron may not be abundantly available. If it is not, the body cannot make up the deficit. Table 22 shows the iron content of a variety of foods.

Table 22. **Iron Content of Foods**

.3-.7 mg/serving				
Fruit: e.g., apples,		Carrots	1 cup	
bananas		Collards	1 cup	
cherries		Potato	1 med	
melons,				
citrus,		*1.5-2 mg/serving*		
pineapple,		Barley	½ cup	
etc.	1 avg. size	Buckwheat	½ cup	
Corn grits	1 cup	oatmeal	1 cup	
Popcorn		Chicken (all cuts)	3-4 oz	
(popped)	1 cup	Bologna	3-4 oz	
Bread (all varieties)	1 slice	Ham	2 oz	
		Dried apricot		
Enriched		halves	6 large	
macaroni,		Green beans	1 cup	
spaghetti, or		Brewers' yeast	1 tbsp.	
noodles	½ cup			
Peanut butter	2 tbsp.	*2-4 mg/serving*		
Mushrooms	⅓ cup	Amaranth	3 ½ oz	
Eggplant	½ cup	Figs, dried	3 med.	
Tomato	1 small	Cooked peas &		
		beans	½ cup	
.1-1.4 mg/serving		Blackstrap		
Rice, cooked		molasses	1 tbsp.	
(brown or		Tofu (soy		
white		curd)	4 oz.	
enriched)	1 cup			
Tortilla (6 in.		*4 - 5 mg/serving*		
diameter)	1	Beef (lean only		
Cream of Wheat	1 cup	all cuts	3 oz.	
Wheatena	⅔ cup	Lamb (lean only		
Wheat germ	1 tbsp.	all cuts	4 oz.	
Dry bulgur wheat	2 tbsp.	Calf's liver	1 oz.	
Pumpkin seeds	1-2 tbsp.	Raisins	½ cup	
Berries (all)	1 cup			
Broccoli	1 cup			

Low calorie diets restrict our food intake, thereby limiting the amount of iron available. On a 1,200-cal diet, a woman would have to eat liver twice a week to meet her iron requirement. Below 1,200 cal, it becomes almost impossible for her to get enough iron from food alone. Therefore, a woman who is constantly dieting is at increased risk for iron deficiency. The lower her caloric intake, the greater that risk.

Consuming large amounts of alcohol will interfere with iron absorption. A woman who is a moderately heavy drinker and limits her caloric intake is in double jeopardy. Since many American women routinely practice calorie control while consuming moderate amounts of alcohol, iron deficiency is common in this population.

Folic acid is another nutrient essential for prevention of anemia. This vitamin, a member of the "B-complex," is essential for normal cell division. The more rapid the rate of multiplication, the higher the requirement for folic acid. The bone marrow cells divide more rapidly than cells located elsewhere in the body. A deficiency of this vitamin will manifest itself primarily by reducing the rate of cell division in the bone marrow. When this rate decreases sufficiently to compromise the marrow's capacity to replace lost red cells, their number in the blood falls. Anemia results. The faster these cells have to be replaced, the greater the need for folic acid. Women replace their red cells quicker than men. Women must constantly make up for the blood losses of menstruation. Thus, women require more folic acid than men. Anemia due to folic acid deficiency is more common in adult women than in adult men. The heavier a woman's menstrual losses, the greater her need for folic acid.

Folic acid deficiency is the most common vitamin shortage in the United States (see Table 23 for foods rich in folic acid). This problem has become so evident that inclusion of this vitamin in bread, cereals, "enriched" flour, white rice, and other refined grain products is now required by government regulations. The level of enrichment will be the amount necessary to replace the portion lost in the milling process. White bread will now have as much folic acid as the whole-grain product currently provides (about 27 mcg per slice). It has long been a common practice for manufacturers to fortify breakfast cereals with folic acid. "Fortified" cereals contain as much as 100 mcg of folic acid per normal serving. The Recommended Daily Intake is 400 mcg for adult men and women.

Table 23. **Folic Acid Content of Foods in Micrograms**

5-20 mcg/serving		*20-50 mcg/serving*	
Carrot	1 med.	Green beans	1 cup
Ear of corn	1 med.	Cucumber	1 sm.
Mushrooms	3 large	Squash	⅔ cup
Potato	1 med.	Strawberries	1 cup
Apple	1 med.	Egg	1 lg.
Hard cheese	1 oz.	Kidney	3 oz.
Grapefruit	½ med.	Shellfish	6 oz.
Milk	8 oz.	Yogurt	8 oz.
Bread	1 slice	Wheat germ	2 tbs.
Sesame seeds	1 tbs.	Orange	1 med.
Lean beef, veal, or pork	6 oz.		

100-150 mcg/serving		*200-300 mcg/serving*	
Avocado (med.)	6 oz.	Brewers yeast	1 tbs.
Breakfast cereals (fortified)	1 oz. (dry)	Spinach	4 oz.
Lentils, cooked	½ cup		
Liver (all)	3 oz.		
Broccoli	2 stalks		
Orange juice	6 oz.		

Unlike iron, folic acid cannot be stored to an appreciable extent, and the requirement increases during periods of great demand for new red cells. Hence, adequate quantities must be consumed daily. Also unlike iron, almost all the folic acid in our diet is absorbed. The excess is simply excreted in the urine.

Because our body has no control over how much folic acid is absorbed, constant calorie control limits the amount of folic acid available from our diet more so than it limits the amount of iron. It cannot extract a higher portion of this nutrient from our food when our reserves are low. Thus, if we are anemic because of folic acid deficiency, our body cannot protect itself by absorbing a greater amount of this nutrient.

Even moderate consumption of alcohol will reduce the amount we absorb, and certain prescription drugs can affect availability of folic acid. Perhaps the most important one, in this respect, is the contraceptive pill. It may both decrease absorption and increase excretion of folic acid. Women who use oral contraceptives are at increased risk for folic acid deficiency. This problem is compounded when women stop taking oral contraceptives to become pregnant. If they succeed, and particularly if they succeed quickly, they may enter the early stages of pregnancy deficient in the vitamin. Because pregnancy is accompanied by rapid cell division in the developing fetus, and because both maternal and fetal bone marrows are very active in making new cells, a woman's folic acid requirement increases dramatically. A deficiency during early pregnancy may be associated with certain types of congenital malformations. Later in pregnancy, a deficiency may lead to anemia in the mother. Therefore, it is recommended that every pregnant woman take folic acid supplements, particularly if she has been on oral contraceptives for a long time. She should begin the supplementation as soon as she discontinues the pill.

Since the conditions necessary for the development of iron-deficiency anemia and folic-acid-deficiency anemia are often similar, some women can become anemic because they lack both nutrients. It is important to diagnose such a condition. Treatment with iron or folic acid alone will not cure this anemia. Fortunately, by examining a drop of your blood, your physician will be able to tell if you have a combined form. As we shall see, this is only one of many reasons self-treatment of anemia is not advisable.

Treatment of a combined anemia is simple—supplementation with both iron and folic acid. Prevention of a recurrence may involve changes in lifestyle, in addition to changes in diet.

Vitamin B12 is another important nutrient in the prevention of anemia. The type of anemia associated with a deficit of it is identical to the anemia that results from folic acid deficiency. Vitamin B12 is necessary for folic acid to work. In essence, a person who has a vitamin B12 deficiency also lacks folic acid, not because the latter is missing in the diet, but because the body cannot properly use it. Vitamin B12 is found in all foods of animal origin. Hence, excepting in pure vegetarians, dietary vitamin B12 deficiency almost never occurs. Vitamin B12 is the only water-soluble vitamin that is stored in the body. Nutritional anemia resulting from a diet deficient in vitamin B12 is very rare. It takes about three years for our normal reserves to be depleted. Hence, anemia caused by a vitamin B12 deficiency takes a long time to develop. Unless there is some abnormality (such as the body's inability to absorb the vitamin), the condition should occur only in pure vegetarians; or, because an "intrinsic factor" in the stomach is required for absorption of the vitamin, in persons that have had surgical removal of most of the stomach.

The mineral *zinc* is also necessary for cell division. Thus, the demand for zinc will increase when the bone marrow is very active and during pregnancy when cell division increases in both the mother and the fetus. Zinc usually occurs in the same foods as iron. Hence, people who are iron deficient may be zinc deficient. Like iron, zinc is stored in the body, and there is some evidence that the state of our zinc reserves influences the rate at which our bodies absorb this mineral from food. Unlike iron, zinc is not a structural element in hemoglobin or any other major blood protein. Blood loss is not accompanied by the loss of large quantities of zinc. However, the response of the bone marrow to blood loss increases the zinc requirement. Thus, women of childbearing age need increased zinc because more red cells have to be made.

As with the other nutrients involved in nutritional anemias, zinc deficiency will result when the increased demand is not met by the diet. The quantity and quality of the food consumed limit the amount in the diet. Again, limiting calories results in an increased risk for zinc deficiency. If the diet is low in foods with significant zinc content, that risk is compounded (see Table 24 for foods rich in zinc).

Table 24. **Zinc Content of Foods in Milligrams**

0.2 to 0.5 mg/serving:		*0.5 to 1 mg/serving:*	
Egg	1 med.	Puffed wheat	1 oz.
Gefilte fish	3½ oz.	Cheddar cheese	1 oz.
Mango	½ med.	Tuna	3 oz.
Applesauce	½ cup	White rice	1 cup
Pineapple juice	8 oz.	White bread	2 slices
Tomato	1 med.	Cranberry-apple	
Potato, cooked	1 med.	drink	8 oz.
		Chicken breast	3 oz.
1 to 1.5 mg/serving:		Milk (whole or skim)	8 oz.
Clams	3 oz.		
Brown rice	1 cup	*4 to 5 mg/serving:*	
Brown rice	1 cup	Beef (lean only)	3½ oz.
Whole wheat Bread	2 slices	Pork (lean only)	3½ oz.
Popcorn	2 cups	Lamb (lean only	3½ oz.
Wheat germ	1 tbs.	Liver (beef and calf) 3 oz	
Bran (cooked, dried)	¾ cup		

Other: 9.4 mg—Pacific oysters (raw) 3 ½ oz.
74.7 mg—Atlantic oysters (raw) 3 ½ oz.

Even if your body is deficient in zinc, you are not likely to become anemic for lack of it. There are two reasons. First, it takes a greater degree of depletion to cause anemia from zinc deficiency than it does from an iron or a folic acid deficiency. Second, zinc deficiency will manifest itself in other ways before anemia occurs. A person with iron-deficiency anemia will often be zinc deficient as well (because the same foods tend to supply both nutrients).

The anemia, however, will be caused by the lack of iron, not the lack of zinc. Even a moderate iron deficiency often rapidly results in anemia. Therefore, iron-deficiency anemia should be treated by increasing your consumption of iron-rich foods (in addition to iron supplements). These foods will incidentally supply enough zinc to replenish your supply of this mineral, and you will establish an eating pattern that may prevent later deficiencies.

Even if you are not anemic, your zinc reserves may be low enough to cause skin problems, taste abnormalities, endocrine problems, and (in children) diminished growth and several maturation problems. Because zinc deficiency is associated with congenital malformations of the fetus, this is particularly important for women of childbearing age. These malformations occur at low serum-zinc levels when other signs of deficiency are absent. Because zinc deficiency is so prevalent in women who are iron deficient, any pregnant woman who is iron deficient should also use zinc supplements. Another consideration is that alcohol reduces zinc absorption and therefore increases our risk for deficiency.

Lack of other nutrients in the diet can cause anemia; but this happens at a very low frequency. Shortages of *copper* and *vitamin E* have been implicated. However, the deficits must be prolonged and severe before the symptoms appear. Only people with unorthodox eating habits are at risk for anemia due to lack of copper and vitamin E.

Anemia resulting from a combination of other nutrient deficiencies is quite rare. Occasionally, a woman who is a pure vegetarian (vegan) may develop an anemia caused by a lack of both iron and vitamin B12. This happens because the best source of iron is meat and other animal products, and vitamin B12 is found only in animals and animal products. However, even small amounts of meat, fish, or dairy foods will satisfy our vitamin B12 requirement. Therefore, the vegan who is anemic is most likely iron deficient, and only rarely deficient in vitamin B12.

The Signs and Symptoms of Nutritional Anemia

The signs and symptoms of nutritional anemia are similar, regardless of the type. They result from the same abnormality, too little hemoglobin in the blood. Hemoglobin is red in color, which is reflected in the body, particularly where the blood comes close to the surface such as the nail beds, the tips of the fingers and toes, the earlobes, and the skin around the eyes. Anyone who is anemic will display a lightening of color in these areas—usually ranging from pink to a grayish-white. As the anemia progresses, a general pallor develops, regardless of our skin color. One way to test for anemia is to press on our nail beds until they become white, and then release the pressure. A prompt return to pink is the normal response. Anemia must be suspected if the pink returns very slowly.

Hemoglobin carries oxygen from the lungs to the tissues. Not enough oxygen reaches the tissues when insufficient hemoglobin is present. Certain signs and symptoms will develop. Tiredness and general fatigue are among the earliest signs. Our attention span becomes shorter and we begin to do poorly at our job, particularly if we work at something that requires concentration.

We become listless and irritable; we lose patience, and the least bit of exertion bothers us. Finally, we can become weak and short of breath. All these symptoms are nonspecific; that is, they can occur with conditions other than anemia. The condition is easily diagnosed by blood tests that reveal the low hemoglobin levels.

Anemia may be a result of causes other than faulty nutrition. Therefore, it is essential that a physician identify the cause. Sometimes it may be a sign of a very serious disease. For example, certain diseases of the blood or bone marrow will produce anemia. The marrow may "break down" and not be able to replace the red cells that are constantly lost. No kind of nutritional treatment will cure this kind of anemia. Sometimes the red cells themselves break down much more rapidly than normal. This condition may be due to genetic abnormalities in the red cells as in sickle-cell anemia, or to certain toxins that cause red cell damage.

Bleeding is the most common non-nutritional cause of anemia. The blood loss may be slow and not easily recognized; for example, bleeding from the gastrointestinal tract. Unlike the anemias mentioned above, that caused by bleeding will respond to nutritional treatment. The anemic condition is due to iron deficiency—not because of insufficient iron in your diet, but because we are abnormally draining our iron stores. Iron supplementation will cure the anemia but not the condition that caused anemia—a very important principle. If it is iron-deficiency anemia, why are you iron deficient? In women, it is usually because their iron intake is not sufficient to meet their normal demands, or because of heavy menstrual periods, or one or more pregnancies that may have drained their iron reserves.

Iron deficiency rarely occurs in men because of too little iron in their diet. An adult male's normal requirement is small. Iron-deficiency anemia in an adult male must be considered a sign of abnormal bleeding; thus, the cause of the bleeding must be established. Self-treatment with iron may temporarily correct the symptoms of iron deficiency, but this delays the diagnosis of the problem and may seriously jeopardize our health.

Anyone who is anemic should see a physician to determine the cause. In a woman who has no other physical problems, the physician may prescribe an iron supplement and recommend a diet high in iron. For a man, a much more extensive series of diagnostic tests may be necessary to determine the cause of iron loss.

Who is At Risk?

The populations mainly at risk for nutritional anemias are women during the childbearing years and children of both sexes during their growing years. In addition, there is some evidence that certain elderly men and women may be at increased risk. Unlike the case of most of the other diseases we have discussed, your race or your family history is not important in determining your risk. There are no known genetic factors that increase a person's chances of developing nutritional anemias. Similarly, other factors such as smoking, high blood pressure, obesity, and lack of exercise— so important in many of the diseases already discussed—do not influence our risk for developing a nutritionally induced anemia. However, for the population groups mentioned above, there are certain other risk factors that can increase their chances of developing nutritional anemia.

During the childbearing years, women go through certain cyclic changes in their physiology that put them at increased risk for nutritional anemias. Primary among these physiologic states are menstruation, pregnancy, and lactation—each requiring specific nutrients. In addition, during this childbearing period, many women have certain lifestyle practices that increase their risk for nutritional anemias. The use of the contraceptive pill increases the need for folic acid; and some diets reduce the availability of iron, zinc, and folic acid. Excess use of alcohol reduces the absorption of the same three nutrients. This combination of life cycle and lifestyles places the adult woman at greater risk for nutritional anemias than the adult man. The extent of that risk depends on how these factors interact. It is important for any woman to establish her own risk for developing anemia. That can be accomplished more precisely with this condition than with any of the other diseases we have discussed.

How heavy are your menstrual periods? This is perhaps the most important question you have to answer. Some women have very light menstrual periods and lose only small amounts of iron. They require only small increases in dietary zinc and folic acid to replace the lost red cells. Other women lose copious amounts of blood with each period and must constantly renew their iron reserves and supply their bone marrow with enough zinc and folic acid. Most women fall somewhere in between.

Naturally, menstruation stops during pregnancy. However, the needs for your blood volume to expand and for the fetus to establish its own new blood supply more than balance this temporary stage. Your bone marrow works much faster during pregnancy; therefore, zinc and folic acid deficiencies are more common at this time. Hundreds of thousands of new red cells are pouring into your bloodstream from your bone marrow and into the circulation of the fetus from its bone marrow. Each of these cells contains hemoglobin and its iron. All the iron must come from the mother—from her reserves, from her diet, or from both. During pregnancy, a woman is more apt to develop anemia than when she is between pregnancies. Equally important, pregnancy can drain her reserves of iron and place her at greater risk for anemia afterward. The more pregnancies you have undergone, the greater your risk for nutritional anemia, particularly if you did not take iron and folic acid supplements during those pregnancies.

If you have had twins or triplets, your risk is increased both during and after pregnancy. Considerable blood can be lost at delivery. For this reason, your physician will determine your hemoglobin and red blood cell count shortly after the baby is born. If these values are low, you will probably be given an iron supplement. However, even if they are normal, your nutrient reserves may have been drained. Remember that anemia is the last stage of iron deficiency. It occurs only after all your iron stores have been depleted. In summation, your risk for nutritional anemia is increased after pregnancy, and the more pregnancies you have undergone, the greater your risk.

Nursing your baby will not increase your risk for nutritional anemia to the extent that menstruation or pregnancy does. Your requirements for iron, zinc, and folic acid will increase, but so will your appetite. The increased food should go a long way toward supplying enough of these nutrients. Nursing women often do not resume menstruating until after the infant is weaned. Blood loss will be minimal; therefore, the nursing period is a good time to replace the nutrient stores lost during pregnancy.

Although *oral contraceptives* have been shown to decrease the absorption of a number of vitamins, including folic acid and vitamin B12, these drugs alone will rarely cause nutritional anemia. However, if a woman is already at high risk, using oral contraceptives may result in the anemia of folic acid deficiency. For some women, on the other hand, oral contraceptives reduce the severity of menstrual periods, in which case the risk for anemia is reduced.

Perhaps the greatest lifestyle factor influencing your risk for nutritional anemia is a *reducing diet*. As you lower your calorie intake, you decrease your opportunity for getting your daily requirement of iron, zinc, and folic acid. Below 1,000 cal per day, it is almost impossible for a woman to get her iron requirement from food alone. If you are continually dieting, your risk for anemia is increased. This is particularly true if the reducing diet is unbalanced. Remember that meat is the best source of iron and zinc, and certain vegetables are the best source of folic acid.

Increasing numbers of American women are practicing some form of *vegetarianism*. A potential problem in this practice is the increased risk of iron-deficiency anemia. Since meat is the best source of iron, a woman who eats little or no meat is at increased risk for iron deficiency. She should manage her diet to provide a maximum source of vegetable iron. If eggs are part of her diet, the yolks are an excellent source of iron.

Alcohol consumed in even moderate amounts can increase our risk for nutritional anemia in two ways. First, it provides calories that are totally devoid of all other nutrients, thus cutting down the total number of nutrient-carrying calories. For example, suppose you are limiting yourself to 2,000 cal. If your diet is varied, it will furnish your daily requirement of iron, zinc, and folic acid. But if you consume 500 cal from alcohol (less than 5 oz per day), this leaves only 1,500 cal worth of food to provide your entire daily requirement. This is much more difficult to achieve.

Second, alcohol directly impairs the absorption of iron, zinc, and folic acid. This reduces the amount your body gets from your food. There is less food to supply the nutrient and poorer absorption from the food you do consume. Alcohol, even moderate amounts, must be weighed as a risk for nutritional anemia.

During the Growth Period of Life

Both genders are at risk during the growth period of life. As our body grows, so does the volume of our blood, and the faster we grow, the more our blood volume expands. To keep pace with the expanding blood volume, the bone marrow must supply red cells faster. More zinc and folic acid are required. Additional iron is required for these new red cells to mature and enter the bloodstream. Thus, the risk for anemia increases during any period of rapid growth. During fetal life, the mother is supplying the nutrients required for the formation of fetal blood so the infant is rarely anemic. However, the first year of life is a period of special risk. This is particularly true if the fetus is born prematurely. For the first few months of life, the infant will consume breast milk or infant formula as its sole source of nutrition. Breast milk contains iron in a highly absorbable form, and folic acid is abundant in her breast milk (provided the mother's diet is well-balanced).

Human breast milk also contains sufficient amounts of zinc. Thus, the breast-fed infant will rarely develop nutritional anemia. If the baby is bottle-fed, an infant formula that simulates breast milk and is fortified with iron is advisable. When the infant is four months old, solid foods may be introduced. However, breast milk or infant formula should still be used until the infant is nearly one year old. Solid foods should emphasize the nutrients needed to prevent nutritional anemia with the emphasis on iron. Many infant cereals are fortified with iron. Meat products and some strained green vegetables are also rich sources of iron. If the infant is a girl, preventing anemia is not enough. It is important also to ensure that her iron reserves are adequate. Otherwise, she will start out in life with a disadvantage.

The preschool years and the early school years are times when growth proceeds at a moderate rate. Therefore, iron, zinc, and folic acid requirements will be somewhat increased. But these years are also a time of major physical activity and hence increased food intake. Rarely is supplementation necessary unless the child is not receiving adequate amounts of a varied diet. If the family is strictly vegetarian, then the child could be iron deficient, and fortified foods or an iron supplement may be warranted.

Adolescence is another time of rapid growth when nutritional anemias are common in both genders. Because of their greater increase in growth rate, adolescent boys develop anemia more often than girls. However, the problem is more serious in girls. The adolescent girl with a nutritional anemia enters adulthood with exhausted reserves, particularly those of iron. Hence, her body is unable to meet the increased demands of menstruation and, later, of pregnancy. By contrast, the adolescent boy will be much more able to make up a deficit as he stops growing (when his demand for iron, zinc, and folic acid drops).

Therefore, both genders have the potential for developing nutritional anemias during adolescence. Children of either sex who are at risk because of their very rapid growth, coupled with diets marginal in iron, zinc, or folic acid, should take preventive precautions. This is particularly true if they have any other risk factors. For example, the adolescent who is constantly dieting is at increased risk, the vegetarian adolescent is at increased risk, and the adolescent who drinks alcohol is also at increased risk. Particularly at risk is the adolescent girl who becomes pregnant. She is growing, her blood volume is expanding because she is pregnant, and her fetus is manufacturing new blood. The nutrients necessary to meet these demands may not be available even if her diet is good. Therefore, any adolescent who is pregnant should receive supplements of iron, zinc, and folic acid.

The Elderly

There is some evidence that older men and women may be more prone to nutritional anemias than young adults. The reasons are not entirely clear. Iron must be converted into its proper form for digestion by the hydrochloric acid in the stomach. Older people have less stomach acidity, and hence proper conversion may not take place. Thus, the iron in their food may not be absorbed sufficiently to meet their needs. Again, in older people, there is evidence that the production the intrinsic factor necessary for the absorption of vitamin B12 is reduced. Thus, an elder person, particularly one who does not eat much meat or meat products may develop anemia due to vitamin B12 deficiency. The evidence for folic acid deficiency is inconclusive. Some studies show that a high proportion of senior citizens are deficient in this vitamin; others do not. Perhaps the biggest problem with determining whether aging is a factor in nutritional anemias is that many older people suffer from chronic diseases of all sorts. Some of these diseases may themselves increase the possibilities for developing anemia. Thus, in any older person, anemia per se may be due not to dietary factors but to an accompanying disease. It is therefore important for any elderly individual who is even mildly anemic to have the cause of that anemia determined by a physician.

Any infant whose birth weight was low and who is growing rapidly would automatically be at high risk. Any infant who was of low birth weight and who suffers an episode of bleeding would be at high risk. Even an infant whose birth weight was adequate but who is growing very rapidly and fed a formula that contained no iron would also be at high risk.

Since you do not know ahead of time whether your infant will grow rapidly or have nosebleeds or experience other forms of blood loss, it would be prudent to take certain precautions to prevent nutritional anemias in your infant. These precautions are simple: breastfeed your child if you can. If you cannot breastfeed, use an infant formula that contains iron. When you introduce solid foods (at around four months), choose those that are rich in iron, folic acid, and zinc.

To score the risk factors for infants, consider

- Birthweight. Infants who weighed five and a half pounds or less at birth are at increased risk for nutritional anemias. Score 3 if your child falls into this category.
- Specific problems at birth. Any infant who has had an "Rh problem" or any other condition necessitating a blood transfusion is at very high risk—score 5.
- Very rapid growth during the first year of life. If birth weight has more than doubled at four months or more than tripled at ten months, score 2.
- Bleeding during childhood. Severe nosebleeds, blood loss due to lacerations, and major surgical operations all increase risk. Score 2 for each.
- Use of any infant formula that does not contain iron and is the sole or major form of nutrition—score 3.

During childhood and adolescence, both genders are equally at risk for nutritional anemias. Pertaining to this stage of development:

- If you were at risk as a child (see above) and did not take preventive measures, your risk as an adolescent increases—score 3
- If your growth rate is very rapid (more than three inches during any year), your risk increases—score 3
- If you have had any episodes of significant bleeding before or during adolescence, your risk is higher—score 2 to 4 (depending on the severity of the bleeding)
- If you are a vegetarian, your risk is increased—score 2
- If you begin your menstrual periods early (before age twelve)—score 3

- If you are on a reducing diet, score 3. If your diet is unbalanced and low in iron, zinc, or folic acid—add 2 more points
- If you are a "regular" user of alcohol, score 2; if you are a heavy drinker—score 3
- If you become pregnant—score 5

A score of 5 or above places an adolescent at high risk. Thus, a person who was at risk as a child, and who undergoes very rapid adolescent growth, is at high risk without any of the other factors being present. A rapidly growing adolescent who becomes a strict vegetarian or decides to go on a reducing diet is also at high risk and should take steps to prevent nutritional anemias. Of course, any adolescent who becomes pregnant is immediately at high risk and should be taking iron, zinc, and folic acid supplements.

For Women During the Childbearing Years

Pertaining to women during the childbearing years, use the following list (a score of 5 or more places you in the high-risk category):

- A history of high risk during infancy and/or adolescence—score 3
- Heavy menstrual period—score 3
- Menstrual periods remaining heavy for more than three days—score 2
- Lasting more than four days—score 3
- Previous pregnancies (including miscarriages and induced abortions)—score 1 for each
- Score 2 for each pregnancy resulting in twins
- Bleeding complications at delivery—score 2
- Other significant bleeding episodes—score 3. Frequent dieting to control weight—score 3
- A pure vegetarian (vegan) diet—score 2

- Use of oral contraceptives—score 2
- Regular frequent consumption of alcohol—score 2
- Heavy alcohol consumption—score 3

As you can see, your previous history is very important. If you were at risk as a child or adolescent and did not take preventive measures, any of the other factors mentioned above automatically puts you into a high-risk category.

Diet for Those at High Risk

We use two main principles in constructing a diet to protect against the development of nutritional anemias. First, the foods must be of high nutrient density for iron, zinc, and folic acid. The nutrient density relates to the quantity of these nutrients per calorie in the daily diet. It should be as high as possible. Thus, a low-calorie food that is only moderately high in iron may be better than a high-calorie food that is very high in iron. Second, certain foods are very rich in these nutrients either naturally, or because they are fortified. Emphasis should be put on incorporating some of these foods into your regular diet.

To achieve the first objective, you need not only to eat certain foods but also to eliminate (or at least markedly reduce) others. Any food that supplies calories without these nutrients should be de-emphasized. For example, alcohol and refined sugar have no nutrients, only calories. Therefore, a moderate reduction in these two "foods" can allow you to eat more nutrient-dense food without increasing your caloric intake. Fat, while carrying certain vitamins and supplying essential fatty acids, does not contain any of the nutrients that are important in protecting you against anemia. Hence, your intake of fat, the most calorie-dense of all the nutrients (9 cal per g), should be lowered substantially.

First, calculate roughly how many calories you are taking in (or wish to, if you are planning to lose weight). Then calculate how many calories you can eliminate by reducing alcohol, sugar, and fat consumption. Finally, decide what foods you will eat to increase your intake of iron, zinc, and folic acid to protect against anemia. In some cases, as we will see, you will not be able to do this without eating fortified foods or taking supplements.

How much iron, zinc, and folic acid are necessary to prevent anemia? If you are not anemic yet, you should take in more iron than you are losing and enough zinc and folic acid to allow your bone marrow to work at maximum efficiency. Supplying more than this amount of zinc and folic acid will have little or no extra benefit. Therefore, any score over 5 would indicate that you should try to supply about one and a half to two times the recommended daily intake. This amount should be more than adequate to meet your needs and allow your bone marrow to do its job. An adult woman's zinc requirement is 12 mg (15 mg during pregnancy); hence, 20 mg per day is more than adequate. Similarly, 1 mg (two and a half times the adult female requirement) of folic acid is adequate.

With iron, however, the situation is quite different. If you replace only the amount you are losing, you will avoid iron-deficiency anemia, but since your reserves are depleted, you will remain at risk for this anemia. To lower your risk, you must rebuild iron stores by taking in more iron than you are losing. How much more depends on how depleted you were initially. Your physician can determine this, but it requires certain complicated tests. A less accurate but adequate method is to use your risk score to determine how much you need to take in. The higher the score, the more depleted you are. A score between 5 and 10 should allow iron rebuilding with slightly more than the recommended daily requirement (18 mg), about 20 to 25 mg. For a person with a score between 10 and 20, 30 mg of iron daily would be reasonable.

If your score is above 20, you should attempt to ingest 40 mg of iron per day. This last figure cannot be met from food alone unless you are consuming large numbers of calories and large quantities of iron-rich foods. A person with that high a score should be taking an iron supplement. Even 30 mg per day (in food alone) would be difficult for a woman, particularly if she is concerned about her calories. The use of iron-fortified foods is one option. If you choose a fortified food containing 100 percent of the recommended daily intake (15 mg for women), then you need only 15 mg from the rest of your diet. Try to get that amount from meat sources—red meats (lean cuts), liver, and egg yolks—since that type of iron is better absorbed. If you do not wish to consume fortified foods, an iron supplement of 20 to 30 mg is needed. If your score is between 5 and 10, you can get the iron you need from your diet if you choose foods carefully; avoid nutrient-poor foods and consume adequate calories. If you are on a reducing diet, you should take an iron supplement. If you are a vegetarian and your score is 5 or above, you should take an iron supplement or eat iron-fortified foods.

The following chart may be useful.

Table 25. **Iron Requirement to Prevent Anemia**

Score	Requirement	Source
5-10	20-25 mg/day	diet, if calories are adequate
10-20	30 mg/day	diet plus fortified foods or supplement
21-30	40 mg/day	diet plus supplement

In planning a diet to prevent anemia, first, decide how much iron you need. Then decide if you need supplementation. If so, choose a supplement at an appropriate dosage (usually 20 to 30 mg per day). If you select fortified foods, pick one (usually a cereal) that contains 100 percent of the RDI for iron (15 mg); it may be fortified with zinc and folic acid as well.

Decide how many total calories you wish to take in each day (between 1,800 and 2,300 for the average woman; up to 2,800 for a very active woman). Decrease foods of low nutrient density (alcohol, refined sugar, fat). From the Tables we have provided, you can pick foods that are high in iron, zinc, and folic acid. Select generously to reach the amount you need. It may sound difficult to do, but it isn't. Suppose you need about 25 mg per day of iron. You have the option of eating a fortified cereal several times per week, liver once a week, red meat twice a week, two to three eggs a week, spinach, collard greens, fish, raisins—all iron-rich foods. Choose the ones you like the best, but ensure your objective. And if the iron you need comes from your diet, you will also get enough zinc. An occasional seafood dinner, especially clams or oysters, will raise your zinc levels even more. Remember, iron and zinc are stored, so you need not get your exact requirement each day. You will want to average what you need over several days. A generous portion of oysters can supply a whole week's zinc requirement. One large portion of liver can supply your iron requirement for several days. Try to meet your requirement for folic acid daily since your body does not store this nutrient. This should be no problem if you eat a variety of foods listed in Table 22. Steps in planning a diet to prevent anemia are listed below:

1. Set your requirement for iron, zinc, and folic acid.
2. Decide on a supplement or fortified food.
3. Decide on your total daily calorie intake.
4. Decrease low-nutrient-density foods.
5. Replace these with high-nutrient-density foods.

If you follow these simple steps, you can lower your risk for nutritional anemias by rebuilding your iron stores and keeping your bone marrow adequately supplied with zinc and folic acid.

If you are a postmenopausal female or an adult male (or suffer from a liver disorder), you should exercise caution in taking supplements which contain iron. If you take a multiple vitamin mineral supplement, maybe you should use one labeled "Silver" or "Senior," etc. (These contain lower level of iron than the standard RDI.) If you use a "one a day" type vitamin supplement, it may be advisable for you to buy the ones without iron. There are some indications that many older people have accumulated too much iron in their bodies and that chronic conditions may be precipitated or enhanced by excessive iron storage. About 1 in 250 Americans has the genes for iron overload, or hemochromatosis (a genetic disorder of metabolism in which excessive levels of iron accumulate in the body). Excessive iron storage in adult men and postmenopausal women may be less rare than the genetic disorder.

Osteoporosis

Every year, more than half a million American women develop osteoporosis (brittle bones)—a very serious and often debilitating disease. Of these women, 200,000 over the age of forty-five will fracture one or more bones. Forty thousand will die of complications following their injuries. Thousands of others will be disabled for the rest of their lives. With its complications, it is the twelfth most common cause of death in the United States. For women, it must be considered a major killer. Yet, with all these impressive statistics, osteoporosis seems to be neglected. An incident such as a woman over sixty-five fracturing a hip is easily dismissed as one of the inevitable consequences of getting older. Possible reasons for this are: one, that brittle bones are a natural result of the aging process; or, two, we have not been much concerned about the health of our older citizens.

Although osteoporosis is, in a sense, an exaggeration of the normal bone loss that accompanies aging in women, we can dispel any notions that it is inevitable.

Osteoporosis is simply a loss of bone. Therefore, to understand how it occurs, it is important to know the processes within our bodies that affect bone growth and bone destruction. Bone is the strongest tissue in our structures but it is not a solid mass. Bones are tubular shaped with a central canal (marrow cavity) surrounded by a complex latticework of protein (collagen) and crystals made of calcium and phosphorus (hydroxyapatite). The marrow cavity contains blood-forming cells which, though housed by bone, constitute a separate organ, the bone marrow. Most of our blood cells are produced there. These cells pass through the bone tissue into the bloodstream by traversing millions of small blood vessels. Bone tissue is not solid. It has passages for numerous blood vessels and nerve fibers.

The blood vessels are not closed conduits passing from the circulation to the marrow. They nourish the bone tissue itself. Bone tissue is in constant contact with the bloodstream. Through this contact, the blood delivers substances to the bone and the bone releases substances into the blood. The intimate relationship between blood and bone is essential. Bone is a living tissue. Its protein matrix is constantly breaking down and rebuilding. As with all body proteins, bone collagen is always in a state of flux, moving new amino acids (building blocks for proteins) from the blood into its structure and releasing used amino acids into the blood.

Within the protein matrix, bone consists of a hard substance made mostly from calcium and phosphorus. This substance, called hydroxyapatite, is constantly remodeling. Like the amino acids, calcium and phosphorus move freely from the blood into the bone and from the bone into the blood. When new bone is constructed, more calcium and phosphorus pass into the structure. When bone tissue is destroyed, more of these minerals move out of the bone. If a similar amount is moving in and out of the bone tissue, there is no net change in bone mass.

Calcium is the key element in maintaining the structural integrity of bone but that is only one of the important functions of this mineral. Calcium is essential for every cell in the body. Without it, nerve cells cannot conduct impulses and muscle cells cannot contract. Calcium is essential for the brain to generate nerve impulses and for the heart to beat. We cannot live unless this essential mineral is available to all the tissues of the body. Ninety-nine percent of it occurs in bone, and only one percent circulates in our blood and other tissues. Yet, this one percent is so critical that the body has evolved a complex machinery to keep the tissues supplied with the precise amount of calcium. This machinery is responsible for regulating calcium within the bloodstream, ensuring that the tissues get an adequate supply. Concurrently, it protects them from receiving too much. Excess calcium within the tissues can have serious consequences. Bone plays a crucial role in this regulatory process.

The calcium in our bones is also a vast reservoir in which excess calcium can be safely stored. If calcium is not available for our tissues, it will slowly be withdrawn from our bones. The more of the mineral withdrawn the thinner our bones become. Eventually they become so thin that the everyday stresses of life are too much. Fractures may occur. When this happens, we are suffering from the effects of osteoporosis.

From the moment a calcium molecule enters our body, the regulatory machinery controls it. First, the amount absorbed is regulated by a hormone (dihydroxy-vitamin D) made in the kidney from vitamin D. This nutrient is obtained from our diet or from a precursor (pro vitamin D) which is activated by ultraviolet light in our skin. The hormone is necessary for calcium to be absorbed by the intestinal cells and passed into the bloodstream. Once in the bloodstream, the calcium molecule becomes part of a pool. If its level should fall below a critical point, the parathyroid glands (four tiny structures at the base of the thyroid gland) secrete parathyroid hormone, which increases the level of calcium in our blood by signaling the kidney to convert vitamin D to its active form. This product increases calcium absorption. It can also stimulate the breakdown of bone to release calcium into the bloodstream.

The body uses another hormone (calcitonin), produced in the thyroid gland, to protect against withdrawal of too much calcium from our bones. We do not understand how this hormone works. Somehow, it inhibits the action of cells within the bone tissues that break down the bone (osteoclasts). These three factors (parathyroid hormone, dihydroxy-vitamin D, and calcitonin) are the principal means for regulating calcium metabolism. They are sensitive to the amount of calcium in the blood, and they interact with each other. Blood calcium levels rarely get too high or too low.

Other hormones within our bodies help in determining whether bone loss will occur.

Unlike the three hormones mentioned above, these do not regulate blood calcium directly. They are secreted for a variety of reasons, but not in response to the level of blood calcium. The most important is the female sex hormone estrogen. Estrogen is a bone-protecting hormone. Yet, it does not have any activity on bone itself. It works indirectly by blocking the action of parathyroid hormone. Thus, when estrogen is present, greater amounts of parathyroid hormone are necessary to cause bone resorption. If estrogen is absent, the brake releases, and even small amounts of parathyroid hormone will release large quantities of bone calcium. When the fine-tuning of the calcium-regulating mechanism is disrupted, more calcium gets into the blood than required. The excess is excreted in the urine and, thereby, lost to the body. Also, estrogen stimulates secretion of calcitonin (the primary bone-protecting hormone). So, when estrogen levels are low, calcitonin levels tend to be low and bone resorption increases. Finally, there is evidence that high levels of estrogen (such as those occurring during pregnancy) stimulate the kidney to convert vitamin D to its active form, thereby increasing the amounts of calcium absorbed. The absence of estrogen will produce an imbalance between the bone-resorbing hormone (parathyroid hormone) and the bone-protecting hormone (calcitonin), in favor of the former. Calcium will be lost from the bones and excreted in the urine. In addition, the one hormone that might reverse this loss, dihydroxy-vitamin D, may not be made as efficiently without estrogen. Therefore, it is not surprising that menopause, when estrogen falls to very low levels, is the key event in the development of osteoporosis in women.

The adrenocortical steroids are another group of hormones affecting bone metabolism. These hormones work directly on bone tissue, causing resorption. Both estrogen and another female sex hormone, progesterone, prevent the action of adrenal hormones on bone tissue. Thus, during menopause when both of these sex hormones decline, the adrenal hormones are given greater license to cause breakdown of bone. Finally, two other hormones affect bone. Growth hormone from the pituitary gland promotes growth of all tissues, including bone, while thyroid hormone promotes bone resorption.

Therefore, bone tissue is under a variety of hormonal influences. Table 26 shows those hormones that promote bone growth and those which promote bone loss. When all of these regulators are in balance, bone growth and loss stabilize so that bone mass does not change. But, if the hormones that regulates bone growth predominate (as during early life), bone mass will increase. If the hormones involved in bone loss predominate (as after menopause), bone mass will decrease. Anything that promotes the action or maximizes the effect of the bone-growth hormones will lower our risk for osteoporosis. Anything that promotes the activity or maximizes the effect of the bone-loss hormones will raise our risk for osteoporosis.

Table 26. **Factors Affecting Bone Growth or Loss**

Bone Growth	Bone Loss
Primary	
Calcitonin	Parathyroid hormone
Dihydroxy-vitamin D	
Secondary	
Estrogen	Adrenocortical hormones
Progesterone	(Cortisone)
Growth hormone	Thyroid hormone

Let us trace the history of a typical bone as a woman goes through her normal life cycle. During infancy and early childhood, the bone-growth hormones predominate, and calcium is deposited into the growing bones. At puberty, estrogen and progesterone levels increase sharply, further promoting bone growth. During pregnancy, levels of estrogen and progesterone again rise, promoting bone growth in the mother and fetus. In addition, the placenta makes dihydroxy-vitamin D during pregnancy, further promoting bone growth. If the mother nurses her infant, the levels of estrogen remain high and bone growth remains good.

A few years before menopause, progesterone levels begin to fall. The balance tips in favor of the bone-loss hormones. At menopause, estrogen levels fall dramatically and the bone-loss hormones become increasingly dominant. The result: bone is rapidly resorbed. At about age sixty-five, adrenal cortical activity lessens and levels of adrenal steroids drop. This tends to correct the imbalance, and bone loss slows down.

Who is at risk?

Who is at risk, and how may that risk be minimized? Osteoporosis relates to several risk factors. Some of these risks are under our control and can be modified by proper diet and certain kinds of exercise. In this sense, this disease is no different from atherosclerosis, hypertension, obesity, diabetes, and some types of cancer. Like them, certain people are more prone to get it than others.

To minimize our risk for osteoporosis, we must take advantage of the times when our hormonal balance favors bone growth. Unfortunately, most women do not become concerned until they are near menopause or later. Then, the balance of hormones is not in their favor. Under these circumstances, osteoporosis often occurs in spite of the preventive measures. Thus, women should do whatever possible to promote maximum bone growth during childhood and the childbearing years.

Certain external forces influence bone growth and resorption. Diet and exercise, particularly weight-bearing exercises, are primary. If we do not get enough calcium in our diet no matter how efficiently our body deposits it, we will not get enough into our bones. A diet deficient in calcium will promote bone loss. The proportion of calcium in our diet that can be absorbed from the gastrointestinal tract is also important. Certain dietary elements promote calcium absorption and indirectly promote bone growth. Other elements of the diet inhibit calcium absorption and indirectly promote bone loss. We will examine these interactions when we discuss eating practices to lower our risk for osteoporosis.

Bones are made to bear weight, and weight bearing increases bone mass. When bones are not supporting weight, they lose mass. Thus, long periods of immobilization or bed rest will result in loss of bone. The importance of weight bearing has become dramatically apparent through studies of astronauts. Even a short period (two weeks) of weightlessness results in measurable amounts of bone loss. This is the most significant medical problem facing our space program. (We still do not fully understand why the state of weightlessness induces such profound changes.)

The first and most important risk factor for the disease is our gender. Women are ten times as likely to suffer from severe osteoporosis as men, largely because of testosterone, the main male sex hormone. Like estrogen, it is a bone-protecting hormone. Whether it works the same way as estrogen is not known. Since men do not undergo menopause, the balance between hormones that promote bone growth and those that promote bone loss is better maintained after men reach middle age. Another reason the ultimate toll of this disease is higher in women than in men is that women live about eight years longer than men. The older we are, the greater our risk. For that reason alone, we can expect more women than men to become osteoporotic. Beyond the sex-hormone differences, males start life with a larger bone mass and lose bone more slowly with age. Their increased weight and muscle mass place more stress on their bones. They also have higher levels of calcitonin.

However, men are not immune to the disease. As male life expectancy increases, more cases of osteoporosis will appear in men. Several of the risks for osteoporosis will pertain only to women. Others will pertain to both genders. If you are male and have enough of these risks, it would be prudent to take preventive measures. The scoring system for osteoporosis, detailed in the next section, places a woman at greater risk than a man. However, some men will reach at least the lower levels of an at-risk category. These men should modify their diets in the same manner as for women who show high risks.

The earlier women undergo menopause, the greater their risk for osteoporosis. Most women experience natural menopause between the ages of forty-five and fifty-one. Of these, about 25 percent will exhibit osteoporosis. If menopause begins before age fifty, the rate is slightly higher, and it is lower if the changes begin after age fifty. Women who have their ovaries removed before natural menopause exhibit a 50 percent risk of developing osteoporosis. Again, the earlier the ovaries are removed, the greater the risk. Estrogen therapy may reduce the risk, but any woman who undergoes surgical removal of her ovaries before undergoing natural menopause must be considered at high risk.

While the actual mechanisms by which our genes affect our bones are unknown, there is no doubt that a strong family history is an important factor. Try to fill in as many branches of your family health tree as possible. Osteoporosis may not be the listed cause of death, so it is not enough to ask what disease a relative died from. We must delve much deeper. Were there any fractures at older ages, particularly fractures of the hip or vertebrae? Did your grandmother limp? If so, at what age did she start? Was there a noticeable shortening of stature in any of your female relatives as they got older? If these symptoms appeared early, your risk for osteoporosis becomes greater. Taking a thorough family history is important for men and women. The genetic effect asserts itself in both genders.

Osteoporosis is less common among African-American women than among white women. African-American women have larger bones at skeletal maturity. They also tend to have larger muscle masses that exert more stress on their bones. African-American women also tend to lose bone at a slower rate than white women, and some studies have shown that they also have higher blood levels of calcitonin. Thus, if you are an African-American woman, you will be doubly protected. You start life with bigger bones and therefore can withstand more bone loss. You lose bone more slowly and, hence, will sustain less loss. Interestingly, there is no such protection for African-American men.

There is less information about other ethnic groups. Women whose ancestors came from the British Isles, Northern Europe, China, or Japan are more likely to develop osteoporosis than those of African, Hispanic, or Mediterranean ancestry. The risks for Jewish women seem to fall somewhere between that of low-risk African-Americans and high-risk whites. Generally, there appears to be an association between skin pigmentation and the degree of risk. The whiter our skin, the higher our risk.

The thinner we are, the higher our risk for osteoporosis. Obese women rarely get the disease. During a woman's reproductive life, the ovaries produce large quantities of estrogen and progesterone plus small amounts of the male sex hormones, androgens. The adrenal glands also make androgens. After menopause, the ovarian output of estrogen and progesterone drops to very low levels. However, the ovaries and adrenal glands still produce the same quantity of androgens. Fat tissue is able to convert these androgens to estrogens. The fatter a woman's body, the more estrogen she will be able to produce before and after menopause. Fat, therefore, reduces her risk for osteoporosis.

If you are small in stature and narrow in build, your risk for osteoporosis increases. You have less bone. Given the same rate of loss, you will reach the osteoporotic, fracture-prone state sooner than your more sturdily built counterpart. This is also true for men. Another reason very thin women (and men) have an increased risk for osteoporosis is that the amount of stress exerted on their bones is less than for heavier people. This results in increased bone loss.

Oral contraceptives contain estrogen and progesterone which stimulate bone growth. Women who take oral contraceptives, particularly if for a long time, seem to have greater bone mass when they enter menopause. Therefore, their risk may be somewhat less than that of women who have not used this form of contraception.

A woman who has never been pregnant has an increased risk for osteoporosis. During pregnancy, levels of estrogen and progesterone are very high and will promote bone growth (if calcium intake is adequate). Since higher estrogen levels increase the production of active vitamin D hormone, and because the placenta makes this hormone, calcium absorption is more efficient during pregnancy. With a diet adequate in calcium, pregnancy can be a time to acquire stronger bones. If her calcium intake is low, the increased demand for calcium during pregnancy will be supplied by the mother's bones, leading to a reduction of bone mass. This happens in developing countries where women whose diets have been inadequate for most of their lives have repeated pregnancies. There is an old adage, "a tooth for every pregnancy." The teeth are not considered to be part of our calcium reservoir, but this extreme can happen.

Although a woman who breastfeeds loses a large amount of calcium each day, there is no evidence that breastfeeding increases her risk for osteoporosis. The reverse may be true. Her hormonal milieu during lactation should promote bone growth. We need more knowledge on the relationship between lactation and osteoporosis, but the fear of osteoporosis is not a valid reason for avoiding breastfeeding. Breast milk will supply an infant the most highly absorbable form of calcium and give the newly forming bones a head start.

If you are confined to bed for a long period, or have to spend much time in a wheelchair, you will be at increased risk for osteoporosis. If you lead a sedentary life, your risk is higher than that of a person who is more active. Weight-bearing exercise is important for several reasons. First, such exercise places physical stress on our bones. Our bones respond by becoming larger and stronger. Second, exercise increases the flow of blood to our bones, thereby increasing the availability of bone-building nutrients. Third, exercise generates mini electrical currents that stimulate bone growth. Fourth, exercise alters our hormonal balance, favoring those hormones that protect the bones. One study showed that middle-aged women had increased estrogen levels after six weeks of moderate exercise. Another study found that middle-aged men who rode exercise bicycles had lower levels of the bone-resorbing adrenal hormones after they exercised.

Measurements of bone density changes resulting from exercise showed—to no one's surprise—that a number of world-class athletes had denser bones than sedentary people. Still unknown, however, is how much exercise is necessary to gain this increase in bone mass. Some studies suggest that regular exercise by middle-aged people over a sustained period of time (one year or more) will prevent the bone loss that would normally occur at this stage of life.

In summary, leading a very sedentary existence will increase our risk for osteoporosis. Regular exercise may increase our bone mass and thereby reduce our risk, or at least delay onset. It is important to note that the type of exercise that gives these results, such as walking, jogging, cycling, basketball, tennis, etc., tends to place a stress on our bones. Swimming, though excellent for cardiac fitness, does not lower our risk for osteoporosis. The buoyancy of the water takes the stress off our bones.

Smoking places you at increased risk for osteoporosis. Women who smoke generally reach menopause about five years earlier than nonsmokers, and early menopause increases their risk for osteoporosis. Smoking affects the potential of the liver for making the vitamin D hormone that increases calcium absorption. Smokers tend to be leaner than nonsmokers, and lean women are more at risk for osteoporosis. However, it is still not clear whether smoking is an independent risk for osteoporosis. We don't know exactly how smoking increases our risk, but there are enough other reasons to stop smoking.

Heavy consumption of alcohol can result in osteoporosis in both men and women. Alcohol has a profound effect on liver function including reduced production of the vitamin D hormone, and it can directly impair the absorption of calcium through the gastrointestinal tract. Men with alcoholism can have severe osteoporosis in their twenties probably because of liver damage, poor diets, and low exercise levels. We are not sure whether moderate consumption of alcohol over long periods of time will increase our risk for osteoporosis. However, if we are already at high risk, this may further stack the cards against us.

Asthma, rheumatoid arthritis, and ulcerative colitis are among several chronic diseases treated over long periods of time with cortisone or derivatives of cortisone (hydrocortisone, prednisone, dexamethasone, etc.). These drugs can promote profound bone loss and result in severe osteoporosis in both genders at early ages. Cortisone and its derivatives appear to act in two ways. They increase calcium excretion and decrease calcium absorption, thus producing a net calcium loss. They also block the formation of new bone. While the osteoporosis induced by these drugs is similar to the form occurring in postmenopausal women, the drug-induced disease is often severe enough to affect bones such as the ribs, which are spared in postmenopausal osteoporosis. The two types of the disease are additive; thus, anyone treated with these drugs for a long time is at increased risk for osteoporosis.

Certain drugs such as phenytoin, phenobarbital, primidone, and phensuximide stimulate the production of enzymes that break down the vitamin D hormone produced by the liver. A relative vitamin D deficiency ensues, and calcium absorption is impaired. The result is bone loss. Anyone taking these drugs is therefore at increased risk for osteoporosis.

Millions of Americans regularly use antacids to alleviate the symptoms of everything from "acid indigestion" to peptic ulcer. Many antacids contain aluminum, which can cause an increase in the rate of calcium excretion. Sometimes antacids, together with corticosteroids, are used to prevent the gastric upset that these drugs often cause. If you often use antacids particularly in the combinations outlined above, your risk for developing osteoporosis increases.

Any illness that keeps us in bed for a long time will increase our risk for osteoporosis, and certain specific illnesses will increase that risk over and above the effects produced by lack of weight bearing. Endocrine diseases such as hyperparathyroidism, hyperthyroidism, and overactive adrenals (Cushing's syndrome) will increase bone loss. Chronic diseases such as diabetes, rheumatoid arthritis, and some forms of kidney disease may also increase our risk for osteoporosis. Certain gastrointestinal problems such as sprue or celiac disease will result in poor calcium absorption from food and, hence, increase bone loss. If you have any of these diseases, your risk for osteoporosis increases.

In some people, periodontal disease may resemble osteoporosis. Bone resorption takes place within the jawbones. Thus, periodontal disease may be a forewarning of osteoporosis.

Of dietary factors that may contribute to the development of osteoporosis, first and most important, is calcium deficiency. No matter how favorable our hormonal balance, if our diet is too low in calcium, our bone mass will decrease. Calcium deficiency is more threatening during certain periods of life, particularly the infant year, than at other times. Bone is being produced at a rapid rate, and hormonal balance is favoring bone growth. The reserves are made ready for later life. If the diet is deficient in calcium, or if calcium cannot be adequately absorbed, the impaired bone growth can never be replaced. Breast milk is the best food for an infant. The calcium it contains is better absorbed than calcium from cow's milk. For mothers who do not breastfeed, an infant formula that simulates breast milk—as closely as possible—is recommended for the first year of life.

Adolescence is another time when inadequate calcium intake can be very risky. It can lead to osteoporosis later in life. An adolescent undergoes the most rapid rate of bone growth that will occur during any period of his or her life. Unfortunately, the eating habits of many adolescents promote calcium deficiency. Some eat only foods that are low in calcium or high in phosphorus (which interferes with calcium absorption). Others diet so rigorously that they do not take in enough food to supply their calcium needs.

Pregnancy is another period when insufficient calcium intake can lead to a reduction of bone mass. The fetal skeleton is rapidly consuming calcium. The mother's body is in a hormonal state that favors bone growth, but, unless adequate calcium is available from her diet, the maternal bones will be the main source of this mineral. Fetal bone growth will take place at the expense of maternal bone mass. A diet adequate in calcium will supply enough for her fetus and concurrently allow the mother's own bones to increase in mass.

If a woman nurses her infant, her milk will have to supply large amounts of calcium. If dietary calcium is inadequate during this period, her bones must supply the calcium. Lactation is a critical time when a lack of dietary calcium can erode bones. Hormones favor bone growth during lactation. If enough calcium is available to satisfy the needs of both her infant and her bones, a woman can finish nursing with an increase in bone mass.

We have seen that the body regulates the amount of dietary calcium absorbed from the intestines into the blood and the amount excreted by the kidneys into the urine. This balance between absorption and excretion determines whether sufficient calcium is available for bone growth, or if calcium must come from our bones to supply our tissues.

Several other constituents of our diet will affect our calcium balance. The first is vitamin D. It is so important that our bodies maintain two methods for supplying it. Our skin contains a substance which, when exposed to the ultraviolet rays of the sun, is converted to vitamin D. In addition, our food supply contains vitamin D, naturally (in fish oils, for example) and through fortification (as in dairy products). However, vitamin D, whether consumed in the diet or converted from the skin, has very little activity within our bodies. To become active, it must undergo two chemical modifications. The first takes place in the liver, which manufactures an intermediate form of vitamin D. This intermediate form is somewhat more active than regular vitamin D, but it is nowhere near as active as the final form made in the kidney. That form, sometimes called vitamin D hormone, is essential for calcium absorption. We have already seen how liver disease or kidney disease, by interfering with the manufacture of vitamin D hormone, can increase our risk for osteoporosis.

However, if insufficient vitamin D is available for conversion to the active hormone, even when our liver and kidneys are working perfectly, less hormone will be made. The results are poor calcium absorption, retarded bone growth, increased bone loss, and greater risk for osteoporosis. It is important, therefore, to get enough vitamin D. Too much, however, is of no advantage. The body converts only as much as it needs. An excess of vitamin D can be quite harmful. It can result in the abnormal deposition of calcium in soft tissues such as the kidney (kidney stones).

The amount of phosphorus in our diet will also affect our calcium balance. Like calcium, phosphorus is essential for life.

Also like calcium, the greatest amount of phosphorus is present in bone. Unlike calcium, however, phosphorus is so abundant in our food that primary phosphorus deficiency almost never occurs. In most American diets, there is such an excess of phosphorus that it can promote negative calcium balance. This happens because calcium and phosphorus are transported from the intestines into the blood by the same system. These minerals do not diffuse passively through the intestinal wall. They are borne by protein molecules specially adapted for this work. These "carrier" molecules have a specific and limited number of sites to which a calcium or phosphorus molecule can attach itself. Phosphorus competes with calcium for transport sites into the body; the more phosphorus we take in (particularly at the same meal in which calcium is consumed), the less calcium we absorb. (The phosphorus in soft drinks cannot be ignored.) The less calcium we absorb, the more negative calcium balance, the slower bone growth, the faster our bone loss, and the greater our risk for osteoporosis.

The high-protein content of most American diets will also induce negative calcium balance. Exactly how this happens is not entirely clear, but studies have shown that subjects fed a very high-protein diet will excrete more calcium in their urine than subjects fed a lower-protein diet. The most concentrated form of protein and phosphorus in our diet is meat. Thus, heavy meat eaters will be at increased risk for osteoporosis. Several studies have shown that vegetarians, particularly ovo-lacto vegetarians, have more dense bones than meat eaters. In one study, bone density was greater in vegetarian women at age seventy than in fifty-year-old women who had consumed meat for most of their lives.

Finally, the large amount of salt ingested by most Americans has a negative effect on calcium balance. The excess sodium must be excreted by the kidneys. In this process, extra calcium is excreted. Though the mechanism is indirect, the more sodium we consume the more calcium we will lose and the higher our risk for osteoporosis.

To start scoring your risks:

- If you are a woman, you are automatically at higher risk than if you are a man. All women therefore begin with a score of 5; all men with a score of 0. Racial tendencies toward osteoporosis pertain only to women, not to men.
- If you are a man, score 0 no matter what your race or ethnic background.
- If you are an African-American woman, score 0.
- If you are of Hispanic, Mediterranean, Eastern European, or Asian-American background, score 1.
- If you are a woman of northern European origin, or of very fair complexion, score 2.
- If your mother or sister or several very close relatives have or have had osteoporosis, score 3.
- If a few aunts or cousins have or have had osteoporosis, score 2; if a scattering of distant relatives, 1; and if nobody in your family was affected, score 0.
- If you are a woman who had surgically induced menopause before natural menopause, score 5. If natural menopause occurred before age forty-five, score 3; if between age forty-five and fifty-five, score 0. Thus, if you underwent surgical menopause before reaching the age of natural menopause, you are automatically at high risk for osteoporosis. Even if you are treated with estrogen, you should still start a program of diet and exercise designed to prevent the disease.
- If you have a large frame and broad bones, score 0; an average frame, 1; and if you are petite and slight of build, score 2.
- Anyone of either gender who is 20 percent or more below ideal weight increases his or her chances of developing osteoporosis. If you fall into this category, score 2; between 10 and 20 percent, score 1. If your body weight is above this figure (even if you are obese), score 0.

- If you have been taking oral contraceptives for a long time, it has given you some protection against osteoporosis. How much protection is unclear. If you are such an individual, subtract one point from your final score. However, if this one point is the deciding factor between whether or not to introduce preventive measures, it would still be prudent to undertake those measures.
- If you are a woman who has never been pregnant, score 3; if you have had one pregnancy, score 1; more than one, score 0. While breastfeeding one or more infants probably offers some protection, we do not know enough about it to assign a risk number. However, if your calcium intake was adequate, you can expect an added bonus in lowering your score.
- If you have been bedridden or confined to a wheelchair for a long time (months or years), score 5; this is a very significant risk factor. Lesser periods of non-weight-bearing time should be scored proportionally. If you live a sedentary existence, score 2; take moderate but occasional exercise, score 1; engage in regular exercise, score 0.
- If you are a heavy cigarette smoker, score 1.
- If you are a practicing alcoholic, you need help for many reasons, only one of which a higher risk for osteoporosis. Whether a man or a woman, if you fall into this category, score 5. If you are a woman, this score will automatically place you in the high-risk category. Heavy drinkers, even if they are not alcoholics, should score 3.
- If you have taken cortisone-like drugs for a long time, score 5; this is a very significant risk factor. It applies to both men and women. For shorter periods on these drugs, adjust your score appropriately, but those short periods can add up.
- Anticonvulsant drugs will increase our risk, but not as much as cortisone and its derivatives. Score 3 if you have been taking anticonvulsants for a long time.

- Antacids also increase our risk. If you regularly use types that contain aluminum, score 2.
- Whether a man or a woman, if you suffer from hyper-parathyroidism, hyperthyroidism, or overactive adrenals (Cushing's syndrome), score 3. If you have diabetes, rheumatoid arthritis, or certain forms of kidney disease (ask your doctor which kinds), score 2.
- If you are a vegetarian, particularly an ovo-lacto vegetarian, score 0. If you eat the "typical" American diet, score 2. Heavy meat eaters should score 3. If you cannot consume foods high in calcium (that is, if you have a lactose intolerance), score 3. If you are a constant dieter, taking in 1,200 cal or less for long periods in your life, score 2.

You are now ready to calculate your risk score for osteoporosis. If the total adds up to 10 or more, you are at enough risk to institute preventive measures. You will see that if you are a woman, your chances for reaching a high-risk score of 10 or more are much greater than if you are a man. This is not surprising. Osteoporosis is much more common in women than in men. For a woman, either surgical menopause or severe alcoholism or chronic ingestion of cortisone-like drugs, alone, is enough to place her in the high-risk category. However, men can also be at high risk. For example, the heavy drinking, very thin, slightly built man who smokes has a score of 10 or higher. Similarly, a man with a strong family history of the disease, whose diet is poor, and who takes certain medications can also be at high risk.

A score of 10 or above places either a woman or a man at high enough risk to alter his or her diet and exercise level. Since it is much easier for a woman to reach this score, many more women will find themselves at this risk level than men. However, for those men who scored 10 or above, the dietary advice is as important as for women.

We cannot estimate risk precisely. The scores allotted to the various categories have been assigned to err on the side of overstatement of risk. Since preventive measures outlined in the next section are without danger and have positive health benefits other than merely lowering our risk for osteoporosis, it would be prudent to institute them more often than not.

Lowering Your Risk

If your score is 10 or above, your risk for osteoporosis is great enough to instigate whatever preventive measures you can. Concurrently, you may wish to undergo tests to determine actual bone density. These tests are available in many hospitals and involve newer forms of tissue-imaging that subject you to little or no radiation. They are helpful in determining if you have already undergone significant bone loss. They are also useful for measuring the degree of probable success of any preventive measures you institute. They are not designed to influence your decision to begin preventive measures. Even though the tests may reveal normal bone mass, if your score is 10 or above, you should begin a preventive program before significant bone loss has occurred. Later tests will tell you if your program is succeeding.

Thoroughly examine your score. Some of the risk factors are under your control and can be eliminated. Once these risk factors have been eliminated, to reduce your risk further, pay special attention to your diet and to the type and amount of physical activity you engage in.

The principles of a diet designed to lower our risk for osteoporosis include: adequate calories to attain and/or maintain ideal weight; a calcium intake of 1 g (1,000 mg) per day or 1,500 mg during periods of high calcium need—such as adolescence, pregnancy, and lactation; a moderately low phosphorus intake; a moderately low protein intake; avoidance of excess dietary sodium; and adequate, but not excessive, amounts of vitamin D.

Calories are important for two reasons. If we are too thin, our risk is increased. Additionally, we are unlikely to fulfill our calcium requirement when we are consuming too few calories.

Women who, for cosmetic reasons, are constantly consuming less than 1,500 cal per day to maintain a weight that is 10 or 20 percent below their ideal weight are endangering their bones. We often assume that the thinner we are the better. If we are at high risk for osteoporosis, this is not true. Being too thin may be as much of a health risk as being too fat.

If you are truly obese, and also are at increased risk for osteoporosis, you will need to follow the regimen outlined in "Obesity." Avoid crash dieting or the use of fad diets. They are often very low in calcium. Emphasize foods of high nutrient density with specific attention to calcium. Choose foods of low-calorie and high-calcium content. For example, skim milk is much better than whole milk; low-fat yogurt is better than sour cream on your baked potato; cottage cheese is preferable to cream cheese. Finally, set realistic goals that you can reach and maintain without constantly restricting calories to unrealistically low levels. If you are overweight but out of the danger zone, you will reap at least one benefit of being slightly overweight. Your risk for developing osteoporosis will be lessened.

The recommended dietary intake for calcium (set by the Food and Nutrition Board of the National Academy of Sciences) for an adult woman is 800 mg per day (1,200 mg per day during periods of increased calcium demand). We recommend that the amounts be slightly higher (see the principles outlined above) because women who are at risk for osteoporosis often begin with a deficit. The levels we set are attainable by eating a proper diet. Calcium supplements are necessary only if you cannot consume adequate amounts of high-calcium foods. Table 27 lists portions that will contribute approximately 300 mg of calcium content per serving.

Table 27. **Calcium Content of Foods**
(Each portion provides approximately 300 mg of calcium.)

Food	Amount		
Almonds	1 cup	Ice cream (regular)	1⅔ cup
Amaranth	4 oz.	Kelp	1½ oz.
Broccoli	2¼ cups	Milk:	
Cheese:		whole, low-fat, or	
Cottage	12 oz.	buttermilk	8 oz.
sandwich-style	1½ to 2 oz.	Tofu (soybean curd)	8 oz.
Custard	1 cup	Tortillas (6 in. diam.)	5
Fish (canned):*		Yeast (brewers')	14 tbs.
mackerel	3½ oz.		
salmon	5½ oz.		
sardines	3½ oz.		

*This calcium level includes the softened bones. If the bones are discarded, the calcium content is greatly reduced.

Most of the high-calcium foods fall into the category of dairy products (Americans normally get about 80 percent of their calcium from dairy products). However, by making careful food choices, we can get the required amount of calcium with a much lower percentage coming from milk and milk products. For example, any daily menu that includes single portions of any two of the following will supply more than half your calcium requirement: almonds, broccoli, canned fish (with bones), kelp, tofu, tortillas, kale, turnip or collard greens, macaroni and cheese, pizza, beef tacos, or cheese or meat enchiladas.

Although the rest of your diet will supply some calcium, you will generally need some dairy foods to reach your requirement. If you cannot eat any dairy products, you should take a calcium supplement. A more complete discussion of calcium supplements will follow.

A diet high in *phosphorus* will inhibit calcium absorption and thereby reduce the amount of calcium getting into our bodies. For optimal calcium absorption, we should strive for a dietary pattern that gives us twice as much calcium as phosphorus. The average American consumes more phosphorus than calcium.

The major dietary sources of phosphorus are meat, particularly red meat, and carbonated soft drinks. These foods contain very little calcium. Thus, the calcium-phosphorus ratio is very low. It should be 2:1. Foods such as beef liver, bologna, fried chicken, corn on the cob, frankfurters, ground beef, ham, lamb chops, and pork chops have a calcium-phosphorus ratio from 1:15 to 1:45. Most phosphorylated soft drinks contain no calcium. By contrast, many green leafy vegetables such as spinach and lettuce have more calcium than phosphorus and hence have a favorable calcium-phosphorus ratio. Dairy products contain significant amounts of phosphorus, and their calcium-phosphorus ratio, although favorable, is not as good as that of some of the plant foods. A diet to lower our risk for osteoporosis should not only be high in calcium, but also be relatively low in phosphorus.

Table 28 is a list of high-phosphorus foods and the average phosphorus content per serving.

Table 28. **Phosphorus Contnt of Selected Foods**

Food	Weight	Mg P			
Beef liver	3 oz.	405	Milk, skim	8 oz.	233
Calf's liver	3 oz.	456	Cottage cheese,		
Lean beef	3 oz.	207	creamed	1 cup	319
Chicken, light	3 ½ oz.	280	Cheddar cheese	1 oz.	136
Chicken, dark	3 oz.	188	Bread, whole wheat	1 slice	71
Pork, lean	3 oz.	185	Bread, white	1 slice	28
Egg, large	1 (57 gms)	103	Peanuts	1 oz.	114
Milk, whole	8 oz-	227	Kidney beans	1 cup	259
Milk, 2% fat	8 oz.	276	Almonds	1 oz.	143

Besides the amount in our diet, the time we eat these two nutrients in relation to each other is important. Because calcium and phosphorus compete for the binding sites on the transport protein ("seats on the train"); the more we separate the intake of these two minerals, the better. The calcium from the sour cream in our baked-potato-and-steak meal is not absorbed as well as the calcium from our late evening ice-cream snack. The meals that emphasize calcium-rich foods are better absorbed if phosphorus-rich foods are not eaten with them. It would be good to emphasize calcium-rich snack foods, which are often eaten separate from our regular meals. An ice cream float is not a good combination!

The very high-protein diets consumed by most Americans will cause more calcium excretion in their urine than occurs in people who consume less protein. Like phosphorus, the main source of dietary protein is meat. The more meat we eat, the more calcium we lose, and the greater our risk for osteoporosis. This does not mean that we have to eliminate meat. It does mean, however, that we should use moderation. Every meal does not have to contain meat. Try to limit your meat intake to one meal a day, and cut down on the size of your portions. Emphasize calcium at other meals and during snacks. If you are consuming dairy products to supply calcium, you will automatically be getting significant amounts of protein and don't need to worry about protein deficiency.

Vegetarians, particularly ovo-lacto vegetarians, have a lower incidence of osteoporosis than meat eaters. This is probably because of the lower protein and phosphorus content of their diets. A well-balanced vegetarian diet that allows milk and milk products is probably the best plan for preventing osteoporosis. The closer you approximate such a diet, the better. However, a pure vegetarian, or vegan, diet (no meat, milk products, or eggs) can be a problem unless nondairy sources of calcium are provided. A vegetarian diet promotes good calcium absorption and low calcium excretion. Therefore, the calcium requirement is probably less than on the typical American diet.

However, even with these factors in your favor, if your risk for osteoporosis is high, you must pay special attention to your calcium intake. Diets which claim to be variations of vegetarianism but are much more restrictive—for example, macrobiotic diets—will increase our risk for osteoporosis. They will be too low in calcium to supply your body's needs. Such diets should be discouraged for several reasons, not the least of which is their tendency to increase our risk for osteoporosis.

A very high-salt intake will force our kidneys to excrete more sodium. In the process, calcium will be excreted. You do not have to go on a low-sodium diet to protect your bones from osteoporosis, but if you are a saltaholic, you should cut back. The mild sodium restriction described in the chapter "Hypertension" is not very limiting and will not place an excessive load on your kidneys. (An occasional transgression can be tolerated without endangering your bones.) Remember the non-dietary sources of sodium such as over-the-counter medications and avoid them when possible.

Most American diets, particularly those adequate in calcium, will be adequate in vitamin D. Thus, a diet for preventing osteoporosis almost always supplies enough of this important vitamin. However, most of our dietary vitamin D comes from dairy products made from milk that has been fortified. If you cannot take more than small amount of these foods, you may need a supplement. Remember that vitamin D in excess amounts can be very dangerous, and since it is stored in the body, its effects can be cumulative. If you must take a supplement, take no more than the RDI (400 IU).

There are two advantages to calcium supplements for people who are at risk for osteoporosis:

1. We can guarantee an adequate amount of calcium for our body's needs.
2. We can consume the calcium in a form and at a time that will promote maximum absorption.

Since there is no known toxicity for moderate doses of calcium, even when they are taken for a long time, we have no objection to using a supplement as an added protection for anyone at risk for osteoporosis. If your diet makes it difficult for you to get enough calcium, if you are an avid meat eater, or if you cannot do without phosphorylated soft drinks, then you need a calcium supplement. If your risk score is 15 or above, we also recommend a calcium supplement. If you cannot give up heavy drinking, you should take a calcium supplement; and if you are constantly cutting calories, a supplement will ensure that you get enough. One gram per day, in addition to that in our food, is more than adequate for our needs.

As you can see, we are advocating that most people at risk for osteoporosis take a daily calcium supplement. If your score is between 10 and 15 and you are able to eat foods that are high in calcium and moderately low in phosphorus and protein, a calcium supplement is optional. If your score is 15 or above, or if you are a heavy user of alcohol, then a calcium supplement should be taken. To minimize the dietary factors that interfere with calcium absorption, the best time to take this supplement is between meals. The use of a calcium supplement is to ensure that you get enough total calcium; it should not be used as a replacement for a high-calcium diet. We believe that a diet high in calcium and low in phosphorus and protein offers considerable protection from osteoporosis. There is no evidence that supplements can replace such a diet. Dietary patterns become habitual. If you can establish a pattern that emphasizes high calcium, low protein, and low phosphorus, you can stay on such a diet for the rest of your life.

Any of the available calcium supplements, with the exception of calcium phosphate, are acceptable. Calcium carbonate is usually the cheapest and contains the most calcium per tablet (several antacid tablets are made of calcium carbonate). Calcium lactate should be avoided by people who are lactose intolerant. Calcium gluconate contains only small amounts of calcium per tablet and, hence, must be taken several times during the day. Calcium chloride irritates the stomach in some people. Bone meal and dolomite are high in calcium but these products may be contaminated by toxic substances, and they contain significant amounts of phosphorus. Whichever supplement you choose, establish a routine and take it at the same time every day.

Exercise

Exercise is important for maintaining healthy bones, especially for anyone at high risk for osteoporosis. The best exercises will combine movement and stress on the long bones. Walking, bicycling, hiking, jogging, rowing, and gymnastics are excellent. But maintaining an active lifestyle is even more important than undertaking a specific exercise program. Walk when you can. Climb that flight of stairs. Stand rather than sit. Let your bones bear the weight of your body. That will lower your risk for osteoporosis.

Excessive exercise, particularly for young women, may increase the risk for osteoporosis. Although the number of women athletes studied is still small, results of tests suggest that exercising to the point where menstruation ceases may increase the risk of bone loss.

It is difficult to say how much exercise is enough. However, a regime such as those advocated for promoting cardiovascular fitness is adequate. You may derive a double benefit from such a regime.

Anyone who is at risk for osteoporosis should have bone mass assessments at regular intervals. For most, the program outlined above will show tangible results. Bone mass will stay the same or regress very slowly. The tests will reinforce your incentive to stay with your diet and exercise program. For some, however, bone loss will progress. At this point, you have to make a difficult decision in consultation with your physician, whether to start estrogen therapy.

Estrogen Therapy

Estrogen therapy can help prevent the bone loss that accompanies natural menopause or removal of the ovaries. It is one of the most effective treatment available, and it can be undertaken when diet and exercise are not adequate in slowing the rate of bone loss. To be effective, estrogen therapy must continue for a long time (ten to fifteen years).

Since this treatment will increase a woman's risk for cancer of the uterus, and perhaps of the breast, it is not a decision to be taken lightly. However, progressive osteoporosis is a very serious problem which can lead to death and disabilities. Thus, you must balance the risk of using estrogen against the risk of not using it. A word of caution: there is an indication that women who are already at high risk for heart disease due to plaque buildup on the arteries may be put at even higher risk for heart attacks by use of HRT (hormone replacement therapy).

The incidence of cancer of the uterus among the general population is about one per thousand. The use of estrogen after menopause increases that risk four to eight times. Therefore, at most, if you undertake estrogen treatment, your risk for developing cancer of the uterus is eight per thousand. Of 1,000 women taking estrogen, 992 will not get uterine cancer. The evidence for breast cancer is not conclusive. Some studies suggest a slight increase with estrogen treatment, some suggest no change in incidence, and some suggest a decrease in incidence. Present evidence suggests that women with a family history of breast cancer, or with other known risk factors for the disease (see "Cancer"), will increase their risk with long-term estrogen treatment. It appears that if only women who show no known risk factors for either breast or uterine cancer use estrogen therapy, their risk for uterine cancer will increase from one per thousand to, at most, eight per thousand. Their risk of breast cancer will not increase significantly.

Balance these numbers against the risk of developing severe osteoporosis and its potentially debilitating fractures. Sometimes the decision is easy. Almost all physicians will treat surgically induced pre-menopausal removal of the ovaries with estrogen. Rapid bone loss in the face of dietary treatment is also an indication for treatment. But how rapid is rapid? In the last analysis, you will have to rely on your physician's judgment. You now know what questions to ask. You can be assured that if you do start estrogen therapy, your increased risk for cancer is very small. In addition, your physician may elect to use progesterone together with estrogen which may reduce that risk.

In summary, if your risk score is below 10, stay alert, but you do not need to take specific measures. If your score is 10 or above, take the following steps:

- Eliminate those factors under your control (alcohol, smoking, and certain drugs).
- Have your bone mass measured periodically.
- Consume a diet with adequate calories to reach or maintain ideal weight; one that is high in calcium, low in phosphorus and protein, and not excessive in salt.
- Maintain regular activities and an exercise program that will place modest stress on your bones.
- Take a calcium supplement (optional for scores 10 to 15; mandatory for scores of 15 and above).

Discuss with your physician the pros and cons of estrogen treatment or more recently developed medications and decide whether such treatment would be best for you.

Combined Nutritional Disorders

Being at risk for one of the nutritionally related diseases does not preclude the possibility that we may be at risk for another. Sometimes, a risk for one increases our chances of being at risk for another. For example, people at risk for obesity are more likely to be at risk for hypertension, hyperlipidemia, and diabetes. All of these diseases seem to run in the same families. Certain environments and dietary factors are common among them. A diet to prevent obesity can be modified to also protect one against hypertension or diabetes or atherosclerosis. Regardless of which combination of risks we have, we can undertake a diet that offers maximum protection without being overly restrictive. In this chapter, we will point out those combinations that are likely to go together and the dietary principles that should be considered in making our food choices.

Two kinds of dietary manipulations can reduce our risks. There are those diseases in which too much of a nutrient or combination of nutrients increases our risk, and there are those attributed to too little of one or more nutrients. Atherosclerosis, hypertension, obesity, diabetes, and cancer are diseases of excess. Osteoporosis and anemia are caused by deficiencies. Thus, to lower our risk for any disease in the first group, we must restrict our intake of certain nutrients. To lower our risk for osteoporosis and anemia, we must increase our intake of certain nutrients. Fortunately, no nutrient that must be reduced to protect us against one illness must be increased to protect us against another. A satisfactory diet can be constructed regardless of how many of these illnesses are rated at high risk for us.

The number of nutrients that must be altered to reduce our risk for all these diseases is small (only seven): calories, fat, salt (sodium), calcium, iron, zinc, and folic acid. A diet low in calories, fat, and salt, and high in calcium, iron, zinc, and folic acid would protect us against all of the diseases. Such dietary adjustments are not only reasonable, but some experts advise that all Americans should use them to lower their risks for all the diseases discussed. The Prudent Diet is an ideal starting plan for most of us.

However, we do not think that everyone has to change his or her diet this way. The major benefits from any of these dietary changes are specific to individuals at high risk for a certain disease. There is no reason to change your diet if it would be of little personal benefit. However, a regimen such as the type advocated above is healthy for everyone, and it can usually be achieved without major inconvenience. Certainly, anyone at risk for more than one disease can simultaneously lower all the risks by changing his or her diet. It is rarely necessary to make all of these changes. Those who are at risk for one disease influenced by excessive intake will probably be at risk for another influenced by the same excess. Those who are prone to a disease influenced by deficient nutrient intake will be prone to any other disease similarly influenced. This is true for several reasons. First, the genetic factors that increase risk for atherosclerosis, obesity, hypertension, and diabetes seem to be linked (occur together). Second, the diseases of nutrient deficiencies (osteoporosis and anemia) occur almost exclusively in women. Finally, the lifestyles of most people generally place them in one group (in which excesses must be avoided) or the other (in which deficiencies must be corrected), but rarely in both. Let us therefore examine these groups from the viewpoint of someone at risk for more than one disease.

The diseases of excess are atherosclerosis, hypertension, obesity, diabetes, and certain cancers. The nutrients are calories, fat, and salt consumed in excessive amounts. Salt (sodium) is specific for hypertension. Thus, if the combination of diseases for which your score was high included hypertension, you must limit your salt intake as outlined in the chapter on hypertension. Calories and fat are inextricably linked. Fat is the most calorie-dense nutrient and hence the major source of excessive calories. Therefore, reducing calories almost always means reducing fat, and reducing fat invariably means reducing calories. For practical purposes, we must reduce the amount of fat in our diet whether we are aiming primarily at fat reduction as regarding atherosclerosis and cancer, or calorie reduction as concerning hypertension or obesity, or both, as applies to diabetes. Once we have done this, we can focus on the calories independent of the fat. Hence, if calories are of primary concern, you may wish to cut them further by reducing your intake of alcohol and refined sugar, and sometimes by reducing your total intake of food particularly foods of high glycemic index (see Table 14, page 118). The steps to be taken are as follows:

- Reduce the amount of total fat (for any combination of diseases).
- Reduce calories further (for obesity, hypertension, and diabetes).
- Reduce sodium (for hypertension).

The most restrictive diet is the one for hypertension, which controls both sodium and calories. By reducing fat as discussed in the chapter on atherosclerosis, we can bring calories into balance. Thus, by only slightly modifying the diet against risk for hypertension, you will be protecting yourself from any combination of diseases. If your risk for hypertension is not significant, regardless of the combined diseases, you do not have to pay specific attention to salt reduction.

The deficiency diseases with which we are concerned are osteoporosis and anemia. Both primarily concern women. A considerable number of American women may be at risk for both. A woman at high risk for osteoporosis and anemia must pay particular attention to consuming foods high in calcium, iron, zinc, and folic acid. Concurrently, she should reduce her phosphorus allowance (particularly at the same meal that supplies a considerable portion of her calcium intake). This type of diet demands the greatest knowledge of the specific nutrients in foods. As we have noted, dietary calcium comes primarily from dairy foods. Fat-free or low-fat dairy foods are more nutrient dense and hence allow us to take in other caloric sources of iron, zinc, and folic acid. Folic acid and zinc requirements have risen only moderately. The inclusion of lean meat, liver, seafoods, and certain green leafy vegetables should meet this increased requirement. As for iron, a risk score above 10 should be treated initially with iron supplements if we are at double risk. To satisfy our calcium requirement, we will be consuming foods that are low in iron (milk, cheese, yogurt, etc.). Thus, we must get our iron from only a part of our diet. If our iron requirement is very high, then it can be achieved only by consuming fortified foods (which also supply calories) or by taking an iron supplement. Conversely, meat is not a particularly good source of calcium and is high in phosphorus. Therefore, a diet that emphasizes meat reduces the availability and the absorption of calcium. Unless we eat dairy products and carefully selected plant foods (see Table 27, page 200), we will have difficulty getting our calcium requirement. Then, we need to take a calcium supplement. The following guidelines should be followed if you are at risk for both osteoporosis and anemia.

- Choose foods rich in calcium, iron, zinc, and folic acid, and low in calories.
- Use low-fat dairy products.

- Favor nondairy sources of calcium that also contain significant quantities of iron, zinc, or folic acid.
- Use fortified breakfast cereals that contain iron primarily, and folic acid and zinc when possible.
- Take a calcium supplement if you cannot achieve your calcium requirement (1,000 to 1,200 mg per day) with the above diet. This will depend on the number of calories you are consuming.
- Take an iron supplement if your risk for anemia is 10 or more.
- If you are deliberately limiting calories (dieting), take a calcium supplement (500 to 1,000 mg per day) and an iron supplement (30 mg per day).

Our goal is to combine a diet that lowers our risk for osteoporosis with one designed to lower our risk for anemia. This can be achieved effectively only if we consume enough food (calories) of the proper nutrient density and if our iron reserves are not too badly depleted. Otherwise, we should take a calcium supplement, an iron supplement, or both.

Occasionally someone, usually a woman, can be at simultaneous risk for one disease from the nutrient-excess group and one from the nutrient-deficient group. For example, she may be at risk for hypertension and anemia. If so, she must keep her weight down by controlling calories, reduce her salt intake, and increase her intake of iron, zinc, and folic acid. To do this, she must pay attention to the foods in her diet. First, how many calories can she take in without exceeding her ideal weight? If the number is below 1,800, she will have a problem getting her iron requirement; below 1,200, she will need an iron supplement no matter how careful she is about her diet. Second, she must pay special attention to the sources of zinc, folic acid, and iron (see Tables 23, 24, and 25, "Anemia"). Finally, she must avoid foods that are either naturally high in sodium or to which sodium has been added.

If cholesterol and saturated fat must be reduced, then our options for iron become fewer because this means reducing our intake of red meats and organ meats (the richest sources of this mineral). Anyone in double jeopardy for a deficiency disease and a disease of excess should consider taking supplements. This will allow us to concentrate on reducing our risks for atherosclerosis, hypertension, obesity, diabetes, or certain cancers (while protecting us against osteoporosis or anemia). Supplements, however, do not eliminate our need to emphasize dietary sources of iron, zinc, folic acid, and calcium. The best way to get these nutrients is from our food. The supplements are simple insurance. For those of you at risk for diseases of both excess and deficiency, the following principles must be observed:

- Decide how many calories you need.
- Reduce calories, fat, and salt as dictated by your risk in the excess category.
- Increase foods as needed if you are in the deficient category.
- Take a supplement—iron, if you are at risk for anemia; calcium, if you are at risk for osteoporosis; iron and calcium, if you are at risk for both of these diseases.

This is rarely a problem for adult men. Adult women may need supplements due to

- High-risk score for nutritional anemia (iron).
- Risk for osteoporosis; inability to consume large amounts of dairy foods (calcium).
- Adolescent pregnancy (iron, folic acid, zinc).
- Any risk score for anemia in a pure vegetarian (iron, zinc, and vitamin B12).
- Risk for osteoporosis and one of the diseases of excess (calcium).

- Risk for anemia and one of the diseases of excess (iron).
- Risk for osteoporosis, anemia, and one of the diseases of excess (iron and calcium).
- Any woman consuming less than 1,200 cal (iron).
- Risk for anemia; heavy alcohol consumption (iron, zinc and folic acid).

Nutrient supplements

Nutrient supplements can be acquired by consuming fortified foods or by taking a pill containing vitamins and minerals.

Vitamins—the body is a versatile chemist. It makes thousands of different substances. There are, however, some things it cannot produce: some of the fatty acids and some of the amino acids. We call these necessary fatty acids and amino acids the "essential fatty acids" (or polyunsaturates) and the "essential amino acids." There are some other complex substances the body needs in small amounts and that it is unable to manufacture. These are called the vitamins. They must be provided by foods (or by "vitamin supplements") or the body will not function at peak efficiency. A serious shortage of one or more vitamins will cause one or more deficiency diseases. Extreme deficiencies are fatal.

Most vitamins are designated by a letter of the alphabet because, at one time, we did not know their chemical structure and could not give them a proper scientific name. In addition, there are vitamins that have proved to be two or more related substances with similar roles in the body. For example, there are several forms of "vitamins D." In some cases, a substance found in food is a "pro vitamin" which, when consumed, is transformed into the needed vitamin itself. For instance, there are various carotenes which, after being eaten, become vitamin A.

The vitamins are usually divided into "water-soluble vitamins," found in the watery parts of cells (and foods), and the "fat-soluble vitamins" which are dissolved in fat or in the fat part of cells. The fat-soluble vitamins are A, D, E, and K. The water-soluble vitamins are the vitamin B complex, in particular B1, B2, niacin, pyridoxine, B12, folic acid, biotin, pantothenic acid, and vitamin C.

Vitamin A is found in nature as the pro vitamin, carotene, in green and yellow plants, and as two forms of the vitamin itself in freshwater fish and land animals on the one hand, and sea fish and animals on the other. It is also found in summer butter, which is butter churned from milk collected in the summer when the cows eat fresh grass full of carotene, the splitting of which in the organism gives rise to vitamin A. Vitamin A then goes on to be secreted in the milk. (In "Golden Guernsey" the splitting is incomplete; some of the yellow pigment is unchanged—hence the golden color of the milk.)

Vitamin A is essential in the growth and maintenance of epithelial tissue which comprises the skin and the covering of internal cavities. It is important in the harmonious development of the bones. It is a constituent in the maintenance of the outside of the eye and is also made into a pigment in the retina of the eye, which enables us to see. This pigment is involved in a complex photochemical process essential to night and twilight vision.

Vitamin D is found in certain foods (fish liver oil, liver, eggs, summer butter) and is also formed when the skin is exposed to the sun. Because cows are exposed to sunshine in pastures, they manufacture vitamin D by conversion of cholesterol. Some of the vitamin D then is secreted into the milk and, (like vitamin A) fat-soluble, ends up in the butter fraction. Vitamin D is necessary for the utilization of the mineral calcium. Milk is often fortified with vitamin D to the level of 400 IU (the Recommended Dietary Intake) per quart.

Vitamin E has a number of important roles that have been described in animals. So far, vitamin E deficiency has not been identified clearly in man, except perhaps in situations where fat absorption is grievously impaired.

Vitamin K, indispensable for the proper clotting of blood, is normally manufactured by bacteria in the intestine. Newborn babies, who do not yet have bacteria in their intestines, often need a supplement of vitamin K.

Vitamin B1, (also called thiamin) is found in whole-grain cereals and meat, among other sources. It is needed for the utilization of starches and sugars. It is also essential to a number of other chemical reactions whereby food is utilized in the body.

Niacin (nicotinic acid and nicotinic acid amide) is necessary for the respiration of the cells. The amino acid tryptophan can be changed into niacin in the body.

Pyridoxine (vitamin B6) is involved in many chemical reactions, in particular in the utilization of protein.

Pantothenic acid and biotin are also known to be necessary factors.

Folic acid and vitamin B12 are needed for the formation of red cells. B12 is also necessary for the maintenance of certain nerves.

Vitamin C (ascorbic acid) found in fruits (particularly in oranges and lemons) and potatoes is necessary for the maintenance of connective tissue—the tissue that binds together the various organs.

Remember that you need vitamins, all vitamins, each day—not C last year and E this year and X or Y or Z next year.

The daily intake levels recommended by the National Research Council are established by subcommittees of the best experts on each vitamin. These are men and women with research experience with these vitamins in clinical nutrition. The recommendations include a generous but reasonable margin of safety to cover individual differences and changing conditions. Large doses (more than 250 percent of the recommended daily intake) should be taken only with the knowledge and advice of your physician. A growing number of prevention oriented physicians are advising their patients to take mega doses (up to 2,000 percent of the recommended daily intake) of vitamin E, vitamin C, and other antioxidants such as beta-carotene. There is growing evidence that these substances can help prevent some of the harmful effects of free radicals (charged molecules) in the body. Perceived dangers of the supplements are almost nonexistent. However, one major concern is that the body can become dependent on them after prolonged use. If you take large doses of these materials and decide to stop (for economic reasons or on the advice of a professional, for example) you should taper off gradually. Abrupt withdrawal of mega vitamin supplements can lead to rebound phenomena which can cause symptoms of vitamin deficiencies even when the intake meets normal requirements.

Minerals—one may not think of food as something to be mined in addition to being planted, bred and hunted, or fished for. But many of man's most important nutrients are scratched from the crust of the earth. Several of these minerals, needed by the body in relatively large amounts, are: calcium, phosphorous, magnesium, iron, *zinc*, sodium, potassium, sulfur, and chlorine.

Throughout our lives we need fresh supplies of calcium to replace that which is constantly called upon to perform necessary functions. Ninety-nine percent of our calcium is in our skeleton, all but one percent of which is in the bones, the rest in the teeth. The remaining one percent which is not in the skeleton makes the muscles, including the heart, contract; aids in blood clotting; and is concerned with the nourishment of cells, the conversion of food to energy, and the supply of an ingredient that facilitates the transmission of nerve impulses.

Closely allied in the body with calcium and vitamin D is phosphorous. It is mostly in the skeleton and accounts for about one percent of body weight. Phosphorous is also essential for the chemical reactions whereby energy is transferred from food for the synthesis of body substances and for changing chemical into electrical energy in the nerves and muscles. We get phosphorous from milk and lean meats, fish, and vegetables. The daily requirement is the same as for calcium: 800 mg per day.

There is about 1 oz of *magnesium* in the body of an adult. Much of it is combined with calcium and phosphorous in the bone. The remainder is in red blood cells and in body fluids. We need magnesium to keep hormones working, to use carbohydrates for energy, and to maintain muscles. There are many sources of magnesium: large amounts in whole-grain cereals (especially oats), milk, fish and shellfish (particularly shrimp), and in meat, fruit, vegetables, and nuts.

Iron is an essential part of hemoglobin, the pigment of red blood cells which loosely combines in the lungs with oxygen and carries it to all the tissues. The most common anemia seen in this country is iron-deficiency anemia. It is seen in infants and young children and in women of childbearing age. It has been found to be more common among the elderly of both genders than previously suspected. Liver and kidney are rich sources of iron. Others include oysters, shrimp, sardines, most meats, dried beans, most nuts, eggs, prunes, raisins, green leafy vegetables, and enriched bread and cereals.

Sodium is found mainly in the blood, lymph, and digestive juices, and the fluid that bathes cells. About a fifth of one percent of the body is sodium, a third of which is in the skeleton. The average American seems to eat about ten times as much sodium chloride (table salt) as he requires. Most people would do well to banish the salt shaker from the dining room table. They could satisfy their needs for sodium from reasonable amounts of milk, meat, eggs, carrots, beets, and spinach.

Chlorine exists throughout the body and particularly in the acid in the stomach, which digests food. You can meet all of your requirement for chlorine from the slightest amount of table salt.

Sulfur used by the body comes from two amino acids (cystine and methionine) each of which contains sulfur. It is an ingredient of hair, nails, bones, tendons, and the fluids of our joints. It performs a function in the process by which the body rids itself of common poisonous substances. Sulfur is provided by lean meat, fish, fruits and vegetables.

The body has about twice as much potassium as sodium and most of it is within the cells. Potassium is vital for maintaining the chemical balance of the cellular fluids. A small additional amount is required for the work of the muscles, especially the heart muscle. There is plenty of potassium in oranges, bananas, dried fruits, tomatoes, leafy vegetables, peas and beans, milk, meats, and fish.

Iodine is what we call a trace mineral. And people who don't get a natural supply of it—by eating seafood, for example—may be afflicted with goiter. This is one of the most clear-cut cases of what can happen when people are deficient in even the tiniest, almost-impossible-to-measure quantities of these essential trace elements or trace minerals.

Iodine is an essential component of the thyroid-gland hormones that regulate the rate at which our tissues breathe. Without it, the tissues use less oxygen, the body slows down, and eventually so does the mind. The thyroid gland enlarges in an attempt to compensate for the lack of iodine, causing the typical swelling of the neck we know as simple goiter. Goiter practically disappeared from the United States when table salt was iodized and when people living in parts of the country where the soil had little or no iodine began eating food from other sections.

About one half of the iodine in the human body is in the muscles. About a fifth is in the thyroid, the rest in the skin, the skeleton, and other tissues. Its important role in the thyroid is to take part in the synthesis of the thyroid hormones that control the rate at which the principal chemical reactions of the body occur. The rest of the trace-mineral story is less simple. Not even the nutrition experts know all they would like to know about trace minerals—how they work, why the body needs them, what foods are rich in them, or even whether we know them all. And our lack of knowledge creates a fertile field for propaganda, confusion, and fear.

Here are some information about several of the other trace minerals:

- *Cobalt* makes up 4.5 percent of vitamin B12, which protects against pernicious anemia. We do not seem to need cobalt as such, only as a component of vitamin B12, which we get from nearly all animal products. The liver and kidneys of ruminants are especially good sources. Yogurt is low in vitamin B12.
- We know that plants need *boron* for growth, but we're uncertain about its importance, if any, to animals and men.
- *Cadmium* is toxic in large amounts and may be essential in tiny ones, but we don't know yet. The same is true of *bromine*.
- *Chromium* in an organic complex known as "glucose tolerance factor" aids insulin in getting glucose into our cells.
- *Manganese* is needed to activate the enzymes that split amino acids off protein, and to obtain energy from the utilization of carbohydrates. The best sources are cereal bran, soybeans, other beans and peas, nuts, tea, and coffee.
- *Selenium* appears to cooperate with vitamin E in preventing certain muscle defects.
- *Molybdenum* may be significant for the working of a number of enzymes. Molybdenum deficiency has been implicated in certain dental deformities in New Zealand.
- *Vanadium* and *Silicon* are known to be essential for the growth of animals, and vanadium again for their reproduction.

We measure the trace minerals in fractions of a millionth of a gram! To understand their role, we must picture each cell in our bodies as a complex factory where thousands of chemical reactions go on at the same time to make us the living, breathing, growing, regenerating organisms we are. In an ordinary factory, such chemical reactions could take place only with highly concentrated compounds at high temperatures. In the cells, they occur at body temperature, in watery fluids with enzymes acting as catalysts. These enzymes, composed of complex protein molecules, have the amazing capacity to bring specific molecules to the right position to react at the appropriate moment. Some of these enzymes contain vitamins as part of their own molecules and many do not function except in the presence of the right trace mineral. Without such activators (and each enzyme requires a particular activator), no reaction takes place. If this happens, you may become anemic, or you do not grow. In extreme cases, you may die.

Fortified foods supply the nutrient with some calories (usually from carbohydrates). Vitamin and mineral supplements usually have no calories. Whichever type you choose, remember that you are taking a supplement for a reason —your diet is low in that particular nutrient. Therefore, decide which supplement you need, and then pick a fortified food or pill containing it. For example, if you need iron and decide to use a fortified breakfast cereal, which brand should you choose? Brand X contains 100 percent of the daily requirement for all the vitamins and 25 percent of the daily requirement of iron. Brand Y contains only 25 to 50 percent of the vitamins, but 35 percent of the daily iron requirement. Brand Y should be your choice even though it is not as high in vitamins. On the other hand, if you need both iron and folic acid, you might elect Brand X, which has 100 percent of the folic acid. Look for the highest amount of the nutrient or nutrients you need. Don't be fooled by ads saying that one cereal provides better nutrition than another cereal because it contains more of certain nutrients, when you do not need extra amounts of those nutrients.

The same principle applies to pills. Pick one that has the right amount of the nutrient you need. The rest of the vitamins and minerals it contains may be extraneous. For example, if you need 30 mg of iron per day, take a pill that contains 30 mg of iron. The amount of B-complex vitamins or vitamins C or A or D the pill contains is not important. If you need only iron, then take only iron. If you need iron and folic acid or zinc, a multivitamin mineral preparation may be appropriate. Ideally, you should take only one pill that contains all three nutrients in the right amounts. Unfortunately, such a pill might not be available. Select a pill with as much of these three nutrients as you need, but avoid pills that are very high in vitamins A and D. These nutrients are toxic if taken in excessive amounts. Another word of caution: heed the warning labels. Iron may seem innocuous to you, but iron supplements can be fatal to toddlers! Keep all pills out of reach of children.

If you need calcium, you cannot depend on fortified foods. None contain sufficient amounts. You will need calcium in pill form. You may have heard that pills do not do any good because they aren't absorbed. But if you have taken one that includes folic acid, did you notice how soon your urine changes color? How could that happen if you didn't absorb the ingredients of the pill? True, some people (particularly the elderly) may not have enough acid in their stomach to dissolve some of the calcium phosphate or other solid form of calcium. In that case, it may be advisable to crush the pills (and possibly mix them with applesauce or other vehicle) before swallowing them. We discussed calcium supplements in the chapter on osteoporosis.

You will occasionally see references to "chelated" minerals, with claims that they are assimilated better. These are organically complexed metals. They bare an analogy to the way iron is contained in the heme molecule and cobalt in vitamin B12, but are usually loosely bound to amino acids or other molecules. The original reason for chelation was the instability of vitamins in the presence of some of the mineral elements such as copper. Organic complexes of the metals did not catalyze the deterioration of vitamins (on the shelf) as did the simple metals. Almost all pills with combined vitamins and minerals include metals in chelated form. The differences in brands are probably minor (except the prices!). One exception may pertain to *magnesium*. Most supplements incorporate this element as an oxide. Several authors have reported that only about 4 percent of the mineral in this form is available for absorption. Magnesium oxide cannot absorb as magnesium oxide. Instead, as with most minerals, the magnesium has to react with an acid turning it in to an absorbable salt. Many people lack sufficient levels of stomach acid as levels drop with age and there is a major overuse of antacids, acid blockers (proton pump inhibitors), carbonates, and oxides in supplements and alkaline waters, all of which further reduce stomach acid reducing mineral absorption. An ionic form of magnesium (such as magnesium chloride) may be necessary— to get the most benefit from the supplement.

Being in "double jeopardy" can be handled with a minimum of inconvenience. For most, it will mean a somewhat more restricted diet. For a few, it will also mean taking supplements. Look at the diets that lower your risk for the particular diseases in question. Combine them. Make a list of the foods to avoid in each disease. For example, if you are at risk for atherosclerosis and hypertension, you will avoid fatty meats, organ meats, eggs, non-skimmed dairy products (atherosclerosis), and luncheon meats, hot dogs, etc. (atherosclerosis and hypertension), and pickled, smoked, and highly processed foods (hypertension). In addition, you will not add much salt during cooking or use the salt shaker at the table. Somewhat restrictive? Of course, you are at risk for two serious diseases! However, you can eat an endless variety of foods: fish, fowl, lean meats, skim dairy products, fruits, vegetables, starches, grains—even wine or other alcoholic beverages in moderation. If you are at risk for obesity, this diet will be low in calories. If you are at risk for breast cancer or uterine cancer, the lowered fat and calories will reduce your risk for those diseases. If your diabetes score is high, the diet will also reduce your risk for that disease. If you are at risk for one or more of these diseases and are also at risk for osteoporosis or anemia, you must choose wisely from the foods that are permitted. In addition, take a calcium supplement for osteoporosis or an iron supplement (if your risk for anemia is high). Finally, if you are at high risk for atherosclerosis, hypertension, obesity, or osteoporosis, you should increase your exercise level (if you are inactive). All the changes recommended are consistent with today's more active lifestyle and can be accomplished without great difficulty. You can continue to prepare gourmet meals at home and to dine in fine restaurants. Some of the finest restaurants now offer choices consistent with the principles outlined above. So, even for those at risk for two or more diseases, there is plenty of room for the enjoyment of good food.

Diseases with Indeterminate Risk

Unfortunately, a precise risk score cannot be formulated for every nutritionally related disease, but we can, sometimes, define certain genetic and lifestyle characteristics that predispose us to a particular disease. If these predispositions raise our risk score above a certain level, we must consider modifying our diet. If our risk score is very low, dietary modification is not necessary. The major diseases discussed in the preceding chapters are fairly predictable.

With some diseases, we know there is an association with diet, but we do not know enough to develop a risk profile. For example, diverticulosis relates to a low-fiber diet, but we are not able to separate people at high risk from those at low risk. Any recommendations for diseases within this category will apply to the general public. They will depend on the prevalence of the disease and our own dietary practices.

To illustrate, suppose a disease affects 20 percent of the population; you have one chance in five of developing it. If your diet puts you in the susceptible category, you may need to change it. By contrast, suppose the disease in question has an incidence of one percent or less. Your chances for getting it are less than one in a hundred. You may elect not to change your diet. Not only will the incidence of the disease influence your choice, but its severity is also important. You may elect to take a one-in-a-hundred chance for one disease, but not for another.

In this chapter, we will discuss some serious diseases for which a risk profile cannot be defined. We will define the disease and outline its prevalence. Then, we will identify dietary practices associated with it. If you have these eating habits, you may want to change them. For anyone who elects to make a change, we will describe the best way to accomplish it.

Diseases of the Large Intestine

The gastrointestinal tract is divided into four discrete regions. The esophagus is the tube passing from the mouth through the thorax and diaphragm to the stomach. It is a tunnel through which the food is helped along by muscular contractions that propel it in the right direction. The stomach mixes the food with fluids that begin the process of digestion. The small intestine is a long, narrow, coiled tube in which most digestion and absorption takes place. The large intestine is a short, wide tube in which water is re-absorbed and the undigested food is processed for excretion. Disease that occurs anywhere along this lengthy tract will often call for a change in diet. The type and consistency of the food passing through the digestive system may alter its condition. In addition, certain diseases within the gastrointestinal tract, particularly in the small intestine, may affect digestion or absorption of specific nutrients, and thereby necessitate a change in diet or the use of a supplement. In this chapter, we will not discuss this type of disease. Although diet is part of the treatment, sometimes the major part, it is not the cause of the disease. Anyone with this type of condition should be under a physician's care.

Some diseases of the gastrointestinal tract, particularly of the large intestine, may be caused by improper diet over a long period of time. To understand how diet may cause these diseases, consider what happens to the residue of our food as it traverses the large intestine. Very little absorption or digestion takes place after the food enters the large intestine. It is simply prepared for excretion. The consistency of the residue and the amount of pressure that must be generated to expel this material depends to a large extent on the composition of the undigested residue reaching the large intestine. When we eat, we consume certain complex carbohydrates that our gastrointestinal systems are unable to digest. These pass intact through the entire system and reach the large intestine in virtually the same condition as when eaten. These undigested complex carbohydrates are called fiber. Fiber comes from cereal brans and various fruits and vegetables. While there are many different types of fiber, they all have one property in common: they trap water.

We've learned that different kinds of fiber help prevent different kinds of illnesses. There are actually two types of fiber: soluble and insoluble. As their names suggest, soluble fiber dissolves in water, but insoluble doesn't. Most plant foods contain both kinds of fiber, but they usually have more of one type than the other. Both soluble and insoluble fiber fill you up, but each one has specific benefits.

Soluble fiber, the kind that will dissolve, helps you feel full and also helps lower your cholesterol and your blood sugar. Soluble fiber is believed to lower cholesterol by linking up with bile acids, which are made from cholesterol stored in the liver, and escorting them out of the body. But the bile-acid supply must be replenished, and this calls for more cholesterol, thus lowering the cholesterol circulating in the blood. Soluble fiber also slows down the body's absorption of carbohydrates, thus restricting dramatic highs and lows in blood sugar.

The best food sources of soluble fiber are apples, barley, beans, carrots, grapefruit, oats, oranges, peas, rice bran, and strawberries. Some breakfast cereals are rich suppliers of soluble fiber, which will help to lower your cholesterol. Select from a wide variety of cereals that contain large amounts of oat and rice bran, two very effective cholesterol-lowering agents. University of Maryland researchers have found, in fact, that the soluble fiber in oat bran is just as effective in lowering cholesterol and far less expensive than some of the commonly used cholesterol-lowering drugs are.

Insoluble fiber, which won't dissolve, comes from the outer, hard shell of grains, and some are also found in most fruits and vegetables. It will help you to feel full and has the added benefit of helping to regulate your bowels by bulking up stools. Insoluble fiber is also believed to help prevent certain forms of cancer, most notably colon/rectal cancer.

This is the kind of fiber you probably know of as the wheat bran in bran muffins and raisin bran cereal. Other excellent sources of insoluble fiber are celery, corn bran, green beans, green leafy vegetables, potato skins, and whole grains.

Increasing the amount of fiber in our diet gets more water into materials passing through the large intestines. The more water, the softer the material and, ultimately, the softer the stool. Thus, one way to prevent constipation (or, for that matter, treat constipation) is to consume a high-fiber diet. Constipation can be a serious problem, particularly for older people. By creating a softer stool, a high-fiber diet will affect the large intestine in two ways. First, it will reduce the amount of pressure necessary to move the stool along for excretion. Second, a high-fiber diet moves the contents of the large intestine more rapidly and generates less pressure.

The large intestine is a muscular tube with an inside lining of specialized cells. Normally there are stronger and weaker areas in the tube. If very high pressure is constantly generated upon the walls of the tube, some areas will balloon and form small outpouchings called diverticuli. If many outpouchings form, we call the condition diverticulosis. This disorder is common in older people. Twenty percent or more of people over sixty-five may have diverticulosis. High pressure over a long time causes the problem. Occasionally food or other debris within the large intestine gets trapped inside one or more of these diverticuli. This creates conditions that favor infection. The diverticuli become inflamed. When this happens, we term the condition diverticulitis. That is a painful and serious condition, and it demands immediate medical attention. We don't know what makes one person more susceptible than another to getting diverticuli. Perhaps minute differences in the nature of the intestinal wall itself cause them. We do know, however, that increasing the amount of fiber in the diet reduces the risk of diverticulosis, and its most serious consequence—diverticulitis.

Should you go on a higher-fiber diet? That depends on how much fiber you are consuming. Table 21 (page 147) lists foods that are high in fiber. How often do you eat these foods? Usually, natural foods are higher in fiber than processed foods, and plant foods are higher in fiber than animal foods. Thus, the closer you are to being a vegetarian, the higher the fiber content of your diet.

Before you decide whether you need more fiber, you should consider another disease that may relate to a low-fiber diet. This disease is much less common than diverticulosis but much more serious: cancer of the colon. It is the second property of fiber in the diet that appears to provide some protection against cancer of the colon.

The more fiber in the diet, the faster the intestinal contents move, and the less chance they have to come in contact with the intestinal wall. If there are substances within the stool that can induce cancer, the exposure time to such substances is shorter on a high-fiber diet. Whether such substances are present in the contents of the large intestine appears also in part to depend on the nature of our diet. The higher its fat content, the higher the risk for colon cancer. Thus, the best type of diet to reduce our risk for colon cancer is one high in fiber and low in fat. The primary sources of fat in our diets are meat and dairy products. These foods are also low in fiber. Increasing the amount of fiber in our diet will almost automatically decrease the amount of fat.

We can summarize the arguments for a high-fiber diet as follows:

- It will keep the stool soft and help prevent constipation.
- It will keep the pressure inside the large intestine low and reduce the risk of diverticulosis.
- It will move the contents of the large intestine more rapidly, reducing contact time with the intestinal wall.
- It will almost always decrease the amount of fat in the diet, thereby reducing the potential carcinogen content of the stool.

How do we know if our diet contains enough fiber? The average American consumes about 12g of fiber per day. The optimal amount is believed to be between 20 and 30 g. Look at Table 21. Add up the amount of fiber that you consume on an average day. Try to increase your consumption of high-fiber foods to approach 30 g. You may find that the quantity of food required to increase the fiber is so high that you can't eat it all. In that case, you may need to cut back more on some of the high-fat foods to make room for them.

It seems ludicrous to suggest that anyone take fiber supplements, but many people do. Maybe they have to restrict their calorie intake to the extent that they feel they cannot consume enough bulky vegetables without giving up too many of the delicious and satisfying animal products. (No foods of animal origin contain fiber!). There are some good supplements to be found in drug stores and elsewhere that were intended to control constipation, but if you think you need them because your diet is too low in fiber, some of them could serve equally well as dietary supplements. There is concern that supplemental fiber may decrease absorption of certain vitamins and minerals. So a multiple vitamin-mineral supplement may be advisable for anyone who takes fiber supplements for prolonged periods of time. Also, if you use any of the powdered fiber supplements, be sure to consume them with plenty of water.

If you make this type of change, do it gradually. If you suddenly take in much more fiber than you are used to, you may feel bloated and suffer from gas pains. Your gastrointestinal tract needs to adapt to the higher fiber content of the foods. Make the change over several weeks, progressively increasing your fiber intake by small amounts each day.

Diseases of the Teeth

One of the great fears of getting old is the prospect of losing one's teeth. One out of every five of our older population has lost all teeth. There is increasing evidence that faulty nutrition plays some role in causing this problem. In early life, diet affects dental caries; in later life, it is related to periodontal disease.

There is no doubt that dental caries are related to diet. Specifically, there is a strong association between the amount of refined sugar we consume and the incidence of dental caries. To understand the nature of this relationship, let us examine how cavities occur.

The mouth is normally a breeding ground for millions of bacteria. The conditions within the mouth, as well as the food eaten, favor the growth of certain types of bacteria. Some of these organisms break down simple sugars such as sucrose (ordinary refined sugar) to a number of products, including organic acids. They also use these sugars to construct a hard substance called dental plaque which adheres to the teeth. Thus, a diet high in simple sugar favors the growth of bacteria that require simple sugars to multiply. These bacteria, in turn, metabolize the simple sugar in a way that releases products that cause dental caries.

The bacteria secrete substances that form plaque. The plaque adheres to the teeth, and the bacteria beneath it are sheltered from your toothbrush. These bacteria continue to break down the simple sugar and in the process secrete organic acids that erode tooth enamel. Soon, a cavity appears which, under the constant exposure to these acids, gets deeper and deeper, finally invading the pulp of the tooth. So far, we have discussed two factors involved in the production of dental caries: sugar and bacteria. A third element must also be considered—the hardness of the tooth enamel itself.

The harder the enamel, the more resistant it will be to the acid secretions of the sugar-metabolizing bacteria. How hard a tooth becomes also depends, to some extent, on diet. Enamel, like bone, depends on calcium for its hardness. Unlike bone, however, enamel is not a calcium reservoir (except under extreme circumstances). Once formed, it holds on to its calcium. Thus, the crucial time for determining the hardness of the teeth is during early childhood when the teeth are forming.

Some studies shown that a diet poor in calcium will result in poor enamel formation and in teeth that are very prone to cavities. It is important, therefore, that the diet of every young child be adequate in calcium. The time to begin is at birth. Breast milk is rich in calcium, in a form easily absorbed by the infant. If your infant is bottle-fed, use a formula that is as close as possible in composition to breast milk. After the child is a year old, whole milk becomes the best source of calcium. Low-fat or skim milk can replace whole milk at about eighteen months of age if you are concerned about fat. Dairy products will continue to be the major source of dietary calcium throughout childhood, but as the child grows older, other foods can contribute significant amounts of it. See Table 26 in "Osteoporosis" for foods that are rich in calcium. Remember, too much phosphorus will reduce calcium absorption. This is a particular problem in children. Many soft drinks contain significant amounts of phosphorus. Read the label. Phosphoric acid means phosphorus. Substitute a drink devoid of phosphoric acid.

Another very important nutrient in determining the hardness of teeth is fluoride, particularly during the early development of the teeth. Fluoride promotes calcium deposition and ensures that it is firmly bound in the enamel. Fluoride is found in minute amounts in some foods and in some water supplies. In the United States, many localities have added fluoride to their water. Others have not. There is no question that the addition of fluoride to water supplies has reduced the incidence of dental caries. Yet, many areas are still reluctant to fluoridate their water because of possible unknown side effects which, supposedly, could manifest themselves after long-term. Many households now use bottled water from which all minerals, including fluoride, have been removed. Some of us have installed filters in our home water supply to remove undesirable odors, or potential hazards. Some of these filters will remove fluorides. To date, we have not seen any long-term hazards from fluoridated water and there is no valid theoretical reason to avoid it.

Breast milk does not contain significant amounts of fluoride. Therefore, breast-fed babies should be supplemented with fluoride. Fluoride is not added to infant formula. Therefore, if you use powdered formulas and the water in your area is not fluoridated, your infant should be supplemented. Fluoride taken in small quantities into the body will get into the teeth only during the first year or so of life. However, larger quantities applied to the teeth are effective throughout childhood. Therefore, we recommend fluoride toothpaste for all children.

To protect your youngster's teeth, the diet must be low in refined sugar, high in calcium, and low in phosphorus, and (during the first year of your child's life) with fluoride added to it either directly or through the water supply. Yet, this type of diet is not enough. The form of the sugar in food may be even more important than the quantity of sugar consumed. If the sugar is in a form that sticks to the teeth such as chewing gum, caramels, candy bars, etc., it is much more harmful than a form that quickly clears the mouth. Therefore, you must pay attention to how you consume your sugar, not just to how much you eat. If it is a sticky type (as in raisins, fruit rolls, and sometimes bread—as well as candies and other "sweets") then it is a good idea to brush your teeth after eating it.

The main points to remember in protecting ourselves and our youngsters from dental caries are:

- Brush often to reduce the bacterial count.
- Reduce the intake of refined sugar.
- Reduce the amount of sugar in a sticky form (and brush after you eat it).
- Consume an adequate supply of calcium.
- Reduce your phosphorus intake, particularly at the same time as you consume your calcium.
- Give your infant a fluoride supplement in the first year of life if you breast-feed or if the water supply in your area is not fluoridated.
- Brush with a fluoridated toothpaste.

Periodontal disease occurs in later life and doesn't directly affect the teeth, but the gums and the bones into which the teeth are anchored. If left untreated, periodontal disease can lead first to a loosening of teeth and then to their loss. Periodontal disease is the major cause of tooth loss in older people, and it is the primary reason that such a high percentage of older people are toothless.

The cause or causes of periodontal disease are not clearly understood. Chronic infection of the gums is one aspect. Erosion of the jawbones is another. Which comes first is not clear. Our best judgment is that usually the chronic infection leads to bone erosion. However, it is possible that sometimes the reverse is true. The erosion that occurs in the bones of the jaw is similar to that seen in osteoporosis. However, the risks associated with osteoporosis do not apply to periodontal disease. It is not more frequent in women. It has no relation to menopause and it does not respond to hormone therapy. Thus, we cannot predict who will be at high risk for it.

Good oral hygiene is very important in preventing periodontal disease. Frequent brushing, the use of mouthwashes, and dental flossing all contribute to the control of chronic infection of the gums. Regular dental examinations will allow treatment to start early enough to control the infection before too much bone erosion has taken place.

Beyond this, there is a role for diet. As with the other bones of the body, the mandible and the maxilla (the two jawbones) participate in the regulation of body calcium. During early life, calcium deposits in these bones. In later life, calcium loss occurs. When more calcium is deposited in these bones during the formative years, more can be lost in later life without seriously affecting bone structure. Thus, the same dietary principles that we discussed for osteoporosis are important in periodontal disease. Unlike osteoporosis, however, there is evidence that sometimes periodontal disease can be reversed by calcium supplementation. Although this approach does not always work, it is worth trying. There is little or no risk to taking a calcium supplement. The potential benefits may be great. The dosage should be between 500 and 1,000 mg daily in the form of calcium carbonate, calcium gluconate, or any non-phosphorus-containing calcium salt.

For those at Low Risk

Suppose your risk for all the diseases we have discussed is low. There are still reasons to consider changing your diet somewhat. That you are at low risk at any given time does not mean that you will remain at low risk for all time. Certain risk factors do not change—your gender, your race, your family history. Others can change rapidly and sometimes dramatically. Suppose you have a serum cholesterol level of 160 and no other major risk factors for atherosclerosis. A year later, you check your cholesterol level and it is 180. Your risk is higher, and the trend is in the wrong direction. Should you alter your diet and increase your activity?

If your diet is high in fat and if your lifestyle is sedentary, the answer is yes. It is this changeability of risks combined with our inability to define specific risk factors in other diseases that has prompted some experts to take a more global approach.

Prestigious authorities have called for all Americans to change their diets. Their argument is that these changes will not harm us and will surely benefit some of us. There are several reasons to refute this argument. *First*, it discourages us from taking responsibility for a major part of our future health. Everyone should determine his or her own risk for those diseases in which such a determination is possible. If our risk is high, then certain changes in our diet may be needed. If our risk is low, we must determine at regular intervals whether that risk has changed. This is our own responsibility. *Second*, not everyone needs to change his or her diet even if risk cannot be established. Only those whose diet is poor in one respect or another need make specific changes. If you are a saltaholic, you should lower your salt intake. If your diet is high in fat, you should avoid certain fatty foods. If you take in very little calcium or iron or zinc, you should take measures to correct the deficiency. While all these recommendations are appropriate for many people, they are not necessary for all people. Examine your own dietary pattern and then look at the recommendations. Make up your own mind about what needs modification and how best to modify it. The recommended guidelines include :

- Consuming the number of calories necessary to achieve and maintain ideal weight.
- Consuming no more than 30 percent of those calories in the form of fat.
- Keeping your salt (sodium) intake moderate.
- Consuming about 55 percent or slightly more of our calories as carbohydrate, with no more than 10 percent as simple sugar.

- Eating abundant quantities of foods containing dietary fiber while including whole grain breads and cereals in place of refined ones.

Do these suggestions look familiar? Some or all of these guidelines were designed for lowering our risk to one or a combination of diseases. Even if your risk is low, they are worth considering if your present diet differs greatly. However, if you do decide to start one or more of these changes, be careful not to unbalance your diet and increase your risk for certain diseases. The woman who decides that she is taking in too much fat, particularly saturated fat, and cuts out all dairy products may induce a calcium deficiency. If she relies heavily on the newly available "fat free" products, she may not get enough vitamin E (a nutrient necessary for healthy skin, for protection of our lungs from environmental pollutants, etc.). Similarly, if she decides to cut out all meats, she may induce an iron deficiency. Unless the diet one is accustomed to is grossly abnormal, radical changes should be avoided, particularly for those at low risk. Any needed changes should be made in a manner that will insure a balanced nutrient intake.

Finally, the first guideline in the list may not be appropriate for many people. In order to achieve and maintain ideal weight, they may have to struggle constantly with calories, thereby increasing their risk for other deficiencies. Perhaps a weight that is 105 percent of your ideal would be easier to achieve and maintain. As we have seen, it is just as healthy and may keep you from constantly dieting.

In order for anyone to change his dietary pattern, adequate food choices must be available. While the United States has the most abundant food supply in the world, our food choices have not always been adequate in nutrient content. It is still not easy to lower our salt intake significantly. Of course, if you salt your food heavily, you can stop. What about the foods themselves?

Until recently as their convenience went up, so did their salt content. TV dinners, canned foods, smoked or pickled foods were usually high in salt. Going on a moderately salt-restricted diet meant a major change in lifestyle. It was difficult to eat in most restaurants, or to take out food or snacks. Not so many years ago, this was true regarding dietary fat. Today, however, there are many alternatives: margarine, safflower, canola or corn oil, skim milk, fat-free or low-fat cheese, etc. We now have many fat-free and low-fat foods on our grocery shelves!

These foods did not appear spontaneously, but because the public demanded them. It is the same with low-salt foods, and we now see a wide variety of high-fiber foods, whole-grain products, and foods rich in calcium, zinc, iron, and folic acid. Increasingly, foods are being sold for the nutrients they contain—diet sodas for their low calories, salmon and sardines for their high-calcium content, skinless chicken for its low-fat content, vegetables that are high in fiber, low-salt spaghetti sauce, and low-fat (or fat free) ice cream. Given the incentive of potentially large profits, the American food industry is extremely innovative.

The more this trend continues, the easier it will be to alter our diets when we need to. Therefore, as more people participate in these dietary changes, the more choices become available. Those at high risk for certain diseases can make dietary changes more easily. As the buying habits of the public move in the direction of healthy dietary practices, it will be easier for all of us to alter our diets when necessary. Beyond that, as more and more products become available, more and more people may find they like them. Our eating patterns may totally change. Diet may no longer be a major risk factor for certain serious diseases.

Motivation

After you have thoroughly evaluated your own health profile, determine whether you need any changes in your diet and lifestyle. If so, decide which plan (or combination of plans) is best for you and your loved ones, and try to motivate yourself and others to develop such a plan and stick with it.

You may ask, "How do I motivate myself to adhere to such a plan?" Here is one strategy that has worked for many individuals, and it may work for you:

Make a list of your strongest desires, regardless of whether you expect them to materialize and no matter how attainable they look on paper. Carry the list with you and add to it any new desires that occur to you. Then, by the process of elimination, decide what you want most. The things you do not truly want will make you drowsy or bored when you think about them. You'll find yourself going to the refrigerator for a snack or something to drink. The things you really want will make you forget about bodily comforts, big meals, or something to drink.

When you concentrate on things you truly, deeply, desperately want, you will forget the clock, creature comforts, vacations, and the nonessentials of life. If you truly want something, your subconscious will furnish you with ample reasons and full power for doing it. Watch your memory in connection with anything you think you want. If you keep forgetting dates, appointments, or tasks related to what you think you want, you don't really have the desire for it. When you have arrived at an awareness of just what you really truly want most, you will find that you must make yourself healthier and more attractive in order to achieve these goals.

Keep your conscious mind on the things you really, truly want to accomplish, and your subconscious mind will guide you to the reasons for achieving them.

Do not adopt measures that may help you in your short-term goals—such as losing five pounds to get into your favorite nightgown for the annual ball, but which will damage your health for your long-term goals. And don't forget that professionals, in addition to your physician, in several medical and paramedical disciplines (psychology, nutrition, physical therapy, etc.), are trained and experienced in guiding persons such as yourself over (or around) the barriers which you will encounter. Do not hesitate to ask for their assistance. There are also several support groups that offer valuable assistance to persons or families with specific health problems, and don't be surprised if you get a tremendous amount of support from your own loved ones. Perhaps, because you share so many genetic and environmental risk factors, your health profiles have many similarities, and, when one person in a family chooses to adopt a new nutritional health regimen, there is a direct spin-off.

The importance of diet and lifestyle becomes more evident to other members. The whole unit begins to improve its eating patterns, and everyone in the household begins to eat in a manner that is closer to the recommended diet. Soon it becomes obvious that these changes are neither difficult nor unpleasant. Often the new experiences are more enjoyable than the old. The principles of good nutrition are particularly important to young people because it is they who will set future trends. They will soon be starting their own families and determining their children's eating patterns.

Appendix A
Exchange Values for Some Prepared Foods

AUNT PENNY'S SAUCES

Food Name	Serving Size	Exchange Information
Aunt Penny's Cheese Sauce	2 tbs.	½ meat and ½ cooked vegetable
Aunt Penny's Hollandaise Sauce	2 tbs.	½ meat and ½ cooked vegetable
Aunt Penny's White Sauce	2 tbs.	½ meat and ½ cooked vegetable

BANQUET BRAND

Food Name	Serving Size	Exchange Information
Beef Stew	8 ounces	2 starch and 1 meat
Chicken and Dumplings	8 ounces	2 starch and 3 meat
Creamed Chipped Beef	5 ounces	1 meat and 2 cooked vegetable
Salisbury Steak with Gravy	5 ounces	2 meat, 1 cooked vegetable, and 1 fat
Spaghetti with Meat Sauce	8 ounces	2 meat, 3 fruit, 1 fat

BETTY CROCKER

Food Name	Serving Size	Exchange Information
Macaroni and Cheddar	½ cup	1 starch and 1 fat
Noodles Almandine	½ cup	1 starch, 1 milk, and ½ fat
Noodles Italiano	½ cup	1 starch and ½ milk
Noodles Romanoff	½ cup	1 starch, 1 milk, and ½ fat
Chili-Tomato Hamburger Helper Mix	⅕ pkg.	2 starch and ½ fat
Hamburger Helper Mix	⅕ pkg.	1½ starch, trace fat
Lasagna Hamburger Helper Mix	⅕ pkg.	2 starch
Spaghetti Hamburger Helper Mix	⅕ pkg.	2 starch
Cheeseburger Macaroni Hamburger Helper Mix	⅕ pkg.	2 starch and 1 fat
Rice Milanese	½ cup	2 starch and 1½ fat
Rice Provence	½ cup	2 starch and 1½ fat
Creamy Noodles'n Tuna or Creamy Rice'n Tuna or Hamburger Helper Mix	⅕ pkg.	2 starch and 1 fat
Dry Hash Brown Potato Mix	¼ pkg.	3 starch
Dry Scalloped Potato Mix	¼ pkg.	3 starch
Instant Mashed Potato Buds	½ cup	1½ starch

BIRDS EYE BRAND

Food Name	Serving Size	Exchange Information
Awake Imitation Orange Juice	½ cup	1½ fruit
Bavarian-style Beans with Spaetzle	½ cup	2 vegetable
Broccoli Spears in Butter Sauce	½ cup	½ vegetable and 1 fat
Broccoli with Cheese Sauce	½ cup	2 vegetable and 2 fat
Broccoli, Carrots and Pasta Twists	½ cup	2 starch, 1 vegetable, and 1 fat
Carrots with Brown Sugar Glaze	½ cup	1 fruit, 1 vegetable, and ½ fat

Chinese-style Vegetables	½ cup	1 vegetable
Cool Whip Nondairy Topping	2 tbs.	¼ milk
Corn in Butter Sauce	½ cup	1 starch and 1 fat
Green Beans & Pasta Curls	½ cup	1 starch, 1 vegetable, and 1 fat
Corn Peas, and Tomatoes	½ cup	2 vegetable
French-style Green Beans with Almonds	½ cup	1 vegetable and ½ fat
French-style Green Beans with Mushrooms	½ cup	1 vegetable
French-style Rice	½ cup	1½ starch, and 1 vegetable
Green Beans in Cream Sauce	½ cup	2 starch, 1 vegetable and 1½ fat
Green Peas and Onions	½ cup	2 vegetable
Green Peas in Butter Sauce	½ cup	1½ veg. and 1 fat
Green Peas and Celery	½ cup	1½ vegetable
Green Peas and Mushrooms	½ cup	1½ vegetable
Malian-style Vegetables	½ cup	2 vegetable
Italian-style Rice	½ cup	1 veg. and 1½ starch
Japanese-style Vegetables	½ cup	2 vegetable
Mixed Vegetables with Onion Sauce	½ cup	1 vegetable, ½ starch, and 1 fat
Oriental-style Rice	½ cup	1 vegetable, 1½ starch
Peas, Shells, and Corn	½ cup	1 vegetable, 1 starch, and 1 fat
Pennsylvania Dutch-style Vegetables	½ cup	1½ vegetable
Rice and Peas with Mushrooms	½ cup	1 vegetable and 1 starch
San Francisco-style Vegetables	½ cup	2 vegetable
Spanish-style Rice	½ cup	1 vegetable and 1½ starch
Creamed Spinach	½ cup	1 vegetable and 1 fat
Wisconsin Country-style Vegetables	½ cup	1½ vegetable
Crinkle or Plain French Fr. Potatoes	3 oz.(1 serv.)	1½ starch and 1 fat
Potato Pattie	3 oz.(1 serv.)	1 starch and 2 fat
Potato Puffs	⅓ pkg.	1 starch and 2 fat
Hash Browns	½ cup	1 starch
Onion Rings	2 oz.	1 starch and 2 fat

BOUNTY (CAMPBELL'S)

Food Name	Serving Size	Exchange Information
Beef Stew	1 cup	1 starch and 2 meat
Chicken Stew	1 cup	1 starch and 1½ meat
Chili Con Carne with Beans	1 cup	1 starch and 1 meat

CAMPBELL'S CONDENSED SOUPS
(All servings ½ can, given in number of prepared ounces)

Food Name	Serving Size	Exchange Information
Asparagus, Cream of	10 ounces	1 starch and 1 fat
Bean with Bacon	11 ounces	2 starch, ½ meat, and 1 fat
Beef	11 ounces	1 starch and 1 meat
Beef Broth (bouillon)	10 ounces	Free Food
Beef Broth and Barley	11 ounces	1 starch and ½ fat
Beef Broth and Noodles	10 ounces	1 starch and ½ fat
Beef Noodle	10 ounces	1 starch and ½ fat
Beef Teriyaki	10 ounces	1 starch and ½ meat

Beefy Mushroom	10 ounces	2 starch and 1 meat
Black Bean	11 ounces	1½ starch, and 2 meat
Celery, Cream of	10 ounces	½ starch and 2 fat
Cheddar Cheese	11 ounces	1 milk and 2 fat
Chicken Alphabet	10 ounces	1 starch and ½ fat
Chicken Broth	10 ounces	1 meat
Chicken Broth and Noodles	10 ounces	½ starch and 1 fat
Chicken Broth and Vegetables	10 ounces	½ starch
Chicken, Cream of	10 ounces	½ starch and 2 fat
Chicken'n Dumplings	10 ounces	½ starch, ½ meat, and 1 fat
Chicken Gumbo	10 ounces	1 starch
Chicken Noodle	10 ounces	1 starch and ½ fat
Chicken Noodle O's	10 ounces	1 starch and ½ fat
Chicken with Rice	10 ounces	½ starch and 1 fat
Chicken with Stars	10 ounces	½ starch and 1 fat
Chicken Vegetable	10 ounces	1 starch and ½ fat
Chili Beef	11 ounces	1½ starch, 1 meat, and ½ fat
Clam Chowder (Manhattan)	10 ounces	1 starch and ½ fat
Clam Chowder (New England made with milk)*	10 ounces	1 starch, 1 meat, 1 fat, and ½ milk
Consommé (Beef)	10 ounces	1 vegetable
Creamy Chicken Mushroom	10 ounces	1 starch and 2 fat
Curly Noodle with Chicken	11 ounces	1 starch and ½ fat
Green Pea	10 ounces	2 starch, 1 meat, and ½ fat
Meatball Alphabet	10 ounces	1 starch, 1 meat, and ½ fat
Minestrone	10 ounces	1 starch and ⅓ fat
Mushroom, Cream of	10 ounces	1 starch and 1 fat
Mushroom, Golden	10 owes	1 starch and 1 fat
Noodles & Ground Beef	10 ounces	1 starch and 1 fat
Onion	10 ounces	1 starch and ½ fat
Onion, Cream of (made with water and milk)•	10 ounces	1 starch, ½ fat, and ½ milk
Oriental Chicken	10 ounces	1 vegetable and 1 fat
Oyster Stew (made with milk)*	10 ounces	½ starch, ½ meat, 1½ fat, ½ milk
Pepper Pot	10 ounces	1 starch, ½ meat, and ½ fat
Potato, Cream of (made with water and milk)*	10 ounces	1 starch, 1 fat, ½ milk
Shrimp, Cream of (made with water and milk)*	10 ounces	1 starch, 2 fat, ½ milk
Split Pea with Ham and Bacon	11 ounces	2 starch, 1 meat, ½ fat
Tomato	10 ounces	1 vegetable, 1 starch, and ½ fat
Tomato (made with milk)*	10 ounces	1 vegetable, 1 star., ½ fat, ½ milk
Tomato Bisque	11 ounces	2 starch and ½ fat
Tomato Rice, Old Fashioned	11 ounces	2 starch and ½ fat
Turkey Noodle	10 ounces	1 starch and ½ fat
Turkey Vegetable	10 ounces	1 starch and ½ fat
Vegetable	10 ounces	1 vegetable and 1 starch
Vegetable Beef	10 ounces	½ starch and 1 meat
Vegetable, Old Fashioned	10 ounces	1 starch and ½ fat
Won Ton	10 ounces	1 starch and ½ meat

*Exchanges based on addition of whole milk

CAMPBELL'S SOUP FOR ONE
(All servings 1 can, given in prepared ounces)

Food Name	Serving Size	Exchange Information
Bean, Old Fashioned With Ham	11 ounces	2 star., ½ meat, 1 fat
Burly Vegetable Beef	11 ounces	1 vegetable, 1 starch, and 1 meat
Clam Chowder (New England made with whole milk)*	11 ounces	1 starch, ½ meat, 1½ fat, ½ milk
Full Flavored Chicken Vegetable	11 ounces	1 starch and 1 fat
Golden Chicken & Noodles	11 ounces	1 starch and 1 fat
Mushroom, Cream of, Savory	11 ounces	1 starch and 2 fat
Tomato Royale	11 ounces	2 starch and 1 fat
Vegetable, Old World	11 ounces	1 starch and 1 fat

*Exchanges based on addition of whole milk

CAMPBELL'S CHUNKY SOUPS (Individual service size, 1 can, undiluted oz.)

Food Name	Serving Size	Exchange Information
Chunky Beef	10¾ oz.	1½ starch and 1½ meat
Chunky Beef with Noodles (Stroganoff style)	10¾ oz.	2 starch, 1½ meat, and 2 fat
Chunky Chili Beef	11 ounces	2½ starch and 2 % meat
Chunky Clam Chowder (Manhattan style)	10¾ oz.	1½ starch, 2 meat, and 1 fat
Chunky Ham'n Butter Bean	10¾ oz.	2 starch, 1½ meat, and 1½ fat
Chunky Old Fashioned Bean with Ham	11 ounces	2 starch, 1½ meat, 1 veg., 1½ fat
Chunky Old Fashioned Veg, Beef	10¾ oz.	1 starch, 1 meat, 1 vegetable, ½ fat
Chunky Sirloin Burger	10¾ oz	1 starch, 1½ meat, 1 vegetable, 1 fat
Chunky Split Pea with Ham	10¾ oz.	2 starch, 1 meat, and 1 fat
Chunky Steak & Potato	10¾ oz.	1½ star. and 1½ meat
Chunky Vegetable	10¾ oz.	1 starch, 1 vegetable, and 1 fat

CAMPBELL'S LOW SODIUM PRODUCTS (1 can, undiluted ounces)

Food Name	Serving Size	Exchange Information
Chicken Noodle	7¼ oz	1 starch and ½ fat
Chunky Chicken	7¼ oz	1 star., 1 meat, ½ fat
Green Pea	7 ¼ oz.	1½ starch, ½ meat, and ½ fat
Mushroom, Cream of	7 ¼ oz.	½ starch and 2 fat
Tomato	7 ¼ oz.	1 starch, 1 vegetable, and 1 fat
Turkey Noodle	7 ¼ oz.	½ starch and ½ fat
Vegetable	7¼ oz	1 starch and ½ fat
Vegetable Beef	7¼ oz	1 vegetable and 1 meat
"V-8" Cocktail Vegetable Juice	6 oz	1 vegetable

OTHER CAMPBELL'S CANNED PRODUCTS

Food Name	Serving Size	Exchange Information
Barbecue Beans	4 ounces	1½ starch and ½ fat
Home Style Beans	4 ounces	1½ stanch and ½ fat
Pork & Beans	4 ounces	1½ starch and ½ fat

Tomato Juice	6 ounces	1 vegetable
"V-8" Cocktail Vegetable Juice	6 ounces	1 vegetable
V-8" Spicy Hot Cocktail Veg. Juice	6 ounces	1 vegetable

CAMPBELL'S PASTA

Food Name	Saving Size	Exchange Information
Macaroni with Cheese	1 cup	1½ starch and 1 meat
Italian Style Spaghetti	1 cup	2 starch
Spaghetti and Ground Beef	1 cup	1½ stanch, 1 meat, and 1 fat
Spaghetti and Tomato Sauce	1 cup	2 starch
Spaghetti and Meatballs	1 cup	1½ starch, 1 meat, and 1 fat
Spaghetti Sauce and Meat	1 cup	1 starch, 1 meat, and 1 fat
Spaghetti Sauce and Mushrooms	1 cup	1½ starch and 2 fat

CHEF BOY-AR-DEE PRODUCTS

Food Name	Serving Size	Exchange Information
Spaghetti Sauce with Meat	½ can (4 oz.)	1 starch, ½ meat, 1 fat
Spaghetti Sauce with Mushrooms	½ can (4 oz)	1 starch, ½meat, 1 fat
Pizza Sauce	2 ounces	1 fat
Mushrooms in Brown Gravy	5 ounces	1 vegetable and 1 fat
Beefaroni	⅓ can (5 oz.)	1 starch and 1 meat
Cheese Ravioli	⅓ can (5 oz)	1½ starch, 1 meat, and 1 fat
Chili Con Came with Beans	⅓ can (5 oz)	1½ starch and 1 fat
Marinara Sauce	½ cup	1 starch
Meatballs with Gravy	⅓ can (5 oz.)	½ star., 2 meat, and 1 fat
Ravioli with Beef	⅓ can (5 oz.)	1½ starch and 1 fat
Spaghetti and Meatballs	⅓ can (5 oz.)	1 starch and 1 meat
Spaghetti Sauce with Meat	⅓ can (5 oz.)	1 starch and 1 fat
Spaghetti Sauce with Meatballs	⅓ can (5 oz.)	1½ starch, 1 meat, and 1 fat
Spaghetti Sauce with Mushrooms	⅓ can (5 oz)	1 starch and ½ fat
Meatball Stew	¼ can (7 oz)	1 starch, 1 meat, 1 fat
Lasagna	⅕ can (8 oz)	2½ starch and 1 fat
Ravioli with Beef	⅕ can (8 oz)	2½ starch and 1 fat
Spaghetti & Meatballs	⅕ can (8 oz.)	2 starch, 1 meat, ½ fat
Pizza Pie Mix (made with water)	¼	2 starch and 1 fat
Spaghetti & Meatball Dinner	⅙	3 starch and 1 meat
Spaghetti with Meat Dinner	⅙	2½ starch and 1 meat
Spaghetti with Mushroom Dinner	⅙	2½ starch
Pizza with Sausage	⅙	1½ starch, 2 meat, and 1 fat
Frozen Beef Ravioli	½ can (8 oz)	2½ starch, 1 meat, and 1 fat
Frozen Cheese Ravioli	½ can (8 oz)	2 starch, 1 meat, and 1 fat
Frozen Lasagna	½ can (8 oz)	1½ starch, 2 meats, and 1 fat
Frozen Manicotti	½ can (8 oz)	2 starch, 2 meat, and 3 fat

CHUN KING CORP.

Food Name	Serving Size	Exchange Information
Chicken Chow Mein,divider-pak..	¼ total mix	2 starch and 2 meat
Beef Chow Mein, divider-pak.	¼ total mix	2 starch, 2 meat, and 1 fat
Mushroom Chow Mein, divider-pak	¼ total mix	2 starch
Meatless Chow Mein	½ can	1 starch

Subgum Chicken Chow Mein	½ can	1 starch
Beef Chop Suey	½ can	1 starch
Chop Suey Vegetables	½ can	Free Food
Chinese Vegetables	½ can	Free Food
Bean Sprouts	½ can	Free Food
Chow Mein Noodles	½ can	1½ starch and 2 fat
Frozen Chicken Chow Mein	½ pkg. (8 oz.)	1 starch and 1 meat
Soya Sauce	--	Free Food

FRANCO-AMERICAN PRODUCTS (Serving size in ounces)

Food Name	Serving Size	Exchange Information
Beef Ravioli in Meat Sauce	7½ oz	2 starch, 1 vegetable, and 1 meat
Beef Ravioli O's in Meat Sauce	7½ oz	2 starch, 1 vegetable, and 1 meat
Beefy O's (O-shaped macaroni and beef in tomato sauce)	7½ oz	1½ starch, 1 meat, 1 fat, and 1 veg.
Cheese O's (0-shaped macaroni in tangy cheese sauce)	7½ oz	1½ starch, 1 meat, and ½ fat
Cheese Ravioli O's in tomato sauce	7½ oz	2 starch, ½ meat, 1½ fat, 1 vegetable
Elbow Macaroni and Cheese	7⅜ oz	1½ starch, ½ meat, and 1 fat
Macaroni and Cheese	7⅜ oz	1½ starch, ½ meat, and 1 fat
Pizza O's (O-shaped macaroni in zesty pizza sauce)	7½ oz	2 starch and 1 vegetable
Spaghetti in Meat Sauce	7½ oz.	1 starch, 1 meat, 1½ fat, 1 vegetable
Spaghetti in tomato Sauce with Cheese	7⅛ oz.	2 starch and 1 vegetable
Spaghetti with Meatballs in tomato Sauce	7⅜ oz.	1 starch, 1 meat, 1 fat, and 1 veg.
Spaghetti O's in Tomato and Cheese Sauce	7⅜ oz.	2 starch and 1 vegetable

GOLDEN GRAIN CO.

Food Name	Serving Size	Exchange Information
Spaghetti Dinner	1 cup	3 starch and 1 fat
Cheese Rice-A-Roni	1 cup	2½ starch, 1 meat, and 1 fat
Spanish Rice-A-Roni	1 cup	2½ starch and 2 fat
Wild Rice-A-Roni	1 cup	3 starch and 2 fat
Twist-A-Roni	1 cup	2½ starch and 1 fat
Scallop-A-Roni	1 cup	2 starch and 1 meat

GREEN GIANT

Food Name	Serving Size	Exchange Information
Broccoli-Cauliflower Medley	½ cup	½ starch, ½ vegetable, and ½ fat
Broccoli Fanfare	½ cup	½ starch, 1 vegetable, and ½ fat
Cauliflower in Cheese Sauce	½ cup	1 vegetable and ½ fat
Okra Gumbo	½ cup	1 vegetable and 2 fat
Rice and Broccoli	½ cup	1 vegetable, 1 starch, and 1 fat
Rice Pilaf	½ cup	1½ starch and ½ fat
White and Wild Rice	½ cup	1½ starch and ½ fat

KRAFT A LA CARTE SINGLE SERVING POUCHES

Food Name	Serving Size	Exchange Information
Beef Stew	one pouch	2 meat, 1½ starch, and 2½ fat
Macaroni and Beef	one pouch	2 meat, 1½ starch, and 1½ fat
Salisbury Steak	one pouch	2 meat, ½ starch, and 1½ fat
Sweet 'n Sour Pork	one pouch	2 meat, 2 starch, 1 fat

KRAFT MIXES

Food Name	Serving Size	Exchange Information
American Style Spaghetti Dinner Mix	1 cup	3 starch and 1 fat
Cheese Pizza Mix	¼ box	1 meat, 2½ starch, and 1 fat
Macaroni and Cheese Dinner Mix	1 cup	½ meat, 2½ starch, and 1½ fat

MORTON BRAND TV DINNERS

Food Name	Serving Size	Exchange Information
Ham (omit applesauce)	1 package	1 starch and 5 meat
Turkey, Beef, Salisbury Steak, Meatloaf, and Fish	1 package	1 starch, 1 vegetable, and 5 meat
Shrimp	1 package	1 starch, 1 veg., 4 meat, and fat

RAGU BRAND

Food Name	Serving Size	Exchange Information
Homestyle Spaghetti Sauce	4 ounces	1 starch and ½ fat
Homestyle Spaghetti Sauce with Mushrooms	4 ounces	1 starch and ½ fat
Homestyle Spaghetti Sauce flavored with meat	4 ounces	1 starch and ½ fat

SWANSON CANNED PRODUCTS

Food Name	Serving Size	Exchange Information
Chunk Chicken	2½ oz.	2 meat
Chunk White Chicken	2½ oz.	2 meat
Chunk Thigh Chicken	2½ oz	2 meat
Chunk Style Mixin Chicken	2½ oz	2 meat and ½ fat
Chunk Turkey	2½ oz.	2 meat
Chicken Spread	2½ oz.	½ meat and 1 fat
Beef Broth	7¼ oz.	Free Food (18 calories)
Chicken Broth	7¼ oz.	1 fat
Beef Stew	7⅝ oz.	1 starch, 1 meat, and ½ fat
Chicken Stew	7⅝ oz	1 starch, 1 meat, and 1 fat
Chicken a la King	5¼ oz.	½ starch, 1 meat, and 2 fat
Chicken and Dumplings	7¼ oz.	1 starch, 1 meat, and 2 fat

SWANSON FROZEN PRODUCTS (MEAT PIES)

Food Name	Serving Size	Exchange Information
Beef	one 8-oz pie	3 starch, 1 meat, and 4 fat
Chicken	one 8-oz. pie	3 starch, 1 meat, and 4 fat
Turkey	one 8-oz. pie	3 starch, 1 meat, and 4½ fat
Macaroni and Cheese	one 7-oz. pie	2 starch, 1 meat, and 1 fat

SWANSON FROZEN HUNGRY-MAN MEAT PIES

Food Name	Serving Size	Exchange Information
Beef	one 16-oz. pie	4 star., 3 meat, 7 fat, 1 veg
Chicken	one 16-oz. pie	4 star., 3 meat, 7 fat, 1 veg
Steak burger	one 16-oz pie	4 star., 3 meat, 8 fat, 1 veg
Turkey	one 16-oz. pie	4 star., 3 meat, 7½ fat, 1 veg

SWANSON FROZEN ENTREES (one complete entree, oz)

Food Name	Serving Size	Exchange Information
Chicken Nibbles with French Fries	5 ounces	2 starch, 1½ meat, and 3 fat
Fish'n Chips	5 ounces	1½ starch, 2 meat, and 2 fat
French Toast with Sausages	4½ oz	1½ starch, 2 meat, and 2 fat
Fried Chicken with Whip. Potatoes	7¼ oz.	2 starch, 2½ meat, and 3 fat
Gravy and Sliced Beef with Whipped Potatoes	8 ounces	1 starch, 2 meat, and ½ fat
Meatballs with Brown Gravy and Whipped Potatoes	9¼ oz.	2 starch, 2 meat, and 2 fat
Meatloaf with Tomato Sauce and Whipped Potatoes	9 ounces	2 starch, 2 meat, and 2 fat
omelets with Cheese Sauce and Ham	8 ounces	1 starch, 2½ meat, and 4 fat
Pancakes and Sausages	6 ounces	3 starch, 1 meat, and 5 fat
Salisbury Steak with Crinkle-cut Potatoes	5½ oz	2 starch, 1½ meat, and 3 fat
Scrambled Eggs and Sausage with Hash Brown Potatoes	6¼ oz	1½ starch, 2 meat, and 5 fat
Spaghetti with Starched Veal	8¼ oz.	1½ star, 1 meat, 2 fat, 1 veg.
Spanish Style Omelet	8 ounces	1 starch, 1 meat, and 3 fat
Turkey/Gravy/Dressing with Whipped Potatoes	8¾ oz.	1½ starch, 2 meat, and 1 fat

SWANSON HUNGRY MAN ENTREES

Food Name	Serving Size	Exchange Information
Barbecue Flavored Chicken with Whipped Potatoes	12 oz**	3 starch, 4 meat, and 3 fat
Fried Chicken with Whipped Potato	12 oz**	2½ starch, 5 meat, and 4 fat
Fried Chicken Breast Portions	11¾ oz**	3 starch, 6 meat, and 4 fat
Fried Chicken Drumsticks	10¾ oz**	2½ starch, 4 meat, and 5 fat
Lasagna and Garlic Roll	2¾ oz	3 starch, 2 meat, and 5 fat
Salisbury Steak with Crinkle-Cut Potatoes	12½ oz	2½ starch, 4 meat, and 5½ fat
Sliced Beef with Whipped Potatoes	12¼ oz	1½ starch and 4 meat
Turkey/Gravy/Dressing with Whipped Potatoes	13¼ oz	2 starch, 4 meat, and ½ fat

** Edible Portion

SWANSON FROZEN MAIN COURSE (One complete entrée, oz.)

Food Name	Serving Size	Exchange Information
Chicken Cacciatore	11½ oz.	½ starch, 4 meat, and 1 vegetable
Chicken in White Wine Sauce	8¼ oz	I starch, 3 meat, and 3 fat
Creamed Chipped Beef	10½ oz.	1 starch, 2 meat, and 3½ fat
Filet of Haddock Almandine	7½ oz	½ starch 4 meat, and 2½ fat
Lasagna with Meat in Tomato Sauce	2¼ oz.	3½ starch, 2 meat, and 3 fat
Macaroni and Cheese	12 ounces	2½ starch, 2 meat, and 3 fat
Salisbury Steak with Gravy	10 ounces	1 starch, 3½ meat, and 3½ fat
Steak and Green Peppers in Oriental Style Sauce	8'/s oz.	½ starch, 2½ meat, and 1 vegetable
Turkey with Gravy and Dressing	9 ¼ oz.	1½ starch, and 4 meat

LEAN CUISINE

Food Name	Exchange Information
Beet and pork cannelloni, Mornay sauce	1½ meat, 1 starch, ½ veg. and ½ milk
Beefsteak Ranchero	1½ meat, 1½ starch, 1 vegetable, and 1 fat
Breast of chicken in Herb cream sauce	2½ meat, ½ starch, ½ vegetable, and ½ milk
Breast of chicken Marsala, vegetables	2½ meat, ½ starch, and 1 vegetable
Breast of chicken Parmesan	2½ meat, 1 starch, 1 vegetable
Cheese cannelloni, tomato sauce	2 meat, 1 starch, and 1 vegetable
Chicken a l'orange, almond rice	2 meat and 2 starch
Chicken & vegetables, vermicelli	2 meat, 1½ starch, I vegetable and ½ fat
Chicken cacciatore, vermicelli	2½ meat, 1 starch, and 2 vegetable
Chicken chow mein, rice	1 meat, 2 starch, and 1 vegetable
Chicken Oriental	2 meat, 1½ starch, and ½ vegetable
Filet of fish Divan	3 meat, ½ starch, ½ vegetable, and ½ milk
Filet offish Florentine	3 meat, 1 veg, and 2 milk
Filet of fish jardiniere, souffled potatoes	3 meat, ½ starch, 1 vegetable, and ½ milk
Glazed chicken, vegetable rice	3 meat and 1½ starch
Lasagna, meat & sauce	2½ meat, 1½ starch, and ½ vegetable
Linguini, clam sauce	1½ meat, 2 starch, and ½ fat
Meatball stew	2½ meat, 1 starch, ½ veg. and ½ fat
Oriental beef, vegetables, rice	2 meat, 1½ starch, and ½ vegetable
Rigatoni bake, meat sauce, cheese	2 meat. 1 starch, and 1½ vegetable
Salisbury steak, Italian sauce, vegetables	2½ meat, 1 starch, 1 veg, and ½ fat
Shrimp & chicken Cantonese, noodles	2½ meat, 1 starch, 1 veg, and ½ fat
Sliced turkey breast, mushroom sauce	2 meat, 1 starch, ½ veg, and ½ milk
Spaghetti, beef and mushroom sauce	1 meat, 2 starch, and 1½ vegetable
Stuffed cabbage, meatand tomato sauce	1½ meat, ½ starch, 2 veg, and ½ fat
Szechwan beef, noodles and vegetables	2 meat, 1½ starch, ½ veg, and ½ fat
Tuna lasagna, spinach noodles and veg.	1½ meat, 1 starch, ½ veg, ½ milk, and ½ fat
Turkey Dijon	2½ meat, ½ starch, 1 veg, ½ milk, and ½ fat
Veal primavera	2½ meat, 1 stanch, ½ veg, and ½ fat
Vegetables and pasta	1 meat, 1 starch, 1 vegetable and ½ milk
Mornay with ham	1 fat
Zucchini lasagna	2 meat, l½ starch, and 1 vegetable

WEIGHT WATCHERS FROZEN ENTREES

Food Name	Exchange Information
Chicken fettucini	2 meat, 1½ starch, 1 fat, and ¼ milk
Stuffed turkey breast	2 meat, ½ starch, 1 fat, and 1½ vegetable
Southern fried chicken patty	3 meat, 1 starch, ½ veg, and 2 fat
Chicken nuggets	2 meat, ½ starch, and 1 fat
Chicken patty parmigiana	3 meat, ½ starch, 1 fat, and 1½ vegetable
Imperial chicken	2 meat, 1 stanch, 1 veg, and ½ fat
Chicken a la king	2 meat, ½ starch, ½ veg, 1 fat, and ½ milk
Sweet' n sour chicken tenders	1½ meat, 1 starch, 1 veg, and 1 fruit
Beef Salisbury steak Roman	2½ meat, 1 starch, 1 veg, and 1 fat
Chopped beefsteak	3 meat and 1 vegetable
Veal patty parmigiana	3 meat and 1½ vegetable
Beef Stroganoff	2 meat, 1 starch, ½ veg, 1 fat, and ¼ milk
Filet of fish au gratin	3½ meat, ½ starch, and 1 vegetable
Oven fried fish	3 meat, ½ starch, ½ veg, and 2 fat
Stuffed sole with Newburgh sauce	2½ meat, 1 starch. ½ veg, 1 fat, and ½ milk
Seafood linguini	1½ meat, 1 stanch, ½ veg, and 1 fat
Broccoli and cheese baked potato	1 meat, 1½ starch, 1 vegetable and ¼ milk
Chicken divan baked potato	1½ meat, 1½ starch, ½ veg. and ¼ milk
Pasta Primavera	1 meat, 1 starch, 1 veg., ½ fat, and ¼ milk
Lasagna with meat sauce	2 meat, 1 starch, 1 veg, and ½ fat
Italian cheese lasagna	2 meat, 1 starch, 1 veg, and ½ fat
Pasta rigati	2 meat, 1 starch, and 1 vegetable
Baked cheese ravioli	2 meat, 1 starch, and 1 vegetable
Spaghetti with meat sauce	1½ meat, 1½ starch, 1 vegetable and ½ fat
Cheese manicotti	2 meat, 1 starch, 1 veg, and ½ fat
Chicken fajitas	1½ meat, 1½ starch, and 1 vegetable
Beef fajitas	1½ meat, 1½ starch, 1 vegetable
Chicken enchiladas Suiza	2 meat, 1 starch, ½ vegetable, and ¼ milk
Beef enchiladas ranchero	2 meat, 1 starch, and 1 vegetable
Cheese enchiladas ranchero	2 meat, 1 starch, and 1 vegetable
Beefsteak burrito	1½ meat, 1½ starch, 1 vegetable and ½ fat
Chicken burrito	1½ meat, 1½ starch, 1 vegetable and 1 fat
Deluxe combination pica	1½ meat, 1½ starch, ½ vegetable
Sausage pizza	2 meat, 1½ starch, and ½ vegetable
Pepperoni pica	1½ meat, 1½ starch, and ½ vegetable
Cheese pizza	2 meat, 2 starch, arid ½ vegetable
Pepperoni French starch pizza	1½ meat, 2 starch, 1 fat, and ½ vegetable
Cheese French starch pizza	½ meat, 2 starch, 1 fat, and ½ vegetable
Deluxe French starch pizza	1½ meat, 2 starch. ½ fat, and ½ vegetable

Appendix B
Exchange Values for Alcoholic Beverages

Beer

Type	Serving Size	Exchange information
Ale, Mild	8 ounces	1½ fat and 1 fruit
Beer	8 ounces	1½ fat and 1 fruit

Wines

Type	Serving Size	Exchange Information
Champagne, Bruit	3 ounces	1⅔ fat
Champagne, Extra Dry	3 ounces	1⅔ fat and ½ fruit
Dubonnet	3 ounces	1½ fat and 1 fruit
Dry Marsala	3 ounces	2 fat and 2 fruit
Sweet Marsala	3 ounces	2 fat and 2½ fruit
Muscatel	4 ounces	2⅓ fat, 1½ fruit
Port	4 ounces	2⅓ fat, 1½ fruit
Dry Red Wine	3 ounces	1⅔ fat
Sake	3 ounces	1 fat and 1 fruit
Domestic Sherry	3½ oz.	1½ fat and ½ fruit
Dry Vermouth	3½ oz.	2⅓ fat
Sweet Vermouth	3½ oz.	2⅔ fat and 1 fruit
Dry White Wine	3 ounces	1½ fat

Liqueurs end Cordials

Type	Serving Size	Exchange Information
Amaretto	1 ounce	1⅓ fat and 1½ fruit
Creme de Cacao	1 ounce	1½ fat and 1 truit
Creme de Menthe	1 ounce	1½ fat and 1 fruit
Curacao	1 ounce	1½ fat and 1 fruit
Drambuie	1 ounce	1½ fat and 1 fruit
Tia Maria	1 ounce	1½ fat and 1 fruit

Bourbon, brandy, Canadian whiskey, gin, rye, nun, Scotch, tequila and vodka are essentially free of carbohydrates. Caloric or fat portion count depends on the proof. Values are rounded off.

Type	Serving Size	Exchange Information
80 proof	1 ounce	1½ fat
84 proof	1 ounce	1½ fat
90 proof	1 ounce	1⅔ fat
94 proof	1 ounce	2 fat
97 proof	1 ounce	2 fat
100 proof	1 ounce	2¼ fat

Index

adipocytes, 69

adipose tissue:

    obesity as a factor, 69

    too large fat cells in, 70

    too many fat cells in, 69

adolescence:

    anemia in, 70

    inadequate calcium intake in, 192

adrenocortical hormones, 183

African-Americans:

    breast cancer among, 142

    diabetes among, 109

    hypertension among, 11

    lactose intolerance among, 13

    osteoporosis among, 187

    sickle-cell anemia among, 165

age:

    at first pregnancy, 143

    and breast cancer, 143

    hypertension and, 52

    at menarche, 148

plaque, dental, 233
Polynesia, obesity in, 25
polyps, colon, 144
potassium, 220
prednisone, 190
pregnancy:
        anemia and, 167
        bone growth during, 184
        breast cancer and, 143
        calcium intake during, 182
        diabetes and, 106
        folic acid deficiency in, 160
        iron deficiency in, 159
        osteoporosis and, 182
        weight gained after, 75
        zinc deficiency in, 161
primidone, 191
prostate cancer, 148
protein:
        calcium excretion and, 194
        in diabetic diet,128
Prudent Diet:
        alcohol consumption in, 45
        at home, 225
        meats in, 224
        plant foods in, 39
        in restaurants, 225
pulmonary hypertension, 78
Pyridoxine, 217
Race:
        breast cancer and, 142
        hypertension and, 50
        osteoporosis and 187
restaurants, sodium restriction in, 65

vitamin B-1, (thiamine), 217
    alcohol consumption and, 18
vitamin B6 (pyridoxine):
    alcohol consumption and, 18
    excessive dieting and, 21
    oral contraceptives and, 19
vitamin B-12:
    anemia and, 153
    folic acid and, 153
vitamin C:
    cancer and, 147
    iron absorption and, 156
vitamin D:

    and calcium, 216
    bone tissue and, 203
vitamin E:
    anemia and, 163
    cancer and, 147
vitamin K, 217
walking,19
water, 7
weightlessness, 185
wine 45
women:
    anemia among 158
    bone loss in, 179
    life expectancy of, 185
zinc:
    alcohol consumption and, 18
    anemia and, 166
    excessive dieting and 21
    menstruation and, 166
    pregnancy and, 161